Business Intelligence in the Digital Economy:

Opportunities, Limitations and Risks

Mahesh Raisinghani
University of Dallas, USA

IDEA GROUP PUBLISHING
Hershey • London • Melbourne • Singapore

Acquisitions Editor:	Mehdi Khosrow-Pour
Senior Managing Editor:	Jan Travers
Managing Editor:	Amanda Appicello
Development Editor:	Michele Rossi
Copy Editor:	Jane Conley
Typesetter:	Jennifer Wetzel
Cover Design:	Lisa Tosheff
Printed at:	Yurchak Printing Inc.

Published in the United States of America by
    Idea Group Publishing (an imprint of Idea Group Inc.)
    701 E. Chocolate Avenue, Suite 200
    Hershey PA 17033
    Tel: 717-533-8845
    Fax: 717-533-8661
    E-mail: cust@idea-group.com
    Web site: http://www.idea-group.com

and in the United Kingdom by
    Idea Group Publishing (an imprint of Idea Group Inc.)
    3 Henrietta Street
    Covent Garden
    London WC2E 8LU
    Tel: 44 20 7240 0856
    Fax: 44 20 7379 3313
    Web site: http://www.eurospan.co.uk

Library of Congress Cataloging-in-Publication Data

Business intelligence in the digital economy : opportunities, limitations, and risks / Mahesh Raisinghani, editor.
    p. cm.
Includes bibliographical references and index.
  ISBN 1-59140-206-9 (hardcover) — ISBN 1-59140-280-8 (softcover) — ISBN 1-59140-207-7 (ebook)
  1. Business intelligence. I. Raisinghani, Mahesh S., 1967-
  HD38.7.B872 2004
  658.4'72—dc22

                          2003022609

British Cataloguing in Publication Data
A Cataloguing in Publication record for this book is available from the British Library.

All work contributed to this book is new, previously-unpublished material. The views expressed in this book are those of the authors, but not necessarily of the publisher.

Dedication

To my angel daughter, Aashna Kaur Raisinghani

"One hundred years from now, it will not matter what my bank account was, how big my house was, or what kind of car I drove. But the world may be a little better, because I was important in the life of a child."

- Forest Witcraft

Business Intelligence in the Digital Economy:

Opportunities, Limitations and Risks

Table of Contents

Foreword

In the past years, research in the field of responsive business environments has had many successes. The most significant of these has been the development of powerful new tools and methodologies that advance the subject of Business Intelligence (BI). This book provides the BI practitioner and researcher with a comprehensive view of the current art and the possibilities of the subject.

Dr. Raisinghani and his colleagues delight us with a breadth of knowledge in Business Intelligence (BI) that ranges from the business executive viewpoint to insights promised by text mining. The expert authors know that BI is about reducing the uncertainties of our business world. A timely and accurate view into business conditions can minimize uncertainty.

The reduction of business and technical risk is the central theme of this text. If data gives us the facts and information allows us to draw conclusions, then intelligence provides the basis for making good business decisions. Information technology can help you seize the information that is available.

Intelligence involves knowing information about your competitors, such as their profitability and turnover rate. The most important thing to gain from intelligence is knowledge of customers and potential customers. This knowledge will help you to better serve customers and ensure that your service offerings align with their needs. Performing an annual survey will not give you this type of information. You need to know why people are or are not your customers. If they are not your customers, whose are they? Have they heard of your company? Are they familiar with your services or are they part of an untapped market?

An IT organization is responsible for putting information in a place where it can be mined by salespeople, product developers, and others within an organization. One way to achieve this is through an information portal. An information portal uses the same technology as Web search engines to find and catalog information within your company giving access to everyone. IT sets up pointers to the information, allowing people to turn it into intelligence.

Business decision makers need rapid access to information about their customers, markets, investors, suppliers, governments, employees, and finances. There are four critical success factors for strategically using and managing IT. First, enterprises must be able to quantify the value of IT. They must know how IT contributes to the creation of the value and wealth of their organization. The second factor involves the ability to collect and organize intelligence, both internally and externally. This intelligence includes information about your market, your customers, and your potential customers. Third, enterprises need to understand the wide spectrum of capability and productivity of IT people within the same skill set. The final success factor is to invest in IT people that can invent and create new tools or services. The internal and external business information problem has existed for centuries — the best hope for the future is the wise use of business intelligence tools.

Thomas L. Hill
Electronic Data Systems (EDS)
Fellow

Thomas Hill has the distinction of being an EDS Fellow, the highest level of technical achievement in the corporation. He brings more than 30 years of extensive experience to EDS' efforts for clients around the world. EDS Fellows are visionary thinkers who represent the top echelon of EDS' thought leadership capabilities. Fellows play a vital role in promoting innovation at EDS and in extending EDS' external reputation as a thought leader and an innovative company through their work and engagements.

EDS, the leading global services company, provides strategy, implementation and hosting for clients managing the business and technology complexities of the digital economy. As the world's largest outsourcing services company, EDS, founded in 1962, is built on a heritage of delivery excellence, industry knowledge, a world-class technical infrastructure and the expertise of its people. EDS brings together the world's best technologies to address critical client business imperatives. It helps clients eliminate boundaries, collaborate in new ways, establish their customers' trust and continuously seek improvement. EDS, with its management-consulting subsidiary, A.T. Kearney, serves more than 35,000 business and government clients in 60 countries. EDS Fellows provide ongoing support to a large number of EDS clients, including General Motors, Sabre, Veterans Administration, Inland Revenue, British Petroleum, First Health and Telecom New Zealand and are integrated into other client-facing engagements. This integration is critical to thoroughly diagnosing their clients' business challenges as well as developing innovative solutions.

Preface

INTRODUCTION
Focus and Content of this Book

Business Intelligence in the Digital Economy: Opportunities, Limitations, and Risks
Wisdom grows in those who help others achieve greatness.
- Colle Davis

Who will build intelligence into your business processes? Organizations that need to gain more efficiency and manage or reduce costs are looking to Business Intelligence (BI) to address their requirements. This book can be used as a tool to explore the vast parameters of the applications, problems, and solutions related to BI. Contributing authors include management consultants, researchers, and BI specialists from around the world. The book has an extensive range of topics for practitioners and researchers who want to learn about the state of the art and science in business intelligence and extend the body of knowledge.

BI is important in helping companies stay ahead of the competition by providing the means for quicker, more accurate and more informed decision making. BI is a general term for applications, platforms, tools, and technologies that support the process of exploring business data, data relationships, and trends. BI applications provide companies with the means to gather and analyze data that facilitates reporting, querying, and decision making. The most agile BI products/services are not confined by industry classification and can create an infinite number of possible applications for any business department or a combination of departments.

Business Intelligence (BI) provides an executive with timely and accurate information to better understand his or her business and to make more informed, real-time business decisions. Full utilization of BI solutions can optimize business processes and resources, improve proactive decision making, and maximize profits/minimize costs. These solutions can create an infinite number of possible applications for finance, competition monitoring, accounting, marketing, product comparison, or a combination of a number of business areas. The most agile BI solutions can be used in any industry and provide an infinite number of value-increasing possibilities for any organization.

The purpose of this executive's guide on Business Intelligence is to describe what BI is; how it is being conducted and managed; and its major opportunities, limitations, issues, and risks. It brings together some high-quality expository discussions from experts in this field to identify, define, and explore BI methodologies, systems, and approaches in order to understand their opportunities, limitations and risks.

The audience of this book is MBA students, business executives, consultants, seniors in an undergraduate business degree program, and students in vocational/technical training institutes.

The scholarly value of this proposed book and its contribution will be to the literature in information systems/e-business discipline. None of the current books on the market address this topic from a holistic perspective. Some are more geared toward knowledge management or artificial intelligence. Others take a more computer science and engineering perspective or a statistical analysis perspective.

CHAPTER OVERVIEW

Chapter I proposes that the initial perceptions of uncertainty and risk relating to the decisions faced are unlikely to be modified, irrespective of the quantity or quality of the information transmitted and processed by the decision maker. Initial risk perceptions and decisions are fairly robust even when confronted with contradictory information. Empirical evidence presented illustrates that the decision maker may also construct his or her decision-making behavior to constrain the opportunity for new information to alter the initial perceptions and choices made. Chapter I thus explores the premise that increased business intelligence reduces the risk inherent in decision making and provides suggestions on the appropriate management of individuals involved in information search activities.

Chapter II presents a high-level model for employing intelligent agents in business management processes in order to gain competitive advantage by timely, rapidly, and effectively using key, unfiltered, measurements to improve cycle-time decision making. It conceptualizes the transition of intelligent agents utilized in network performance management into the field of business and management. The benefits of intelligent agents realized in telecommunications networks, grid computing, and data visualization for exploratory analysis connected to simulations should likewise be achievable in business management processes.

Chapter III describes the different flavors of data mining, including association rules, classification and prediction, clustering and outlier analysis, customer profiling, and how each of these can be used in practice to improve a business' understanding of its customers. The chapter concludes with a concise technical overview of how each data-mining technology works. In addition, a concise discussion of the knowledge-discovery process — from domain analysis and data selection, to data preprocessing and transformation, to the data mining itself, and finally the interpretation and evaluation of the results as applied to the domain — is also provided along with the moral and legal issues of knowledge discovery.

Chapter IV provides a German industry perspective with a good balance of business and technology issues. Although system performance and product efficiency are continuously increasing, the information and knowledge capability of the enterprise often does not scale to the development of business requirements. This often happens due to complex company structures, fast growth or change of processes, and rising complexity of business information needs on one hand and a slow and difficult IT-improvement process on the other hand. The chapter illustrates which system architecture to use, which logical application structure to develop, how to set up and integrate the implementation project successfully, how to operate and improve these environments continuously, and how to configure, improve, and maintain the reporting, OLAP and HOLAP environments.

Chapter V presents an Intelligent Knowledge-Based Multi-Agent Architecture for Collaboration (IKMAC) to enable such collaborations in B2B e-Marketplaces. IKMAC is built upon existing bodies of knowledge in intelligent agents, knowledge management, e-business, and XML and web services standards. This chapter focuses on the translation of data, information, and knowledge into XML documents by software agents, thereby creating the foundation for knowledge representation and exchange by intelligent agents that support collaborative work between business partners. Some illustrative business examples of application in Collaborative Commerce, E-Supply Chains, and electronic marketplaces and financial applications — credit analysis, bankruptcy analysis — are also presented. IKMAC incorporates a consolidated knowledge repository to store and retrieve knowledge, captured in XML documents, to be used and shared by software agents within the multi-agent architecture. The realization of the proposed architecture is explicated through an infomediary-based e-Marketplace prototype in which agents facilitate collaboration by exchanging their knowledge using XML and related sets of standards.

Chapter VI takes a closer look at text mining that is a collection of broad techniques for analyzing text, extracting key components, and restructuring them in manner suitable for analysis. As the demands for more effective Business Intelligence (BI) techniques increases, BI practitioners find they must expand the scope of their data to include unstructured text. To exploit those information resources, techniques such as text mining are essential. This chapter describes three fundamental techniques for text mining in business intelligence: term extraction, information extraction, and link analysis; an outline of the basic steps involved; characteristics of appropriate applications; and an overview of its limitations. The limits and risks of all three techniques center around the dependency on statistical techniques — the results of which vary by the quality of available data, and linguistic analysis that is complex but cannot yet analyze the full range of natural language encountered in business environments.

Chapter VII makes a step-by-step analysis of how one retail giant moved quickly to solve a very real problem facing industry executives today, i.e., getting and manipulating necessary data from a large variety of diverse legacy systems running on heterogeneous operating systems and platforms. The case study shows how the organization evaluated available software packages against internal development and nimbly adopted internal development to yield an integrated system that gathers and manipulates data from diverse systems using a common system architecture. The chapter also provides a valuable insight into the area of reclamation of advertising revenue that is valued at 3% of retail sales. The imperative this company faced was the loss of that revenue due to the expiration of the claim period unless its proposed solution came online as planned. The analysis shows, in detail, how a variety of systems' data were linked in a highly unique but effective manner to create the system that has value far greater than the sum of its parts.

Chapter VIII explores the opportunities to expand the forecasting and business understanding capabilities of Business Intelligence (BI) tools by using the system dynamics approach as a complement to simulate real-world behavior. System dynamics take advantage of the information provided by BI applications to model real-world under a "systems thinking" approach, improving forecasts and contributing to a better understanding of the business dynamics of any organization. It discusses how BI tools can support system dynamics tools, supplying "analyzed and screened data" to models of real-world situations that are illustrated by application examples such as Customer Relationship Management (i.e., supporting the processes of acquiring, retaining, and enhancing customers with a better understanding of their behavior), Value-Based Management (i.e., understanding the dynamics of economic value creation in an organization), and Balanced Scorecard (i.e., modeling a balanced scorecard for a better insight of enterprise performance drivers).

Chapter IX explores data mining and its benefits and capabilities as a key tool for obtaining vital business intelligence information. It includes an overview of data mining, followed by its evolution, methods, technologies, applications, and future. It discusses the technologies and techniques of data mining, such as visual, spatial, human-centered, "vertical" (or application-specific), constraint-based, and ubiquitous data mining (UDM) for mobile/distributed environments. Examples of applications and practical uses of data mining as it transitions from research prototypes to data-mining products, languages, and standards are also presented in this chapter.

Chapter X focuses on the factors necessary for strategic BI success from a managerial perspective. BI results from the various information and human knowledge source systems, as well as the holistic view of the business processes within an organization, with its goal being to maximize the resources, and minimize the inefficiencies that are systematic within an organization. The interrelated and non-sequential factors for BI success are discussed. The chapter discusses the critical success factors that enable strategic BI success, i.e., business process of BI within an organization, managerial understanding of data systems, accountability for BI, and execution on BI.

Chapter XI discusses the role of text mining (TM) in BI and clarifies the interface between them. BI can benefit greatly from the bulk of knowledge that stays hidden in the large amount of textual information existing in the organizational environment. TM is a technology that provides the support to extract patterns from texts. After interpreting these patterns, a business analyst can reach useful insights to improve the organizational knowledge. Although texts represent the largest part of the available information in a company, just a small part of all Knowledge Discovery applications are in TM. By means of a case study, this chapter shows an alternative of how TM can contribute to BI. The case study presented, with the methodological approach described and an adequate tool, can be used to guide an analyst in developing similar applications. A discussion on future trends such as the approach that uses concepts instead of words to represent documents supports the effectiveness of TM as source of relevant knowledge.

Chapter XII is an explanatory study of a CRM application in a financial services organization to understand decision-making in data warehousing and related decision support systems (DSS), the authors find the DSS provided by these systems limited and a difference in strategy selection between the two groups of user, analysts and advisors, related to incentives. They recommend an extended version of the DSS-decision performance model that includes the individual characteristics of the user as a construct to better describe the factors that influence individual decision-making performance and includes metadata, explanations and qualitative data as explicit dimensions of the DSS capability construct.

Chapter XIII is a two-part survey exploring the role of data integration in E-CRM Analytics for both B2B and B2C firms. The first part of the survey looks at the nature of the data integrated and the data architecture deployed and the second part analyzes technology and organizational value added with respect to the e-CRM initiative. Interestingly, (and as one's intuition may lead one to believe) they find that an organization that integrates data from multiple customer touch points has significantly higher benefits, user satisfaction, and return on its investment than organizations that do not do so. They propose an e-CRM Value framework as a model for generating greater total benefits for organizations engaging in e-CRM projects.

Mahesh Raisinghani, PhD, CEC
Editor
October 2003

Acknowledgment

The editor would like to acknowledge the help of all involved in this project (both directly or indirectly) from the idea generation to the final publication of this book, without whose support the gap between my intent and implementation could not have been bridged satisfactorily. A special note of thanks goes to the publishing team at Idea Group Publishing, whose contributions throughout the whole process have been invaluable.

I wish to thank all of the authors for their insights and excellent contributions to this book. I also want to thank all of the people who assisted me in the reviewing process. Most of the chapter authors also served as referees for articles written by other authors. Thanks go to all those who provided constructive and comprehensive reviews. Finally, I want to thank my family for their love and support throughout this project.

Mahesh Raisinghani

Chapter I

Reducing Risk in Information Search Activities

Clare Brindley, Manchester Metropolitan University, UK

Bob Ritchie, Manchester Metropolitan University, UK

ABSTRACT

This chapter proposes that the initial perceptions of uncertainty and risk relating to decision making are unlikely to be modified irrespective of the quantity or quality of the information transmitted and processed by the decision maker. It argues that initial risk perceptions and decisions are fairly robust even when confronted with contradictory information. The chapter begins by offering definitions of the key terms such as risk, uncertainty, and the components of the digital economy. The authors then provide an overview of risk assessment and associated management processes before moving onto an examination of the contribution of intelligence and information to risk resolution. A case scenario provides a practical illustration of the issues raised.

INTRODUCTION

Information technologies have been deliberately targeted toward enhancing database access, analytical powers, and the communications capacity of managers. The justification for these efforts has been based on the premise that more and better quality information will result in reduced uncertainty and improved risk perceptions in decision situations. In short, the outcome would be reflected in "better quality" decisions in terms of risk assessment and resolution. A countervailing outcome is that the digital economy itself may enhance the riskiness of the business situation through a more dynamic and rapidly changing environment and fundamental changes in the structures, processes, and relationships involved in business. The whole emphasis in managing business risks is undergoing significant change.

An overview of the risk assessment and management process is presented, highlighting the key dimensions. The changes in business structures, operations, and relationships as a consequence of the digital economy are examined and the implications for risk assessment and management are assessed. Investigating the accepted wisdom that increasing information will improve risk assessment, the chapter proposes that the initial perceptions of uncertainty and risk relating to the decisions faced are unlikely to be modified, irrespective of the quantity or quality of the information transmitted and processed by the decision maker. Initial risk perceptions and decisions are fairly robust even when confronted with contradictory information. Empirical evidence will be presented that illustrates that the decision maker may also construct his or her decision-making behavior to constrain the opportunity for new information to alter the initial perceptions and choices made. This outcome is used to conclude that a change in emphasis is needed that provides more attention to managing risk. Key topic areas discussed in the chapter include:

a.   Defining risk and uncertainty;
b.   Examining the individual/organizational response to resolving risk while recognizing that it may not be possible to fully eliminate the risk extant in any decision situation;
c.   Addressing the contribution of intelligence and information gathering toward resolving some of the uncertainty and improving the identification, measurement, and management of risk;
d.   Evaluating the more usual approach to risk resolution through information search and processing;
e.   Recognizing the limitations of this approach, such as, the ability to search and source relevant information, the issue of quality assurance of the

information available through the Internet, and the individual's capacity to process and manage increasing volumes of information;

f.   Assessing the factors associated with individual characteristics and their influence on risk perceptiveness, intelligence gathering, and risk taking in business decisions;

g.   Understanding why investments in corporate intelligence and information processing may not yield significant improvements in decision quality;

h.   Identifying the alternative approaches to managing risk more effectively through business intelligence and relationship management in the digital economy; and

i.   Developing a conceptual model of risk resolution and risk management within the context of the digital economy.

The chapter thus explores the premise that increased business intelligence reduces the risk inherent in decision making and provides suggestions on the appropriate management of individuals involved in information search activities and risk management. A short case scenario is introduced at appropriate stages in the chapter to provide a practical illustration of some of the issues raised. The case is designed to be illustrative rather than exhaustive, and caution needs to be exercised in suggesting that the solution proposed in this scenario may be equally appropriate in alternative scenarios.

THE DIGITAL ECONOMY

The term "digital economy" reflected in the title of this chapter may be viewed from a variety of perspectives. *Figure 1* illustrates the key dimensions of this term underpinning the discussion in this chapter.

1.   *Technology developments,* especially those relating to the digital communication of data and information, are usually considered as the primary driver in the creation of the digital economy. Increases in speed, improvements in capacity, accuracy, reliability, general quality, and ease of use are all features that have enabled the widespread adoption and development of digital technologies. The developments in audiovisual communication technologies and wireless technologies are opening up further opportunities for the transmission and exchange of business intelligence.

2.   *Socio-economic changes* have been equally influential in the rapid adoption of the new technologies. Individuals of all ages, educational and social backgrounds are prepared to regularly use mobile communications,

Figure 1: Components of the Digital Economy

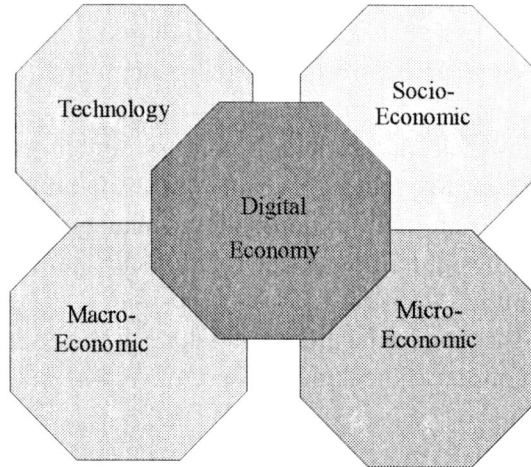

access the Internet and engage in interactive video communications, often with friends and family in different parts of the globe. We should not underestimate the impact that these changes in individual and group social behaviors have had on the rate of adoption of new technologies. The reasons underlying such changes are multifaceted and complex and beyond the scope of our present discussion, though they have been influenced broadly by individual social and economic needs.

3.   *Micro-economic factors* at the level of the individual organization have been responsible for "pulling" and "pushing" organizations and their management towards increased attention and adoption of the digital economy. Significant "pull" factors include demands from end-users of the product or service (e.g., requests for more detailed information on the product/service, prior to and subsequent to the purchase, in terms of performance, maintenance, modifications, upgrades). Intermediaries in the supply chain (i.e., retail distribution channels) also require this type of information to facilitate their specific role within the supply chain. The "push" factors are typically associated with the business organization seeking to maintain its competitive position by offering services equivalent to its main competitors, especially if these may be viewed as providing a distinctive competitive advantage (e.g., providing detailed product information via the Web and enabling customers to order direct). Some of the issues involved will be discussed further in later sections of the chapter.

4.   *Macro-economic factors* are particularly significant in enabling the development of the digital economy though they are often less evident in exploring individual product/market developments. Changes in legislation

affecting consumer rights, guarantees of financial transactions, security of information held on computer systems, and commercial contracts negotiated via the Internet are all examples of the changes in the macroeconomic environment needed to facilitate and support the development of the digital economy. Without such changes, individual organizations and customers might consider the risks of such commercial transactions to be too high. In essence, the responsiveness of governments and other similar institutions have lagged behind many of the demands placed on them by the rate of change in the digital economy. An example has been the slow responsiveness of the Chinese authorities, both nationally and locally, to the changing needs of an economy driven by digital communications.

It may be argued that defining the term the digital economy remains problematic due to the number of perspectives from which this term may be viewed and due to the number and interactive nature of the variables involved.

OVERVIEW OF RISK AND RISK MANAGEMENT

The fields of risk and risk management are exceedingly diverse and straddle almost every conceivable discipline including those of decision making and information management, which are the subject of the present discussion. The approach adopted in this section seeks to address some of the key elements in the risk field, including: defining risk and uncertainty; examining risk resolution; investigating the role of information search, including the contribution of the digital economy; and considering individual characteristics before finally noting some interim implications for the management of risk.

Risk and Uncertainty

Attempts at defining the seemingly simple term "risk" have proved diverse and problematic — evidence the broad themes emanating from various academic disciplines. For example, since the 1920s risk has become a popular element in research literature in the economics fields (Dowling & Staelin, 1994). This is further illustrated by the study of gambling being used to test economic theories such as risk taking (Clotfelter & Cook, 1989). Subsequently, the concept of risk has formed part of management, environmental, insurance, and psychological studies, each focusing on a particular aspect but normally contextualized within the area of decision making, i.e., when the individual or organization is faced with making a decision. Commonalities in these paradigms relate to their definition of risk, which relates to the issues of unpredictability, decision making, and potential loss. Risk perceptions have antecedents in economics and behavioral decision theory according to Forlani and Williams (2000). For example, Sitkin and Pablo (1992, p.9) define risk as "the extent to which there is uncertainty about whether potentially significant and/or disappointing outcomes of decisions will be realised." Similarly, MacCrimmon and Wehrung (1986) identified three components of risk: the magnitude of loss, the chance of loss, and the potential exposure to loss. For March and Shapira (1987), the variation in how these "losses" may be perceived is why risks are taken or not. In Knight's (1921) seminal work on risk, risk was seen in terms of assessing the likelihood of incurring losses. Later work, such as Blume (1971) stressed a more positive definition of risk centered on the possibility of gains, which, it could be argued, is a more realistic definition given that individuals and organizations usually make decisions to try to gain some reward.

Uncertainty is defined as the absence of information concerning the decision situation and the need to exercise judgment in determining or evaluating the situation, alternative solutions, possible outcomes, etc. (Rowe, 1977). An important tenet of the field of risk management is the integration and interaction of the terms risk and uncertainty within the commonly used term of risk itself. Uncertainty typically reflects the ambiguity surrounding the decision, possibly in terms of the precise nature of the situation, its causes, possible solutions, and the reaction of other stakeholders to the implementation of the solution.

The literature in regards to risk definition may be categorized into three types. Firstly, that risk propensity is a result of a particular personality trait or quirk, the manifestation of which is contingent. Secondly, risk is a sociological construct that can be learned or shaped by the individuals' environment. Thirdly, risk is a behavioral construct where risk manifests itself in action or not.

Risk Resolution

If it is assumed that risk is inherent in decision contexts and that the risk may result from both internal and external sources, then the next question to pose is can this risk be resolved or managed? A natural reaction by decision makers facing uncertainty and risk is to seek to resolve the risk inherent in the decision situation by essentially seeking to understand the parameters of the decision and the degree to which these may be predicted. Firstly, it must be recognized that the organization may not have the capability to eliminate or ameliorate many of the external risks (e.g., changing political/economic climate in key export markets) that are impinging upon it. Moreover, gathering corporate intelligence may aid in identifying the potential sources and consequences of the risks involved and provide some reassurance. Secondly, there is the issue of whether the individual decision maker is aware of his/her own personal characteristics that may be impinging upon the conceptualization of these risks. What is therefore needed is a process to manage the risk, to position the organization, and develop appropriate strategies to manage the impact of such events (Bettis, 1982) and their consequences in terms of the organization's strategic objectives to the individual decision maker to have the necessary management tools to aid his or her task. The management of such risks poses new challenges for the business organization, particularly in terms of the increasing complexity and multitude of relationships consequent to the digital economy being in evidence.

Case Scenario:

Fleur PLC manufactures and distributes a range of female and male cosmetics and perfume products. The company is a multimillion dollar sales organization currently operating in the US and Europe. Although the company is not one of the top twenty in terms of market sales, its management is regarded as very innovative in terms of both products and markets. The company considers itself to be one of the leaders in the industry in relation to Information and Communication Technologies (ICTs), though it has not managed to capitalize on this in terms of a perceived distinct competitive advantage in the marketplace.

The Company's management has identified the markets in China and the Asia-Pacific region as the next key strategic development for the business. The current and potential growth in these consumer markets is viewed as exceptional, though the cost of establishing a physical presence in these markets may prove impractical and uneconomic due to the wide geographic area involved and the diversity of cultural and behavioral norms present. The management undertook to explore the nature and effectiveness of a strategy more fully employing the digital economy.

Information Search and Corporate Intelligence

In order to make decisions, it is normal to search for, analyze, and process relevant information. This information is then used (consciously or unconsciously) by the decision maker in a way that satisfies that the risk of the decision has been removed, reduced, or resolved. If the decision maker is not satisfied that he or she has achieved sufficient resolution of the risks involved, then further information searches, analysis, and processing will occur. The circles in *Figure 2* represent the layers of information present in any decision situation. By exploring each of the subsequent layers of uncertainty and risk in a given situation (i.e., moving successively outwards in the figure), the decision maker will potentially improve his or her understanding and resolution of the risks involved in the given situation. However, the stripping out of successive layers through the process of intelligence gathering need not necessarily result in improved understanding and risk resolution. The uncovering of more influencing variables may cause perceptions of greater uncertainty, both as a consequence of uncovering new influencing variables and an increasing sense of complexity. Ritchie and Marshall (1993) argued that the quality and sufficiency of the information available would influence the perception of risk by those involved in the decision-making process. Thus, risk perception is both the consequence of information search and analysis and its determinant (Ritchie & Brindley, 1999). The issue of when the decision maker has reached the stage of sufficient resolution to move to the decision-making stage is analyzed later in this chapter.

Case Scenario:
   The proposed China and Asia-Pacific strategic development by Fleur PLC would require a significant investment in information search and corporate intelligence gathering, relating to a number of dimensions:

* *Macro-economic factors and the extent to which they facilitate market entry from foreign investors, the general economic forecasts, the preparedness to accept foreign direct investment, any financial or strategic constraints imposed, and the quality of the general infrastructure to support commercial development. Each of these dimensions would have implications for the strategic risk profile.*
* *Micro-economic factors that impact on the existing business and its capacity to initiate and sustain a new strategic development are key*

Figure 2: Information Search and Corporate Intelligence: A Conceptual Model

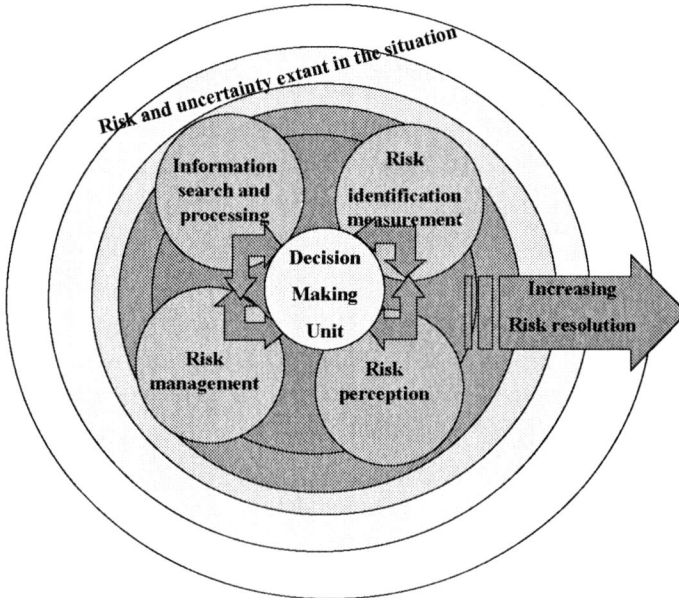

contributors to the risk profile of the emerging strategy. The nature of the existing market in terms of structure, distribution channels, market shares, channel pricing structures, consumer preferences, etc., will pose potential risks for the Company.

- Socio-economic factors will be particularly influential in assessing and managing the risks involved in the strategic development. Differences in fashion, taste, cultures, and consumer behavior are all likely to generate new risks for Fleur PLC, influencing decisions concerning both the level and profitability of sales.

- Technology may generate further risks, assuming that established competitors are already adopting technology solutions to manage their business and supply chains. Alternatively, technology may itself provide solutions that may ameliorate the other risks involved, for example, strengthening the links in the supply chain with local distributors or possibly local manufacturers.

In each of these cases, the management of the company needs to identify the risks involved, assess the likelihood of their occurrence, *and then assess the potential strategic consequences. Although this list is not intended to be exhaustive, it should illustrate the diversity and importance of high quality business intelligence as a means to resolving risks.*

Digital Economy and Risk Resolution

If it is accepted that information is a risk reduction or risk insulating tool, then it could be argued that more and better information would result in more effective risk management. Thus, if one studies the rapid and unrelenting rise in ICT developments (Rycroft & Kash, 1999; Kalokota & Robinson, 2000), it follows that both individuals and organizations have easier access to more information, information that is more time-frame specific, and arguably more relevant information. Indeed, Swash (1998, p.242) argued that the Internet "can no longer be regarded as a peripheral information resource." The decision makers can therefore access through their own desktop, internal data, external market reports, competitor information, etc. It can therefore be seen why Swash (1998) recognized that it is essential to overcome the problem of information overload by ensuring the Internet is used frequently, thus improving the users' surfing proficiency and their knowledge of "useful" sites. Zsidisin and Smith (2002), in examining the impact of the Internet on supply chain decisions, suggested that:

> *when organizations and their suppliers work together as part of ESI (Electronic Supply Interchange) projects, it is natural that information exchange improves. With better exchange of information comes better knowledge of the situations surrounding the dynamics of a supply relationship, and with that information comes greater potential for detecting, averting, and managing supply risk. (p.15)*

Individual Characteristics and Risk

Chung (1998) views differences in risk perception as resulting from differences in information processing styles, i.e., there is a difference in the individual's approach to risk cues. For example, women assigned significantly more weight to risk cues. Indeed, Chung (1998) found that women tended to assign more importance to all cues than men, which offered direct support to the issues that women are more detailed information processors than men. Chung (1998) found that women made significantly more risk-averse judgments than men. Some findings suggest that propensity varies according to entrepreneur's gender (e.g., Birley, 1989; Sexton & Bowman-Upton, 1990), while Masters and Meier (1988) found no difference in risk propensity in male versus female entrepreneurs, a departure from findings prior to the 1970s.

Busenitz (1999, p.329) argues that increasing "evidence indicates that individuals vary in the way they deal with risk" (see, for example, Shapira, 1995). As Busenitz (1999) asserts, there is much uncertainty at the start-up of a business, and it is the individual's use of biases and heuristics that can be the basis on which the decision to go into business is made. For example, overconfidence itself may be seen as a bias or indeed a conscious or subconscious decision to ignore the risk signals present and the information supporting them. It may be postulated that overconfidence is a result of personality or social constructs and may, for example, occur in certain social groupings more readily. In other studies it is implicit that risk-taking propensity varies according to personality type, but McCarthy (2000) argues that the shortcomings of personality trait theory have been well-documented, even though it has been a major approach to the study of entrepreneurial risk.

For Stewart, Watson, Carland, and Carland (1999), an awareness of an individual's risk behavior could help not only existing entrepreneurs in their business planning but also potential entrepreneurs in assessing their suitability for entrepreneurship. The idea of suitability is also developed by Forlani and Williams (2000, p.306), who argue "that a better understanding of risk and its role in new venture decision making has the potential to improve the quality of decision making in the risk-charged environments which most prospective founders of new firms face." Forlani and Williams (2000) further posit that if individuals are aware of their own risk propensities, they are able to determine whether their assessment of new venture opportunities have been influenced by their propensity to take risks. This raises the issue that if propensities differ, as a result of say gender, but individuals are not aware of this, then an underassessment of the venture's competitiveness may be made. Such bias can be ameliorated through the use of structured decision aids (see Ghosh & Ray, 1997) or utilizing information on outcomes from a broader range of decisions (Kahneman & Lovallo, 1993). Forlani and Williams (2000, p.319) also argue that "providing would-be entrepreneurs with tools, techniques, and analytical frameworks for reducing the variability in their forecast of new venture outcomes can play an important role in facilitating their pursuit of potentially attractive, but risky, opportunities."

Case Scenario:

> *Fleur PLC faced with a major strategic decision needs to be particularly aware of the individual and group characteristics in terms of their perception and preparedness to take risks. For example,*

- *If the standing or esteem of the principal executives in the organization is reflected by the growth of the business or its presence in major markets, then there exists the potential for such executives to be biased in favor of the China strategy. This may be reflected in the initial perception of the risks involved, an unwillingness to give consideration to any negative intelligence, and the likelihood that they may be more prepared to take higher risks.*
- *Functional bias towards particular strategies is not uncommon, and in Fleur's case, the fact that the proposal was generated by the Marketing function could lead to a more favorable interpretation of the market feasibility studies and information.*
- *Another pressure that often impinges on the decision process at this stage is that of time. Executives in an organization such as Fleur will be particularly conscious of the rapid changes in the situation and especially the strategic developments by competitors.*
- *As Fleur discovered, the dynamics of the situation and the recognition that delay in making a decision itself may add further to the risk perceived. The organization needed to "manage" the risks, the collection of appropriate business intelligence, and the decision process itself.*

Business Intelligence and Risk Resolution

Seeking to amalgamate the strands of our discussion in terms of risk and the role of Business Intelligence in the digital economy leads to the conceptual model presented in *Figure 2*. This illustrates the three dimensions of individual/group/organizational behavior when confronted with risk in given decision situations:

- Risk perception influences the desire or willingness to seek further resolution of the decision situation faced, both in terms of the context and the decision specific variables (i.e., understanding changes in the competitive environment in general will resolve risks for a number of decisions, though the influence of these may be contingent on the specific decision variables involved).

- Desire to identify and measure the risks in some way, either objectively or subjectively, as a means to increasing confidence/reducing risk.
- Information search and processing viewed as the natural approach to aiding the decision makers in identifying and measuring risks and consequently changing their risk perception (i.e., seeking to enhance resolution of the risks faced).

These three dimensions are closely interrelated in the sense that changes in one may result in activities in the other. For example, intelligence gleaned about a particular competitive development is likely to modify the existing risk perception, leading to further information search, risk identification, and measurement. The final parameter included in the *Figure*, risk management, is increasingly viewed as an integral element of the risk and decision making by individuals and organizations. Risk management may be undertaken prior to the decision itself (e.g., insuring against certain risks) or after the decision (i.e., effective management of relationships with customers to reduce the likely incidence of disputes).

Risk Management Consequences

These uncertainties and risks place new demands on the field of risk management, indicating that the conventional methods of managing uncertainty (e.g., buffer stocks, spare capacity, quoted lead times) are likely to be less effective in meeting the new demands and uncertainties. Managers may find it more difficult to avoid the risks resulting from increased global competition in their home or local markets. The preparedness of the decision makers and the consequences for their behavior when undertaking decisions relating to global and international competition are seen as significant consequences of the expected developments.

INDIVIDUAL DECISION-MAKING BEHAVIOR

Three perspectives of individual behavior in decision making are examined in this section: the process of making a decision and the impact on risk measurement and perception; the factors that influence and modify risk perceptions; and impact of information processing on the individual's risk resolution.

Modifying Risk Perceptions

The analysis of decision-making behavior may be divided into three elements: risk perception, risk propensity, and risk preparedness. It is often the case that studies focus on one of the three elements rather than taking an integrated approach. There is also no general agreement on whether risk is the result of a particular personality trait, a social construct, or a behavioral construct. However, it seems apparent that risk is present in the decision situation context, personality traits, and the specific decision (personal/individual). Yet, the studies on risk implicitly suggest that changes in the context or changes in access to opportunities and/or support mechanisms can facilitate change. The assumption that the changes in attitude/behaviour are simply a product of risk factors is misleading. There are obvious changes occurring in the external world, i.e., in terms of social structures that influence risk. Personality traits may possibly reinforce other risk influences.

The process of decision making may be configured in a variety of ways depending on the purpose of the analysis, though the key elements are common. The approach adopted in this chapter and illustrated in *Figure 3* identifies the major components in the corporate decision process to purchase a product or service. Selecting a particular product or service and committing expenditure to acquire this involves elements of uncertainty and risk for the consumer.

Figure 3: Modifying Risk Perceptions

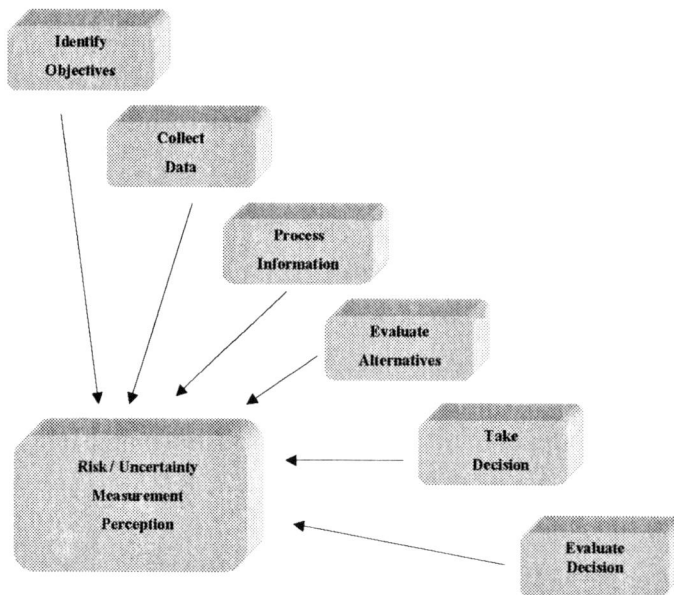

Arguably, the more significant the purchase (either in financial terms or in personal authority terms), the greater the uncertainty and risk associated with the purchasing process (e.g., Helliar, Lonie, Power, & Sinclair, 2001).

The key proposition, originating from the Risk Management field (Ritchie & Marshall, 1993), is that the uncertainty and risk perceived is influenced at every stage in the process of decision making and in the post-decision analysis. This proposition rests on the view that uncertainty/risk perception will evolve as the decision process itself develops, the key being the use of information or intelligence by the decision maker both in terms of the data provided and the assimilation methods employed. The latter stages in the process may involve a degree of post-decision rationalization of the decision made and the uncertainties/risks involved. The decision maker will seek to manage or fully resolve any residual risks as the decision is implemented and may also seek the necessary evidence to support the initial decision (i.e., a form of self-reinforcement that the correct decision was made, combined with a personal insurance policy should the decision fail to deliver the desired outcomes). The development of experience and learning resulting from the decision process is somewhat complex and untested as few studies have really focused on the learning process and its effect on uncertainty/risk. It is nevertheless an important dimension influencing repeat decisions and recommendations to others facing potentially similar decision situations.

Factors Influencing Risk Perception

Throughout this process, the individual is seeking information to remove the uncertainties and to resolve the risks involved in the decision. There are, however, a series of factors that will reduce the individual's effectiveness and efficiency in achieving these goals and gaining enhanced confidence concerning the decision. The factors that contribute to the uncertainty and risk perceived by the individual may be represented in the form shown in *Figure 4*.

Six main groups of components have been identified in the figure:

- *Direct implications:* The costs, benefits and other outcomes to the decision situation that are directly attributable to the decision and may be assessed with a reasonable degree of certainty.
- *Decision attributes:* There are a further set of outcomes to any decision that are known with less certainty (e.g., the reactions of peers and colleagues to given decisions and the manner in which the decision was addressed).

Figure 4: Factors Influencing Risk Perception

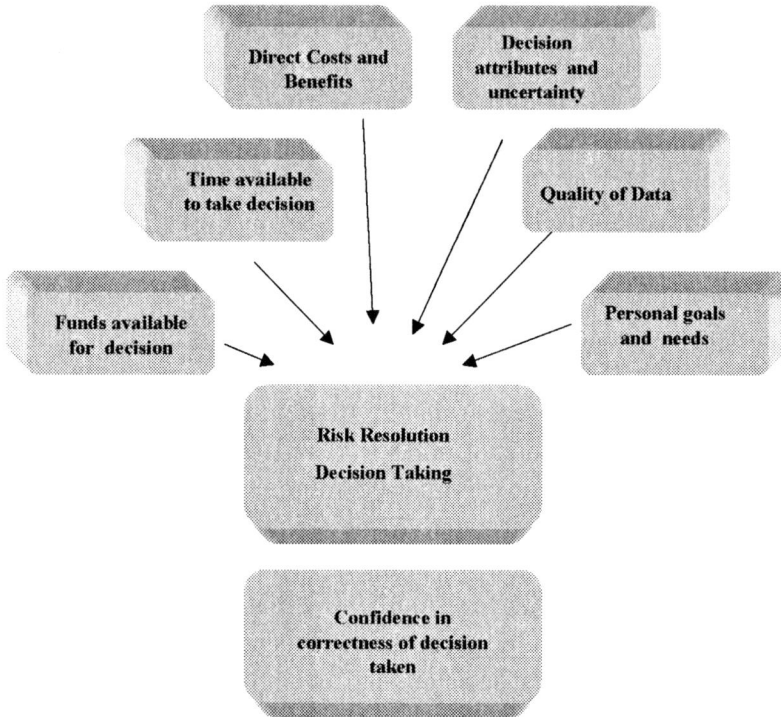

- *Time availability:* Most decisions are made within a constrained timeframe, though there is often evidence that this may be dictated more by the individual in terms of time management than imposed from outside.
- *Money available:* A further constraint on any decision is the funding available to undertake the research, analysis, and evaluation processes involved. The decision maker may often have a view of the information and the analysis he or she wants to undertake but may be constrained by the cost implications. Clearly, the advent of the digital economy has transformed many of the parameters associated with cost and availability of information.
- *Personal Goals:* The requirement to satisfy a diverse range of non-complementary goals tends to enhance the feeling of risk associated with the decision.
- *Quality of the Data:* Data quality may significantly influence the nature of the risks perceived and enhance or alternatively diminish the uncertainty perceived. *(Ritchie & Brindley, 2000)*

The integration and interaction of many of these components increase the complexity of the model (represented in *Figure 4*) in terms of risk perception and decision behavior. For example, although funding may be available to undertake intensive research, the pressures of time to respond to a given situation may preclude such activities even though they may be considered desirable. For example, the decision to hire a taxi may often be a reaction to time pressures, precluding consideration of other forms of less expensive transport.

Two other important dimensions to this model (*Figure 4*) should be noted. Each component has the capacity to generate new potential options for the decision makers' consideration. For example, the investigation of personal banking services may reveal a range of possible alternative services, each satisfying different dimensions of the consumer's needs. Equally, the components themselves may identify new sources of risk or make the scale of already identified risks more evident. This process of searching for solutions will generate more options and simultaneously more risks, thus making the decision process potentially more complex. For this very reason we might expect the decision maker to limit or constrain this search process to limit the options for consideration, to leave uncovered certain risks, and to keep the decision model less complex. An important conclusion would be that the decision process might become more complex as more dimensions of the decision are explored through the corporate intelligence systems available. Indeed, it is possible to envisage a situation in which decision makers may become frustrated at the increased complexity and uncertainty arising from their own decision to undertake a more rigorous search.

Information Processing and Risk Resolution

Developing the discussion in the previous section towards the information processing behavior of the individual could result in the process described in *Figure 5*. In seeking to resolve the risks in a given situation, the decision maker will search for appropriate information, process, analyze, evaluate, and synthesize this with other information relating to the situation. The contribution of the Digital Economy is most evident not only in providing the initial intelligence but in assisting the decision maker to process and manipulate the data prior to the decision-making stage. It is suggested that the decision maker either consciously or subconsciously assesses whether the risks have been sufficiently resolved or not. In many respects, this may be posing the question concerning one's own degree of confidence in proceeding with the decision, though it may also be influenced by the factors identified in *Figure 3*, discussed earlier.

An assessment that the risks had not been adequately resolved would normally result in further information search, analysis, synthesis, etc., repeating this cycle until the individual believed the risks had been sufficiently resolved to proceed. It is unlikely that the decision maker would achieve the situation where he or she was fully confident concerning risk resolution. The probable outcome, even after seeking further risk resolution, is that of having to make the decision even though the risks are not fully resolved as a consequence of time constraints, lack of resources to pursue further information, or the feeling that further search is unlikely to prove cost-effective. This is probably a very common outcome reflected in the statements of many decision makers that "there are many other angles that we ought to explore, but we no longer have the time to do so."

In situations where the decision maker considers that the risks have been adequately resolved one might conclude that the normal procedure would be to proceed with the decision. Another possible outcome could be suggested where the decision maker decides to delay the decision. This may be simply a reluctance to commit oneself even if one is fairly clear and confident of the decision to be made. Alternatively, the delay may reflect a more deliberate tactic of waiting for changes in the decision situation in order to assess the likely responses of other participants in the competitive situation or perhaps with the hope that someone else may take on the decision-making responsibility.

The making of a decision is no longer viewed as the concluding stage in the process. Attention is increasingly being addressed at the post-decision activities; these are undertaken to ensure that the opportunity is taken to avoid potential risks anticipated in the decision process, to avoid risks seen as less likely to impact on the situation, and to minimize the likelihood and consequences of those risks seen as more likely to occur. A generic term for these activities is *Risk Management* (see *Figure 5*). Examples of Risk Management activities include:

- Insuring against the financial consequences of particular outcomes;
- Developing formal contractual arrangements with trading partners to limit scope for non-predicted behavior;
- Training and staff development;
- Communication of intentions within the appropriate internal and external networks to ensure involvement and commitment (e.g., relationship marketing);
- Detailed planning, monitoring and control at all stages; and

Figure 5: Information Processing and Risk Resolution

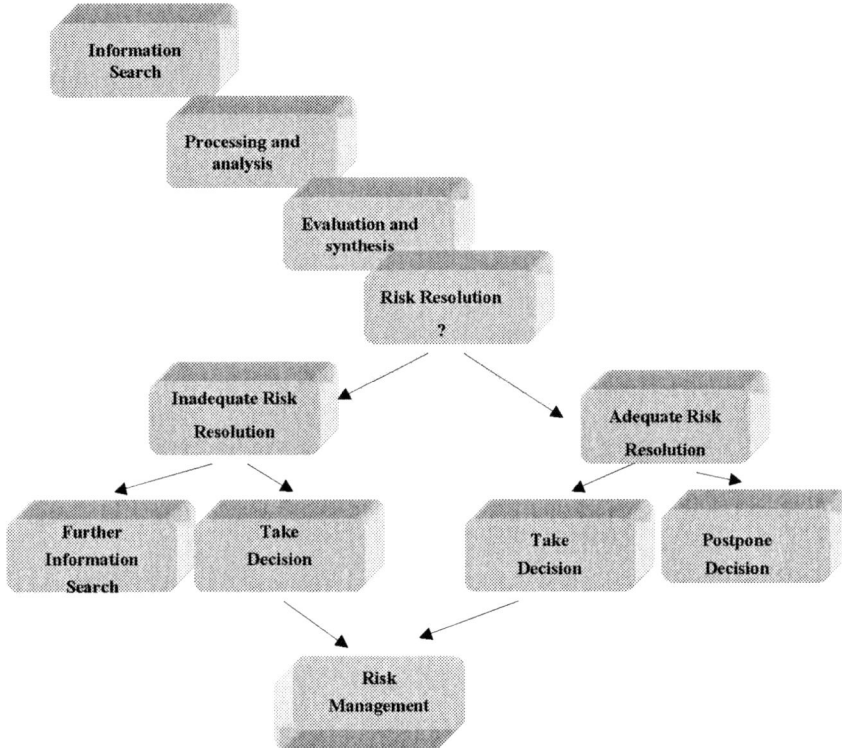

- Building close relationships with key partners to generate a sense of common purpose and trust (e.g., partnering).

An important element in developing more effective Risk Management strategies is the ability to communicate effectively at all levels, both within the organization and with external partners. The Digital Economy and the associated ICT developments have provided improved capability in this respect.

The elements of all three perspectives (i.e., modifying risk perception; the factors that influence and modify risk perceptions; and the impact of information processing on the individual's risk resolution) of the decision-making process and behavior outlined in *Figures 3*, *4*, and *5* were the subject of an empirical research study. Although the research itself was centered on a specific strategic decision scenario, the findings should have application within a much broader set of decision situations within organizations. Empirical studies (e.g., Ritchie & Brindley, 2001) have revealed significantly different search behavior patterns reflecting a number of the components outlined previously in *Figure 4*. For example, some individuals might perform a rigorous and methodical search of the entire database available, while others might be content to skim the database exploring only a very few elements in depth. Others display particular preferences for types of information, some displaying a preference for externally oriented information while others preferred internally available data. Such information search behavior patterns are probably a reflection of the individual's personality traits, prior knowledge/background, and perhaps not totally surprising. Evidence seems to suggest that prior knowledge, understanding, and analytical skills were important factors in determining the depth of the interrogation undertaken. However, the overwhelming reason seems to relate to the individual's decision-making style and experiences. Another significant finding from previous studies was the robustness of the original risk perceptions made by individuals, even in the light of highly contradictory information. This suggests that decision makers are less likely to modify initial impressions of a given situation and the associated risk perceptions made. The consequences for business intelligence and the Digital Economy itself are perhaps less certain. Search patterns will not follow any predictable pattern in generic terms, and many users will only "skim" the data available, not only because of a real lack of time or prior knowledge but also because of their normal search behavior patterns. Interestingly, all of the participants in the empirical study (Ritchie & Brindley, 2001) declared themselves satisfied with their data search and analysis. All of them displayed a relatively high degree of confidence in the decision made and very few would have wished to spend more time or effort in researching the decision or the alternatives available. In the process of post-decision rationalization many of those involved had formulated in their own minds the possible contingency strategies to adopt if certain predicted events or situations did not materialize as they had predicted. These actions were in essence risk management strategies (e.g., change own pricing strategy in response to aggressive pricing strategy from competitors).

CONCEPTUAL MODEL OF RISK RESOLUTION AND RISK MANAGEMENT WITHIN THE DIGITAL ECONOMY

The developments of the Digital Economy are likely to fundamentally alter the basis of competition for organizations and enhance their risk exposure. This will impact on organizations irrespective of their size, geographic location, or sector. The Digital Economy will also facilitate solutions and opportunities for these organizations to resolve and manage the new risks. These changes in the nature of the business operations and risks are likely to lead to specific challenges for the organizations in the Digital Economy:

1. There are potentially fundamental changes in the marketplace as a consequence of providing more direct communications with the consumer. For example, we may anticipate greater rather than lesser heterogeneity in the market in terms of consumer needs and behavior and a movement in the balance of power towards the consumer as opposed to the manufacturer or service provider. The potential consumer is likely to be in a position to access identical information concerning potential goods and services via the Web from across the globe and to undertake negotiations on quality, delivery, and payments at first hand, irrespective of where the supplier is based geographically. Likewise, other members of the existing supply chains may access such business intelligence as a prelude to developing their own strategies and tactics for disintermediation, including direct access to the final customer.

2. The expectation that the individual/organization will seek to resolve risks in a rational and structured manner is unlikely to occur. Conventionally, the emphasis has been on information search, corporate business intelligence, and evaluation of information and hence changes in risk perception leading to a decision. If the demand for corporate intelligence is less predictable in terms of occurrence, search patterns, and the impact of the information gained, this will have significant implications for the development and design of business intelligence systems.

3. The prediction that the Digital Economy will lead to improved decisions by providing improved access to information and processing capabilities may be less sustainable given the other confounding issues present (e.g., individual decision-making behavior patterns).

4. Changes in the modus operandi of competitive and business relationships within the Digital Economy will in themselves change the nature and extent of risks faced. Significantly, for organizations this may mean exposure to new types of risk that they have not previously experienced (e.g., competition from international organizations operating in different sectors) and that are likely to occur with much greater speed.

5. The capability to manage these new risks is not solely dependent on the information available and its accessibility. Development and training of the individual in terms of the appropriate knowledge, skills, and behavior

patterns (i.e., the manner in which information is sought and processed) is a necessary prerequisite to utilizing the potential intelligence available on the Web.

6.   The nature of what constitutes "effective" risk management may well change in the Digital Economy. There is evidence (e.g., Ritchie & Brindley, 1999) to demonstrate that the whole nature of the competitive structure is undergoing fundamental change. This has implications for risk management and associated dimensions of relationship marketing.

The Digital Economy removes a number of barriers that were founded on the lack of business intelligence or more precisely the access to it. The ability of all to access relatively similar data sources with no significant cost differentials poses new threats, opportunities, and challenges to all existing competitive situations and business relationships. The net effect is a fundamental change in the nature of the risks faced and the likelihood that the marketplace will become increasingly turbulent (i.e., the degree of predictability and hence confidence based on previous knowledge and experience may no longer be an asset for the decision maker), unstable, and risk prone. Managers now need to be equipped with improved knowledge, skills, and understanding to be able to identify, analyze, and manage these developments and to assess the consequences and risks arising from the more diverse range of market contexts. Equally important is the need to develop and employ a wider set of risk management strategies to ameliorate the consequences of the incidence of risks and their consequences. Fortunately, ICTs and the Digital Economy provide the necessary resources and solutions to facilitate this improvement in risk management.

REFERENCES

Bettis, R.A. (1982). Risk considerations in modelling corporate strategy. *Academy of Management Proceedings*, 22-25.

Birley, S., & Westhead, P. (1994). A taxonomy of business start-up reasons and their impact on firm growth and size. *Journal of Business Venturing*, 9, 7-31.

Blume, M.E. (1971). On the assessment of risk. *Journal of Finance*, 26(1), 1-10.

Busenitz, L.W. (1999). Entrepreneurial risk and strategic decision making: It's a matter of perspective. *The Journal of Applied Behavioral Science*, 35(3), 325-340.

Chung, J.T. (1998). Risk reduction in public accounting firms: Are women more effective? *International Review of Women and Leadership*, 4(1), 39-45.

Clotfelter, C.T., & Cook, P.J. (1989). *Selling Hope*. Cambridge, MA: Harvard University Press.

Dowling, R.G., & Staelin, R. (1994). A model of perceived risk and intended risk-handling activity. *Journal of Consumer Research*, 21(1), 119-25.

Forlani, D., & Mullins, J.W. (2000). Perceived risks and choices in entrepreneurs' new venture decisions. *Journal of Business Venturing*, 15(4), 305-322.

Ghosh, D., & Ray, M.R. (1997). Risk, ambiguity and decision choice: Some additional evidence. *Decision Sciences*, 28(1), 81-104.

Helliar, C., Lonie, A., Power, D., & Sinclair, D. (2001). Attitudes of UK managers to risk and uncertainty. *Balance Sheet*, 9(4), 7-10.

Kahnemann, D., & Lovallo, D. (1993). Timid choices and bold forecasts: A cognitive perspective on risk taking. *Management Science*, 39(1), 17-31.

Kalakota, R., & Robinson, M. (2000). *e-Business*. Reading, MA: Addison-Wesley Longman.

Knight, F.H. (1921). *Risk, Uncertainty and Profit*. Boston and New York: Houghton Mifflin Company.

MacCrimmon, K.R., & Wehrung, D.A. (1986). *Taking Risks: The Management of Uncertainty*. New York: Free Press.

March, J.G., & Shapira, Z. (1987). Managerial perspectives on risk and risk taking. *Management Science*, 33(11), 1404-1418.

Masters, R. & Meier, R. (1988). Sex differences and risk-taking propensity of entrepreneurs. *Journal of Small Business Management*, 26(1), 31-35.

McCarthy, B. (2000). The cult of risk taking and social learning: A study of Irish entrepreneurs. *Management Decision*, 38(8), 563-575.

Ritchie, R.L., & Brindley, C.S. (2001). The information-risk conundrum. *Marketing Intelligence and Planning*, 19(1), 29-37.

Ritchie, R.L., & Brindley, C.S. (1999). Relationship marketing as an effective approach to organisational risk management strategies. *Proceedings of the Fourth International Conference on the Dynamics of Strategy*, (April 22-23, Surrey, 1, pp. 313-323).

Ritchie, R.L., & Marshall, D.V. (1993). *Business Risk Management*. London: Chapman and Hall.

Rowe, W.D. (1977). *Anatomy of Risk*. New York: Wiley.

Rycroft, R.W., & Kash, D.E. (1999). *The Complexity Challenge*. London: Pinter Publishers.

Sexton, D., & Bowman-Upton, N. (1990). Female and male entrepreneurs: Psychological characteristics and their role in gender-related discrimination. *Journal of Business Venturing, 5*(1), 29-36.

Shapira, Z. (1995). *Risk Taking: A Managerial Perspective*. New York: Russell Sage.

Simon, M., Houghton, S.M., & Aquino, K. (2000). Cognitive biases, risk perception and venture formation — Implications of interfirm (mis)perceptions for strategic decisions. *Journal of Business Venturing, 15*(2), 113-134.

Sitkin, S.B., & Pablo, A.L. (1992). Reconceptualizing the determinants of risk behaviour. *Academy of Management Review*, 17(1), 9-38.

Stewart, W.H., Watson, W.E., Carland, J.C., & Carland, J.W. (1999). A proclivity for entrepreneurship — Determinants of company success. *Journal of Business Venturing*, 14(2), 189-214.

Swash, G. (1998). UK business information on the Internet. *New Library World*. 99(1144), 238-242.

Zsidisin, G.A., & Smith, M. (2002). Early supplier involvement as an approach to reducing supply risk in supply chain risk: A Reader. (forthcoming).

Chapter II

Intelligent Agents for Competitive Advantage:
Requirements and Issues

Mahesh Raisinghani, University of Dallas, USA

John H. Nugent, University of Dallas, USA

"The test of a first-rate intelligence is the ability to hold two opposed ideas in mind at the same time and still retain the ability to function."

- F. Scott Fitzgerald

ABSTRACT

This chapter presents a high-level model for employing intelligent agents in business management processes, much like has been successfully accomplished in complex telecommunications networks, in order to gain competitive advantage by timely, rapidly, and effectively using key, unfiltered measurements to improve cycle-time decision making. The importance of automated, timely, unfiltered (versus "end of period" filtered) reports is highlighted, as are some management issues relative to the pressures that may result concerning an organization's employees who must now take action in near real time. Furthermore, the authors hope that understanding the underlying assumptions and theoretical constructs through the use of employing intelligent agents in business management processes as a sub element of, or tool within Business Intelligence (BI), will not only inform researchers of a better design for studying information systems, but also assist in the understanding of intricate relationships between different factors.

INTRODUCTION TO MEASUREMENT AND REPORTING SYSTEMS

Since 1494 and the appearance of the double-entry accounting system (the development of which is accredited to an Italian by the name of Pacioli), those involved in business have attempted to measure business performance in an organized manner. As many accounting functions are repetitive in nature (e.g., payroll, inventory, etc.), accounting was one of the first business disciplines to which early computing technology was applied. From this humble beginning, today we see comprehensive enterprise models that have been incorporated into ISO Standards in an attempt to build quality, capability, and uniformity into business enterprise systems. Supporting these models and systems is an effort to also launch the Extensible Business Reporting Language (XBRL), such that metadata models gain uniformity and make business information more readily accessible across systems and enterprises.

Yet despite all the gains and improvements in models and systems capabilities, many in management today are still dealing with stale data — that is, data presented at the end of a reporting period (month, quarter, year) versus as it is taking place. And even those entities that are slightly more advanced require their professionals to proactively seek out data between "end of period" reporting periods via making system requests for such data ("dynamic query").

This chapter addresses a concept for transitioning from an "end of period" reporting model to one based on "push agents" delivering to the pertinent manager information that is key to managing the enterprise in near real time in order to gain a substantive competitive advantage. The high-level model in *Figure 1* demonstrates the suggested movement from an "end of period" model to an automated push agent model, with an intermediate step already utilized in some enterprises that is a dynamic query model.

Comparing where we are today in business reporting practices with those practices being used in the virtual real time management of many telecommu-

Figure 1: Migration of Reporting Models for Competitive Advantage

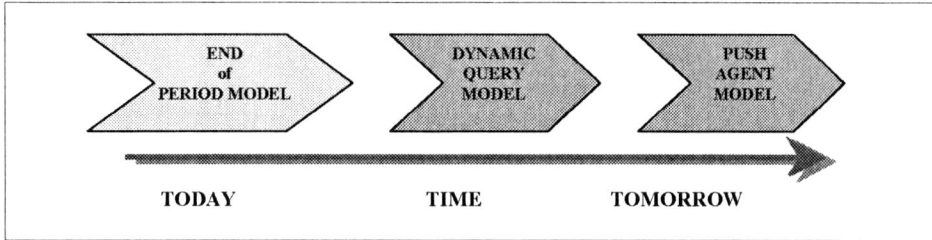

nications and IT networks, we see that comprehensive management tools have made great inroads in the efficient management of technical networks. For instance, Computer Associates (www.cai.com), perhaps the first to offer comprehensive, automated agents that forewarn of impending network trouble, introduced some time ago neural agents ("Neugents") that measure current states as they change against historical databases of past network activity in order to discern conditions that may be reoccurring and are similar to those that caused problems previously. Such detections may involve equipment failure to circuits becoming overloaded, with automated warnings and recommendations as to corrective actions being sent to the appropriate manager via the chosen message system (email, voicemail, paging, etc.).

Such "heads up," automated, near real-time reporting of impending conditions permits network operators to be proactive in addressing problems before they occur. So too in business reporting, it is becoming ever more important to gain insight into where the enterprise stands at any given moment in order to more competitively and effectively gain cycle-time advantages with near real-time reporting and alerts relative to deviations from plan. Such real-time network feedback requires an enterprise to develop "key performance indicators" (KPIs) or key measurements that it wishes to track against plan and run the enterprise. Here, many products are on the market that address the principles for such KPIs and go by such names as "Cockpit Charts," "Digital Dashboards," and "Balanced Scorecards." The secret of the balanced scorecard and the reason it has gained such wide acceptance is primarily due to the fact that it allows organizations to reach their full potential by putting strategy — the key driver of results today — at the center of the management process in organizations facing uncertain equity markets, an accelerating pace of change and increased expectations for productivity and concomitant results. However, just having a strategy is not adequate; rather implementing strategy for results in a strategy-focused organization is the key. These traditional KPI

Table 1: Comparative Characteristics of Reporting Models

	Business Models				Network Model
Type of Reporting	End of Period	Dynamic Query	Push/Pull Agents		Pull/Push Agents
Timeliness of Data	Stale	Near Real time	Near Real time		Near Real time
Potential for Managerial Filtering	Yes	Yes	No		No
Delivery Choice	No	Not Typically	YES		YES
Alerts	No	Not typically	YES		YES
Silo Issues	No	Possibly	No		No

identification and management processes lack the removal of people, delay, potential human filtering, and massaging of information from the reporting process of this enterprise critical function. The comparative characteristics of reporting models are listed in *Table 1*.

Instead of waiting for end of period reports, critical measures can be monitored in near real time as a function of the KPIs assigned to each measure as seen in *Figure 2*.

BENEFITS OF EMPLOYING A BUSINESS MANAGEMENT PROCESS INTELLIGENT AGENT TOPOLOGY

Erik Thomsen, Distinguished Scientist at Hyperion Solutions Corporation (2002) defines the term "agent" as "a solution-oriented ensemble of capabilities including natural language processing, autonomous reasoning, proactive com-

Figure 2: Simplified Intelligent Agent Push Model

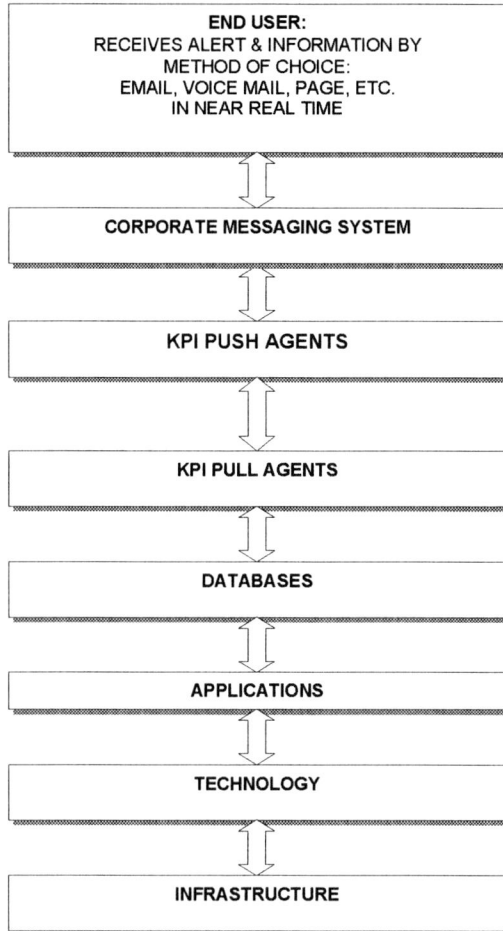

```
┌─────────────────────────────────────────┐
│              END USER:                   │
│   RECEIVES ALERT & INFORMATION BY        │
│           METHOD OF CHOICE:              │
│    EMAIL, VOICE MAIL, PAGE, ETC.         │
│          IN NEAR REAL TIME               │
└─────────────────────────────────────────┘
                  ⇕
┌─────────────────────────────────────────┐
│      CORPORATE MESSAGING SYSTEM          │
└─────────────────────────────────────────┘
                  ⇕
┌─────────────────────────────────────────┐
│            KPI PUSH AGENTS               │
└─────────────────────────────────────────┘
                  ⇕
┌─────────────────────────────────────────┐
│            KPI PULL AGENTS               │
└─────────────────────────────────────────┘
                  ⇕
┌─────────────────────────────────────────┐
│              DATABASES                   │
└─────────────────────────────────────────┘
                  ⇕
┌─────────────────────────────────────────┐
│             APPLICATIONS                 │
└─────────────────────────────────────────┘
                  ⇕
┌─────────────────────────────────────────┐
│              TECHNOLOGY                  │
└─────────────────────────────────────────┘
                  ⇕
┌─────────────────────────────────────────┐
│            INFRASTRUCTURE                │
└─────────────────────────────────────────┘
```

puting, discourse modeling, knowledge representation, action-oriented semantics, multimodal interaction, environmental awareness, self awareness, and distributed architectures." He describes the following five areas where the potential impact of intelligent agents on the logical functionality and physical performance of traditional business analytic systems can be positive:

1.   Agents should help move Business Intelligence (BI) from being application centric to being truly process centric and provide a single point-of-access to distributed information. This is operationalized in intelligent agent solutions by self description of individual modules that is made available to the system of agents as a whole and a user's personal agent being able to query all librarian agents responsible for various data sets in an organization for specific information.

2. An active dialog between the software and the user to seek out and learn user wants and be able to anticipate/predict user wants in future. Thus in addition to tailoring client layers to individual users and enhancing BI applications with options and preferences, the software/intelligent software agent plays an active role in querying the user.
3. As attention shifts to business process as much as data states, the number-centric BI applications will have to provide more integrated text and multimedia handling. One of the focal points of intelligent agent solutions is merging this multimedia data within the context of a single interaction.
4. Intelligent software agents can provide personal analytic "coaching" for higher level business processes by observing, learning about, and interacting with users. Agent applications within an overall BI/Business Process Management (BPM) framework can be deployed to encode horizontal and domain-specific analytic knowledge (i.e., how to select dimensions for a particular business problem, or how to perform sensitivity analysis on the choice of weighting factors for a particular indicator).
5. Last but not the least, the server side of most BI applications is very complex due to the changes in the load patterns/factors and the wide range of physical tuning options. Intelligent physical optimizers can evaluate their own physical organization and, optionally, interact with an administrator before performing any reorganization.

A survey by Lederer, Mirchandani, and Sims (1998) indicates that businesses adopting Web-based information systems (WISs) responded that the most important benefit of being on the Web was to "enhance competitiveness or create strategic advantage." Intelligent online agents can help simplify complex Web environments acting as artificial secretaries (Maes, 1994). Nwana, Rosenschein, Sandholm, Sierra, Maes, and Guttman (1998) define agents as "software entities that have been given sufficient autonomy and intelligence to enable them to carry out specified tasks with little or no human supervision." There is no standard definition for intelligent agents, but they are generally described (Decker, Pannu, Sycara, & Williamson, 1997; Hendler, 1996; Specter, 1997) as programs that act on behalf of their human users to perform laborious and routine tasks such as locating and accessing necessary information, resolving inconsistencies in the retrieved information, filtering away irrelevant and unwanted information, and integrating information from heterogeneous information sources.

Business-intelligence (BI) software using intelligent agents and BI technologies such as data marts/warehouses, data mining, website analytics, modeling and predictive tools, and data visualization tools can help analyze customer data to make connections that can boost sales, increase efficiency, and keep customers. The BI server connects to the data sources and provides analytical services to clients, who access the BI server through a Web interface or other desktop client. An application server typically provides the Web interface and often runs on the same server as the BI software. For example, a research company used BI tools to correlate the prescriptions written by doctors based on such esoteric variables as the weather and day of the week. Armed with that information, the company provided valuable marketing data to pharmaceutical companies. Also, a Fortune 500 insurance company used BI tools to create new products targeted at specific demographics within their existing customer base.

The key benefits of employing a business management process intelligent agent topology are as follows:

- Timeliness of reports;
- Automated measurements against planned goals;
- Unfiltered information; and
- Delivery based on the end-user's preference.

The key features that should be analyzed when evaluating BI reporting tools are as follows:

- *Analysis:* The ease in creating reports and the end-user's ability to manipulate the report once distributed;
- Formats and data sources supported;
- *Data access:* Preferably provide data-attribute-level security; and
- *Price:* This can be compared based on a given number of users, administrators, report creators, and server deployment on a specific hardware configuration.

To enable enterprises to better track and manage cross-departmental performance, BI vendors are rolling out frameworks designed to help them integrate and leverage multiple existing BI systems and analytic capabilities. Theoretically, this enables a powerful enterprise-wide management tool for optimizing performance and profits. However, in practice, there are challenges associated with these frameworks that range from data acquisition, cleansing, and metadata management to aligning models and delivering performance management BI capabilities scalably, securely, and flexibly across diverse user interfaces, dashboards, and portals.

POTENTIAL DRAWBACKS OF EMPLOYING A BUSINESS MANAGEMENT PROCESS INTELLIGENT AGENT TOPOLOGY

The pressures on the management team to act in near real time on automated business measurements without detailed analysis are intense. Executives often struggle to integrate multiple data sources that can then be analyzed and synthesized for financial reporting. For example, inventory data may be stored in the data warehouse while sales information is housed elsewhere. Or an executive may want to link financial reports from multiple divisions and compare them with industry benchmarks as part of financial reporting. In addition, executives may want to close their books as often as daily, without having to wait until the end of the month to address a problem that could affect revenue or earnings forecasts.

Business intelligence tools are best suited for allowing executives to drill down into the source of financial reports to review their accuracy. For example, if an employee forgets to book an order in an order management system but later makes the adjustment in the general ledger, a BI tool could help find the discrepancy in the revenue figures. In this situation, the source of the information may be a flag to start investigating further and if anomalies are found, it is critical to drill into the support data to determine the reason. However, a majority of BI systems would be hard-pressed to catch someone intent on committing fraud if the data was entered correctly in the data capture system.

Enterprise application vendors also are adding analytics to back-end financial systems to help companies better leverage raw transactional data. For example, PeopleSoft has embedded analytics in its financial module designed to report to executives on a daily basis the status of KPIs. Executives and line managers can receive color-coded reports highlighting any variances from performance goals, and cost controls can be embedded in the system to ensure that budgetary limits are not exceeded.

Executives have little time to analyze data before senior management inquiries begin, and they need visibility across the internal and extended supply chain to have the control in their organization. As making BI accessible across the enterprise becomes increasingly important, embedding analytics into enterprise applications — as SAP AG, Siebel Systems Inc., and PeopleSoft Inc. have already done or are working to do — is gaining popularity. With a broader audience, the need for more detailed intelligence will drive analytics that are targeted not only at specific vertical industries, but at specific departments and roles. However, the dangers of creating more analytic silos cannot be overemphasized, and it is pertinent to ensure that business rules and metadata remain consistent across all applications.

It is prudent to remember that pressure to act may result in erroneous actions. As the economic downturn of the last couple of years has illustrated, business survival depends on an infrastructure that can adapt to changing market conditions. With companies focused on leveraging existing resources and increasing efficiency, infrastructure is no longer just an operational cost of doing business. Meta Group predicts "infrastructure development will be a key strategic IT discipline through 2005" with special emphasis on adaptability, robustness, and affordability (Burriesci, Kestelyn, & Young, 2002). Solution providers are paying attention to this growing need for intelligent infrastructure, with companies such as Network Appliance Inc. and WebMethods Inc. partnering with BI vendors to bring new abilities to their solutions, such as storage analytics and business activity monitoring, that can help companies realize the full potential of their resources.

CONCLUSION

This chapter conceptualizes the transition of intelligent agents utilized in network performance management into the field of business and management. A tiered IA system could be implemented at many levels of management and could be the key for successful, timely knowledge-management strategies and successes. Clearly the tools exist today to implement an IA system to monitor and timely report on KPIs in virtual real time, just as is done today in network monitoring and management with tools such as Computer Associates' "Neugents." Such a system would be timely, unbiased, and objective, and should provide significant competitive advantages. Moreover, such a system could leverage existing assets and provide a single objective measure of employee performance at appraisal time.

Although there has been some progress in increasing the number of users in the area of query and reporting, a lot more progress needs to be made in closing the loop between decision making and operations. Employees should be provided with some additional time to link decisions to operations via rules engines or rules transport — necessary for a closed loop system. IA benefits realized in telecommunications networks, grid computing, and data visualization for exploratory analysis connected to simulations should likewise be achievable in business management processes.

REFERENCES

Burriesci, J., Kestelyn, J., & Young, M. (2002). *The top 10 trends for 2003*. Retrieved on December 17, 2002 from http://www.intelligententerprise.com/030101/602news1.shtml.

Decker, K., Pannu, A., Sycara, K., & Williamson, M. (1997). Designing behaviors for information agents. *Proceedings of Autonomous Agents '97*, Marina del Rey, California (February 5-8, pp. 404-412).

Hendler, J. (1996). Intelligent agents: Where AI meets information technology. *IEEE Expert*, 11(6), 20-23.

Lederer, A. L., Mirchandandi, D.A., & Sims, K. (1998). Using WISs to enhance competitiveness. *Communications of the ACM*, (41)7, 94-95.

Maes, P. (1994). Agents that reduce work and information overload. *Communications of the ACM*, 37(7), 30-40.

Nwana, H., Rosenschein, J., Sandholm, T., Sierra, C., Maes, P., & Guttmann, R. (1998). Agent-mediated electronic commerce: Issues, challenges and some viewpoints. *Proceedings of the 2nd International Conference on Autonomous Agents*, Minneapolis, Minnesota (May 9-13, pp. 189-196).

Spector, L. (1997). Automatic generation of intelligent agent programs. *IEEE Expert*, 12(1), 3-4.

Thomsen, E. (2002, September 17). Agents uncovered. *Intelligent Enterprise*, 5(15), 45.

Chapter III

Data Mining and Knowledge Discovery

Andi Baritchi, Corporate Data Systems, USA

ABSTRACT

*In today's business world, the use of computers for everyday business processes and data recording has become virtually ubiquitous. With the advent of this electronic age comes one priceless by-product — **data**. As more and more executives are discovering each day, companies can harness data to gain valuable insights into their customer base. Data mining is the process used to take these immense streams of data and reduce them to useful knowledge.*

Data mining has limitless applications, including sales and marketing, customer support, knowledge-base development, not to mention fraud detection for virtually any field, etc. "Data mining," a bit of a misnomer, refers to mining the data to find the gems hidden inside the data, and as such it is the most often-used reference to this process. It is important to note, however, that data mining is only one part of the Knowledge Discovery in Databases process, albeit it is the workhorse. In this chapter, we provide a concise description of the Knowledge Discovery process, from domain analysis and data selection, to data preprocessing and transformation, to the data mining itself, and finally the interpretation and evaluation of the results as applied to the domain.

We describe the different flavors of data mining, including association rules, classification and prediction, clustering and outlier analysis, customer profiling, and how each of these can be used in practice to improve a business' understanding of its customers. We introduce the reader to some of today's hot data mining resources, and then for those that are interested, at the end of the chapter we provide a concise technical overview of how each data-mining technology works.

INTRODUCTION

In today's business world, the use of computers for everyday business processes and data recording has become virtually ubiquitous. With the advent of this electronic age comes one priceless by-product — *data*. Virtually every large corporation now records all transactions that take place, no matter how small or insignificant, and stores them in a large and complex data warehouse.

These data warehouses are growing at an ever-increasing rate, and there is no end in sight. Due to their sheer bulk, data warehouses are generally impossible to directly analyze by humans looking for interesting patterns or trends. In most cases, the data contained in the data warehouses is too valuable to simply purge or expire. Paradoxically, the data itself is worthless unless there is a method of analyzing it from the "big picture" perspective. Only from this perspective can the researcher or business person gain the very valuable secrets locked deep within the data.

Hence, there is an urgent need for tools that can analyze the data and search for interesting patterns or information that may be embedded below the surface. It is important to note that, in most large databases, there are virtually an infinite number of patterns available to extract, and extracting all of them would be no more helpful than browsing the large collection of raw data itself. The key is to mine the data for interesting patterns. These are the less obvious patterns in the data, those that provide some insight into underlying market trends, customer preferences, fault and fraud detection, and so forth.

To fulfill this need, researchers from the fields of artificial intelligence and database systems collaborated to design various approaches in the field of knowledge discovery to extract hidden patterns from data. In this chapter, we describe the knowledge-discovery process and highlight the procedures followed, which correspond to each knowledge-discovery step. The analysis of knowledge discovery focuses mainly on data mining and interpretation-evaluation steps.

As more and more executives are discovering each day, companies can harness data to gain valuable insights into their customer base. Data mining is the process used to take these immense streams of data and reduce them to useful knowledge.

Data mining has limitless applications, including sales and marketing, customer support, and knowledge-base development, not to mention fraud detection for virtually any field, etc.

Let's take a quick look at one of the sales and marketing possibilities using data mining. Consider Wal-Mart and the thousands if not millions of sales the company makes each day. Each sales receipt contains not just one item — most contain one or two-dozen items. You can bet that people have analyzed individual receipts to correlate what items people typically purchase together. Many are obvious, like cereal and milk. Others are less so, such as diapers and beer (yes, this trend has been found in past research of this type).

Obviously, this type of research can only be done on a small scale, and not for the billions of sales receipts that Wal-Mart has printed in the past, right? No! Knowledge Discovery in Databases/Data Mining, in this case mining for *association rules*, is the answer. With this technology, computers can quickly, effectively, and intelligently find these patterns that can then help Wal-Mart better lay out its stores, set its prices, and manage ordering for maximum profitability.

Knowledge Discovery in Databases

The application of the knowledge-discovery process to large databases for the purposes of extracting hidden patterns or knowledge in the data is called Knowledge Discovery in Databases (KDD). Generally, KDD is used in databases whose large size prevents humans from manually identifying the underlying patterns and extracting valuable knowledge.

Although still in its infancy, KDD is one of the fastest growing fields in computer science research and industry. KDD is currently employed for a multitude of applications, such as marketing, fraud detection, customer profiling for targeted advertising, new market trend discovery, and data classification. This list is growing rapidly as researchers discover new uses for this powerful data analysis method.

Formally defined by Fayyad, Piatetsky-Shapiro, Smyth, and Ramasamy (1996b, p.84), KDD is "the nontrivial process of identifying valid, novel, potentially useful, and ultimately understandable patterns in data." Note that, in this context, data are a collection of facts, and pattern is a higher-level expression that describes the data or some subset thereof.

In further analyzing the data, one comes across the qualifier on patterns that KDD identifies — they must be valid, novel, potentially useful, and ultimately understandable. A valid pattern is one that correctly describes the training data and also correctly describes new data with some degree of certainty. The stipulation that patterns be novel and potentially useful is intuitive; what good is a system that points out obvious yet irrelevant redundancies?

Finally, it is desirable for the discovered patterns to be ultimately understandable so they can be analyzed further to study their causes and effects.

KNOWLEDGE-DISCOVERY STEPS

According to Fayyad et al. (1996b), KDD is the process of using the database — along with any required selection, preprocessing, subsampling, and transformation of the data — to apply data-mining methods (algorithms), to enumerate patterns from the data, and to evaluate the products of data mining to identify the subset of the enumerated patterns deemed "knowledge." The KDD process can be divided into seven discrete steps, as shown in *Figure 1.*

Figure 1: KDD Process

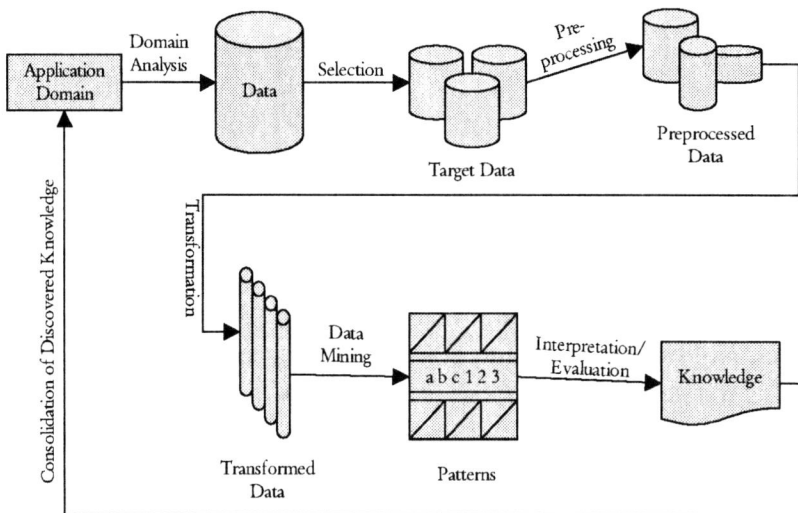

These seven steps, which collectively form the methodology of the KDD process, are explained as follows:

1. *Domain Analysis:* the nature of the data in the domain is analyzed and the goals of the discovery are considered. If any prior domain knowledge exists, it is evaluated.
2. *Selection:* the data is reduced to a target data set containing the desired data to analyze, which can mean eliminating fields or rows in the data, or both. The kind of discovery to be performed is also analyzed in this step.
3. *Preprocessing:* data is cleaned to remove noise, methodologies are defined to handle missing data fields, and so forth.
4. *Transformation:* a data representation is chosen that is compatible with the data-mining algorithm to be used. The data are analyzed to find useful features to represent the data depending on the goal of the task. Optionally, the data representation is then modified to account for temporal or spatial intricacies in the data.
5. *Data Mining:* a data-mining algorithm is chosen and applied to the preprocessed and transformed data to search for patterns of interest. Note that the performance and results of this step are greatly dependent on the quality of the preceding steps. Since the data-mining step is the workhorse of the KDD process, data mining will be explained further in this chapter.
6. *Interpretation and Evaluation:* the patterns discovered by the data-mining algorithm are interpreted by a human and evaluated for interestingness. They are then recorded in some easy-to-understand form.
7. *Consolidation of Discovered Knowledge:* the discovered patterns are put to good use. Plausible uses include incorporating the knowledge into another system for further action, documenting the patterns and reporting them to interested parties, and even reapplying KDD to the database using the new background knowledge.

Data Mining

This section concentrates on "data mining," the fifth step of the KDD process (see *Figure 1*). Data mining is the component of the KDD process that applies an algorithm to a preprocessed dataset to search for hidden patterns.

One category of data mining is predictive data mining. In predictive data mining, the goal is to find correlations between data fields; that is, predictive data mining uses a set of known variables to predict other unknown of future variables. Although predictive data mining is very important in some applications, it is not as important in KDD as is descriptive data mining.

Descriptive data mining is the second major category of data mining. In describing data mining as a step in the KDD process, attention is focused on descriptive data mining. The purpose of descriptive data mining is to discover, within the data, embedded patterns that describe the data.

Data mining is a broad field of data analysis and pattern discovery; in fact, there are numerous subfields of data mining. The list below outlines some of the major subcategories.

1.   *Classification:* learning a function *f* that, when given as input in a set of variables to represent a data record, maps (classifies) the record into one of several predefined classes (Hand, 1981; McLachlan, 1992; Weiss & Kulikowski, 1991). Classification is probably the most common application of data mining in business. Fraud detection, for example, is a prime candidate for the classification data mining. In this scenario, the classifier typically tries to identify transactions as being either legitimate or suspect. Other typical uses of classification data mining include credit scoring, customer profiling, and so forth. There are no limits to the possible uses of classification or the number of "buckets" into which the records can be classified.

2.   *Regression:* learning a function *f* that, when given as input in a set of variables to represent a data record, maps the record to a real-valued prediction variable. Note that regression is very similar to classification, with the exception that the function is mathematically more complex due to its non-discrete nature.

3.   *Clustering:* discovering groups (clusters) of similar items in the input data.

Clustering is useful in business because it can "look" at large collections of data and, on its own, begin to "sort out" the different groupings of similar records. This can be a useful step as a preamble to classification, i.e., to give guidance to the user as to the buckets for the classifier, or it can be used by itself for any number of purposes. For example, if clustering is applied to a list of user profiles, a framework of the different "types" of customers can be built. This has potential uses in marketing, customer support, and even fraud detection (i.e., if a cellphone user's behavior profile immediately jumps from one cluster to another, this could indicate a cellphone theft or cloning).

4. *Summarization:* finding a model that more compactly describes a part of the input data. Summarization data mining is used whenever a company wants to gain general insights, such as market trends, from their database. This is the type of data mining that most people think of when they think of data mining.
5. *Dependency modeling:* developing a model that describes significant structural or numerical dependencies between fields in the input data (Glymour, Scheines, Spirtes, & Kelly, 1987; Heckerman, 1996).
6. *Change and deviation detection:* keeping track of historical data and looking out for drastic changes. This task is often employed in the fraud detection.

TECHNICAL REVIEW OF DATA-MINING TECHNOLOGIES

This section describes the different methods of data mining and some systems that implement each of these methods.

Classification

Classification systems, useful in a wide variety of applications that deal with prediction, traditionally function as decision makers for a single attribute of the data. For a classifier to be used, it must first learn a mapping from a set of input variables and their values to the predicted output values for the decision variable. Once this mapping is learned using the training data, the classifiers can then be used to predict the value of the decision variable using the input values.

One method of implementing classifiers is a decision tree learning algorithm. Decision trees mirror the commonly used "flow chart" concept; that is, a decision tree represents a hierarchy of decisions, each of which leads to more decisions until the data can be classified. Traditionally, decision tree induction algorithms work on the concept of information theory, where attributes for splitting the tree are selected based on how much splitting the attribute separates the values of the classification variable. One such system that is widely used is the C4.5 algorithm (Quinlan, 1993). One pitfall of decision trees is that variables need to have a small number of possible values so that they can be effectively split, making decision trees ill-suited for continuous-valued numeric data. Although it is possible to work around this obstacle by dividing the range of possible values into a few discrete ranges, this introduces a loss of information.

Decision tables (Kohavi & Summerfield, 1998) are also popular for classification. Simpler than decision trees, decision table classifiers essentially compare the new data with training data, searching for training items that match the new items in terms of a small subset of input variables. These decision variables are chosen in the learning stage based on how well they split the classification variable into separate classes.

Another useful method for performing classification is the inductive logic programming (ILP) technique. ILP is the process of learning general theories from specific examples within the framework of causal logic. The popular ILP systems today approach the problem with a "separate-and-conquer" strategy (Quinlan & Cameron-Jones, 1995, p.288). In this method, each iteration looks for a new theory that describes a number of previously undescribed positive examples, without also erroneously describing negative examples. This methodology can be further subdivided into top-down and bottom-up approaches.

The top-down approach, where general rules are created first and then become more specific through multiple iterations, is employed by the FOIL system (Quinlan & Cameron-Jones, 1995). Interfacing with a Prolog database, FOIL takes in as input a set of all desired target relations as well as any available background knowledge. The resulting output is shown as a set of output clauses, also in Prolog notation.

GOLEM (Muggleton & Feng, 1992), on the other hand, takes the bottom-up approach to first order ILP by first generating specific rules for small sets of positive tuples and then generalizing these tuples in subsequent iterations. Another popular ILP system, Progol (Muggleton, 1995), has since replaced GOLEM. Progol takes a top-down approach like FOIL but also employs a mechanism called inverse entailment, which helps derive the most specific clause that entails a given example.

According to Quinlan and Cameron-Jones (1995), both top-down and bottom-up approaches have successfully processed very large databases at much higher speeds than early ILP systems. This large speed differential exists because these early ILP systems are based on a successive revision method, which can be likened to a brute-force exhaustive search.

Clustering

Clustering is a form of unsupervised learning that involves searching the input database for naturally occurring separations between data items. These separations divide the data into logical groups called clusters. Clusters are often employed for change and deviation detection, where the goal is to find data items that do not fall within the norm, or the clusters. Change and deviation detection applies to a multitude of fields, such as detecting fraudulent transactions (e.g., telephone or credit card fraud), detecting inappropriate medical treatment before it is too late, or noticing new market trends.

One particularly robust implementation of clustering is the Autoclass system (Cheeseman & Stutz, 1995), which employs a special form of clustering called Bayesian Clustering. Bayesian clustering works on the concept of automatic class discovery, where the goal is to find the most probable set of class descriptions (clusters) for the given input data and background knowledge; that is, Autoclass does not explicitly assign data items to clusters; rather, it assigns a membership probability for each item and class pair.

Association Rules

Association rules are designed to facilitate summarization (and classification in some cases) of the input data. Association rules accomplish these tasks by describing patterns that occur between variables; that is, they show how to predict the values of various fields in the data using the other fields. Association rules are expressed as implications between equality statements, such as: A=3 and B=5 $\rightarrow$ C = 4. Intuitively, it is apparent that they can be used for classification if the rules generated have the classification variable in the right-hand side of the implication. To describe association rules, the support of an itemset must be defined as the percentage of items in the database that are in the itemset, and the confidence of a rule (A $\rightarrow$ B) as the percentage of items in the set of items containing A that are also in the set of items containing both A and B.

Traditional association rule learners start by generating itemsets with minimum support and then growing these itemsets over multiple iterations. The growing is performed by adding another item from the input data to the itemsets at each iteration. After all the itemsets with minimum support are collected, rules are generated between these itemsets for all combinations of itemsets that generate rules with minimum or greater support and confidence.

The Apriori algorithm (Agrawal & Srikant, 1994) is the benchmark among association rule learning systems. Apriori takes the same basic approach as the traditional association rule algorithms described above, except that it does not look back at the input data when iterating to grow the itemsets with minimum support. Agrawal and Srikant noticed that, for any itemset with minimum support, every item-subset inside it must also have minimum support. Taking advantage of this clever realization, Apriori was made to only look at size k-1 itemsets (from the previous iteration) with minimum support when generating size k itemsets, rather than looking at all the input items again. This dramatically reduces the runtime of Apriori without reducing the quality or completeness of the results output by the algorithm.

Association rules are very useful in basket data analysis, where the goal is to try to notice associations or correlations between a set of items or objects in database transactions. They are not, however, very good at working with multi-valued attributes in databases. Furthermore, association rules tend to have the same pitfall described earlier for classifiers — they do not lend themselves well to continuous-valued attributes in the input data without discretization in preprocessing.

A GLANCE AT SOME POPULAR DATA MINING RESOURCES

As our background is primarily in designing and using our own data-mining algorithms, it is beyond the scope of this chapter to provide a review of popular commercial data-mining systems. That having been said, in this section we will attempt to introduce the reader to some popular resources and tools.

KDNuggets

KDNuggets.com is the authoritative source for everything "Data Mining, Knowledge Discovery, Genomic Mining, Web Mining." That is, at this great website, you can navigate your way to reading everything you ever wanted to know about knowledge discovery, at however technical a level you desire. You can find data-mining jobs, or data-mining professionals looking for them. Looking for data sets to test your data-mining system? They've got it. Want to find out what the most popular data-mining tools are out there? They list them.

Last but certainly not least, KDNuggets provides a newsletter that can keep you posted on the latest trends, news, and products in the Knowledge-Discovery community.

SPSS Clementine

Judged the most popular data-mining tool by KDNuggets polls for multiple years running, this application is touted to be the best because it is designed not around the data mining but around the business processes first. It has a full array of data-mining functionality built in like any other data-mining suite, but its "trump card" is supposedly its ability to best integrate this technology into real-world business intelligence.

Excel/Spreadsheets

Believe it or not, a lot of data mining gets done without a specific data-mining tool at all. According to the most recent KDNuggets poll, spreadsheets are still the fourth most popular data-mining tool used by knowledge-discovery professionals today. This indicates to us that flexibility of data manipulation is still paramount, and people still like to visually see and arrange their own data. This is an inefficient approach, however, as spreadsheets, while more powerful by the day, still cannot compete with true data-mining algorithms in terms of efficiency.

MORAL AND LEGAL ISSUES OF KNOWLEDGE DISCOVERY

All of KDD's awesome features do not come without a price. It is imperative that, when practicing KDD methods, scientists and industry users of the technology respect the privacy of individuals. Most database transactions in data warehouses are composed of relations between people, or between people and items. When mining these data, a scientist might discover things about people (subjects) described by the data that, perhaps, the subjects do not wish to be shared.

Because of privacy concerns, in many cases the data warehouses themselves are locked up and access to them is only granted to high-ranking individuals within the company. These individuals will, in most cases, sign some sort of nondisclosure agreement stipulating that they will not share the data with others outside the company (e.g., competitors). This can become a major roadblock for KDD professionals because it becomes difficult for them to get the data. Note that, when they do procure the data, they are responsible for respecting the privacy of the individuals described by the data, perhaps by hiding the real names and other identifying fields in the final discovered patterns.

In the context of personal business transactional data, these moral and legal issues are paramount. The data being analyzed are not only very revealing about specific users' habits, but also, once mined, they provide valuable secrets about the company's sales and supply infrastructure.

CONCLUSION

With the ever-increasing ubiquity of large databases in business, data mining, or more generally speaking Knowledge Discovery in Databases, can be a very powerful tool for the business user. It allows business to take these immense streams of data — their large databases — and reduce them to useful knowledge. This knowledge can be relating to the customer base, the product offered, or any combination thereof; there are no limits.

REFERENCES

Agrawal, R., & Srikant, R. (1994). Fast algorithms for mining association rules. *Proceedings of the 20th International Conference on Very Large Databases*, Santiago, Chile (September).

Baritchi, A. (1999). *Knowledge discovery in telecommunications data.* Masters Thesis, University of Texas at Arlington.

Baritchi, A., Cook, D. J., & Holder, L. B. (2000). Discovering structural patterns in telecommunications data. In the *Proceedings of the 13th Annual Florida AI Research Symposium.* Menlo Park, CA: AAAI Press/The MIT Press.

Cheeseman, P., & Stutz, J. (1995). Bayesian classification (AutoClass): Theory and results. *Proceedings of the First International Conference on Knowledge Discovery and Data Mining.* Menlo Park, CA: AAAI Press/The MIT Press.

Cook. D. J., & Holder, L. B. (2000). Graph-based data mining. *IEEE Intelligent Systems,* 15(2).

Fayyad, U.M., Piatetsky-Shapiro, G., & Smyth, P. (1996a). Knowledge discovery and data mining: Towards a unifying framework. *Proceedings of the Fourth Knowledge Discovery and Data Mining Conference.* Menlo Park, CA: AAAI Press/The MIT Press.

Fayyad, U.M., Piatetsky-Shapiro, G., Smyth, P., & Uthurusamy, R. (1996b). *Advances in Knowledge Discovery and Data Mining.* Menlo Park, CA: AAAI Press/The MIT Press.

Glymour, C., Scheines, R., Spirtes, P., & Kelly, K. (1987). *Discovering Casual Structure.* New York: Academic Press.

Hand, D. J. (1981). *Discrimination and Classification.* Chichester, UK: John Wiley & Sons.

Heckerman, D. (1996). *Bayesian Networks for Knowledge Discovery: Advances in Knowledge Discovery and Data Mining.* Menlo Park, CA: AAAI Press/The MIT Press.

Kohavi, R., & Sommerfield, D. (1998). Targeting business users with decision table classifiers. *Proceedings of the Fourth Knowledge Discovery and Data Mining Conference.* Menlo Park, CA: AAAI Press/The MIT Press.

McLachlan, G. (1992). *Discriminant Analysis and Statistical Pattern Recognition.* New York: Wiley.

Muggleton, S. (1995). Inverse entailment and progol. *New Generation Computing Journal, 13.*

Muggleton, S., & Feng, C. (1992). Efficient induction of logic programs. In S. Muggleton (Ed.), *Inductive Logic Programming,* (pp. 281-298). London: Academic Press.

Quinlan, J. R. (1993). *4.5: Programs for Machine Learning. The Morgan Kaufmann Series in Machine Learning.* San Francisco, CA: Morgan Kaufmann.

Quinlan, J. R., & Cameron-Jones, R.M. (1995). Induction of logic programs: FOIL and related systems. *New Generation Computing, 13,* 287-312.

Weiss, S. I., &. Kulikowski, C. (1991). *Computer Systems that Learn: Classification and Prediction Methods from Statistics, Neural Networks, Machine Learning, and Expert Systems.* San Francisco, CA: Morgan Kaufmann.

Chapter IV

Enterprise Information Management

Ulfert Gartz, PA Consulting Group, Germany

ABSTRACT

Although capacity and functionality of information management systems increased remarkably in the last years, the information and knowledge supply in most enterprises is still not sufficient. Using the framework of enterprise information management, organizations are able to align their existing data warehouse, business intelligence, knowledge management, and other information systems to their business processes and requirements. This means a consolidation on one hand and continuous processes to manage change on the other to improve these systems' sustainability and to decrease costs the same time.

INTRODUCTION

In comparison to other chapters in this book, the following will focus on the dependencies and impacts between business objectives and technology usage in the field of Information Management and Business Intelligence (BI). Because of changing business requirements and based on a substantial industry experience, there are several forces affecting the future development and usage of BI. This particularly applies to enterprises anticipating the opportunities of the Digital Economy.

Working for PA Consulting Group, my colleagues and I have helped many organizations to improve and optimize their Information Management and BI portfolio. In this chapter, we will summarize our project experience, key findings and recommendations for successful enhancement of enterprise decision support, and explain our approach of Enterprise Information Management (EIM).

After one decade of investment in Business Intelligence, the usage of tools and solutions for all aspects of decision support, planning, forecasting, and reporting has become a commodity in most industrial organizations. As experienced with operational systems before, the lack of flexibility to accommodate changing processes and increasing costs of operation for growing heterogeneous systems lead to disaffection both on the IT and business side.

The majority of data warehouse projects and BI initiatives still don't realize the perceived benefits. To make matters worse, in difficult economical times it has become more difficult to invest in BI projects because benefits are often non-financial or not measured easily and spread across different departments in the organization.

Taking into account the opportunities and the business environment of the Digital Economy, where Information Management and fast reaction to changing customer behavior are crucial for economic success, the efficient management of information and Business Intelligence is more important than ever.

The changing business rules are threatening lots of enterprises who underestimate the importance of corporate information and knowledge as a key factor to sustainable success.

To overcome the technical and organizational challenges and to be prepared for the opportunities and risks of new business models, successful enterprises have to achieve substantial changes in their BI environment in the coming years.

In the following chapter, we will take a closer look at how common BI solutions are implemented and maintained in the industry today. We will investigate new business requirements and business imperatives that have to be considered.

The structure and development of the BI market will give us hints for future improvements and possible changes in adoption of technology.

Based on that, we will analyze BI in terms of the current organizational and technical problems and their impact on profitability and competitive position of enterprises in the old and the new economy.

Finally, we will derive an approach for sustainable BI strategy, BI implementation, and BI operation and will briefly look at the horizon for solutions to come in the next years.

BUSINESS INTELLIGENCE HAS BECOME A COMMODITY FOR MANY ENTERPRISES

To understand the challenges of Information Management projects we have to understand the history of Business Intelligence (BI), data warehousing, and Information Management as well as the market development first. Business Intelligence is, as defined by Gartner, the process of transforming data into information and through discovery transforming that information into knowledge (Dressner, 1989). This means it is the process of providing insights that will enable business managers to make tactical decisions, as well as to establish, modify, or adjust the business strategies and business processes in order to achieve competitive advantage and improve business operations and profitability. The following sections will summarize the last decade of Business Intelligence and Information Management and give a structured view on the BI Market.

The First Wave of Information Management Projects is Completed

The first wave of data warehouse and BI projects started in the early nineties and most of these solutions are running and are maintained continuously.

As Watson and Hayley (1998) stated, in the first turn, the majority (52%) of organizations assessed the expected benefits, but only a fifth of them calculated real costs and financial benefits. Key problems to overcome in this stage *have due to this report been* poor data quality, missing financial and human resources, poorly defined goals, technical limitations, understanding of base data, lack of support/training, and management of expectations.

On one hand, many of these projects where based on "informational needs" such as better or faster access to more and more detailed information, the need for a single source of data and, to a minor part, to support other applications. These key drivers led to technology-founded, large-scale data warehouse initiatives collecting every transactional data available in fast-growing data stores. Consequently the poor quality of data became visible and lots of integration and consolidation issues occurred that have been solved — more or less.

In contrast, the "decision-making" departments such as controlling, senior management, marketing and sales, or purchasing developed or bought focused and tailored applications for specific decision needs. These solutions are often integrated badly into the IT environment, sometimes maintained by non-IT staff and only appropriate for dedicated needs. To fulfill the various requirements, different specific solutions have been elected for each purpose. Thus, several isolated instances of BI solutions, so-called BI silos, do exist in parallel today and are well-established. System users as well as information recipients got used to specific deliverables derived from heterogeneous IT-Systems and BI solutions. Product vendors have been very diligent to sell their BI solutions to single departments instead to central IT units.

The parallelism of technology-driven and business-oriented BI deployment led to remarkable initial and growing ongoing costs. The growth of the analytic systems led to increasing costs not balanced by the business. Often the given objectives in these projects were not really related to business expectations. As a result, a positive return on investment could not be shown clearly and was, in many cases, captured by other, business-related projects. Surveys show that:

- 41% of respondents say their organizations have experienced at least one project failure, and only 15% claim that their data warehousing efforts to date have been a major success. Additionally, only 27% of overall companies indicated they feel 'confident' with data warehouse technology. (Cutter Consortium, 2003)
- As many as 41% of data warehousing projects fail because they do not meet the business objectives of the company or because they ignore what users really need out of a data warehousing application. (Conner, 2003)
- Only 17% of companies say they have carried out ROI studies on data warehouse applications, and only 13% have established metrics to support application planning and development. (Hall, 1999)

As budgets are decreasing, analytical applications are suffering a vicious cycle. The increasing informational needs of process owners are often still not proven by a business case and, therefore, necessary investment in infrastructure cannot be justified properly. On the other hand, former spending on the analytical environment is often put into question because of a missing benefits analysis.

The Business Intelligence Market is Still Individualized and Volatile

In recent years, the BI market has experienced a consolidation process eliminating lots of smaller vendors and niche players covering the functionality of reporting, On Line Analytical Processing (OLAP) and forecasting functionality. End-user access via web clients has become common with remarkable and evident advantages concerning security, deployment, and remote availability of the application components. This migration has, on the other hand, suffered from a lack of functionality and efficiency, especially for OLAP-components and ad hoc reporting. The OLAP market has turned slowly from isolated multidimensional (MOLAP) and relational (ROLAP) OLAP implementations to integrated and hybrid (HOLAP) solutions. The market consolidation and acquisition led to richer product suites, so-called Enterprise BI suites (EBIS) and, in the second step, to integrated tools for data modeling, security administration, and metadata management for both OLAP and reporting applications. Today suppliers tend to cover the core functions and adjacent areas of functionality while retaining the uniqueness of their products. Functionality from many related product categories such as ETL tools, document and content management, enterprise portals, knowledge management, or data mining are integrated and vice versa.

To cope with rapidly increasing user needs in terms of process adoption, usability, and duration of implementation, vendors started offering packaged business applications. Currently, the market is split up into two large market segments: The EBIS-segment providing an integrated portfolio of OLAP, analysis, and reporting and the market of BI platforms, which focuses on standardized OLAP-infrastructure and packaged applications. The following figures show the actual Gartner Magic Quadrants reflecting the position of key players in the respective market.

The Magic Quadrant is copyrighted by Gartner, Inc. and is reused with permission. Gartner's permission to print its Magic Quadrant should not be deemed to be an endorsement of any company or product depicted in the quadrant. The Magic Quadrant is Gartner's opinion and is an analytical representation of a marketplace at and for a specific time period. It measures vendors against Gartner-defined criteria for a marketplace. The positioning of vendors within a Magic Quadrant is based on the complex interplay of many

Figure 1: Gartner Magic Quadrant EBIS and BI-Platforms (Dressner, Hostmann, & Buytendijik, 2003)

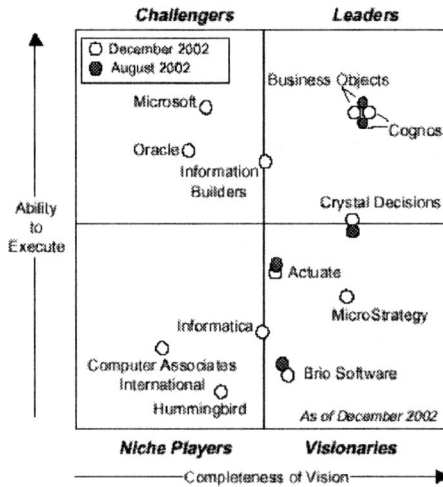

Source: Gartner Research

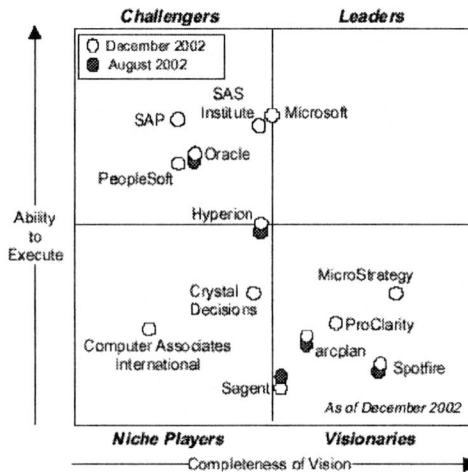

Source: Gartner Research

factors. Well-informed vendor selection decisions should rely on more than a Magic Quadrant. Gartner research is intended to be one of many information sources and the reader should not rely solely on the Magic Quadrant for decision-making. Gartner expressly disclaims all warranties, express or implied of fitness of this research for a particular purpose.

While the EBIS market is characterized by market maturity in the BI platform and applications market, real leaders are just aborning. In addition, the position of many vendors is weakened due to their current shareholder value. New competitors are appearing as well.

Therefore, enterprises have to choose carefully which vendors to rely on. New technological opportunities, which will be discussed later, are on their way to maturity and should be adopted as soon as possible to realize competitive advantages.

A NEW APPROACH FOR BUSINESS INTELLIGENCE IS NEEDED TO OVERCOME EXISTING PROBLEMS

As described, the BI and Information Management endeavors have resulted in strategic, economical, and technological impacts and issues. We will look at these aspects both from the commercial and from the technical side, especially considering new "digital" business models. To overcome existing complications, enterprises do need a comprehensive approach, driven by business objectives and economic benefits and implemented following standardized and durable IT architectural principles. The approach of Enterprise Information Management (EIM) described in earlier enables organizations to achieve sustainable competitiveness by realizing the potentials of Business Intelligence and Information Management.

Lots of Expectations and Requirements Have Not Been Fulfilled

Although the BI environments are maturing, enterprises are faced with several implications to handle in the future. First of all, current BI infrastructures often do not reflect strategic expectations or anticipate the fast change in business requirements. The growing importance of digital and web-based processes in particular completely changes the transactional structure and the requirements derived from that. The current solutions are growing unconsolidated, and information overload is heavily increasing.

Current Solutions Do Not Cover Economic Development and Strategic Expectations

The expectations of decision makers and knowledge workers have changed because of rapidly changing business objectives and an improved understanding of technology. The strategic importance of having the right information at the right time aligned to flexible processes has gained especially high importance. As summarized by Gabriel (1998), the strategic relevance of analytic systems is underpinned by several user defined quality criteria like:

- Focused and in-time information research enabling the user to find and visualize relevant, actual, and consistent information;
- Access to information based on changing and multidimensional criteria;
- Multidimensional techniques for access and usage of information;
- Fast and flexible data aggregation and data-mining functionality;
- Business- and problem-oriented visualization and consolidation of information;
- Real world modeling of issues and problems;
- Comprehensive representation of findings in various manners such as raw data, text, graphics, pictures, and speech;
- Enhanced representation and evaluation of company knowledge using knowledge-based systems;
- User-specific information delivery and presentation; and
- Empowerment of employees and management achieved by informed and precise decision making on all relevant levels in the organization.

To overcome the challenges of continuously increasing competition, changing client requirements, and growing client awareness businesses have to plan, analyze, control, and change their business strategies comprehensively with powerful, fast, and focused tools.

Business users expect their BI solutions to achieve unification, simplification, and business orientation of all required information sources. Companies can only deliver a product competitively if they have the right information (and *only* the right information) as fast as possible. This applies, for example, to former public companies being exposed to increasing international competition and having high transaction volumes (e.g., telecommunication or utility companies).

In addition, increasing collaboration issues with customers and suppliers force enterprises to take advantage of automated cross-company processes. These expectations are, to a certain extent, already fulfilled by the ERP and SCM solutions and apply to BI solutions as well. Decision processes have to be balanced between cooperating business partners to achieve, for example, optimized production, storage, and delivery processes or focused promotion activities.

The information derived from analytical systems is more and more valuable input for other commercial and operational applications like CRM, Call Center, or supplier collaboration solutions. This loop-back has not been foreseen in many implementations.

Looking at the concentration processes taking place in different industry sectors, business leaders are challenged by another important need. The integration of several companies must be supported by a fast and flexible integration of the information flow of the involved business units. When merging companies, the successful integration of operational resources and IT solutions depends heavily on the type of business to be integrated. A fast integration of the Information Management environment delivers a consolidated financial view and is always strongly recommended. Without an integrated view of financial and operational activities of the new integrated enterprise, expected opportunities can hardly be achieved. Therefore, a unified taxonomy, consistent breakdown structure, and consolidated visualization of business activities have to be delivered as fast as possible by the BI infrastructure.

Digital Business Processes Lead to Changing Requirements

Looking at new business models, we are identifying another, new, increasingly important set of requirements. The number of companies offering their services and products via the Web is increasing rapidly. These companies cope with specific challenges to drive their business successfully:

- Competitors are much closer to the customer, making quality and services are much easier to compare.
- The need for competitive differentiation is increasing.
- The customer churn rate is higher.
- The volatility and unpredictability of business development in the old economy is also reinforced by digital processes and increasing transparency.
- Much more information is available about clients and potential clients (e.g., click stream data), increasing the need to capture and validate this information to identify business opportunities and avoid mistakes.
- Customer loyalty has to be achieved by technology rather than human customer services.

These challenges lead to specific needs and to information overload as well. Successful enterprises need integrated and focused information and knowledge about their current business and future development based on their own transactional data as well as external sources.

Current Business Solutions are Stamped by Unconsolidated and Fast Growth

As described earlier, the two ways of information delivery using BI silos and full-scope data warehouse systems are well established in most companies. With these two infrastructures, IT and business managers find that it is much more difficult to maintain and improve an analytical system environment than to build one. In most cases the environment is growing fast in terms of data available, load and transformation processes, and specific analytical requirements to satisfy. The databases used are normally able to scale with this growth. But in most cases, this leads to a collection of all information available, increasing research time and complexity of the analytical applications.

More and more data sources are opened up for analytical purposes and the data collection is growing fast. Large-scale data warehouses tend to double their size every 15 months because, in most cases, it is difficult or impossible to delete transactional data and to keep aggregated information consistently. The growth of any analytical application increases the spending for successful and secure operation of the environment. That is, on one hand, a success story for product vendors; on the other hand, it underpins the tendency to collect increasing amounts of data that do not stay valuable over time.

Due to that, information overload is becoming critical to enterprises in terms of costs not related to business benefits. For example, according to Inc. magazine (1999), 80% of information filed is never used; an average person spends 150 hours a year looking for lost information; 40% of executives' working time is being spent reading; 44% of managers do believe the cost of collecting information exceeds its value to the business.

Load processes that collect data from several operational data stores are performing complex cleansing processes, which often lead to artificial representations of the enterprise. The timeframes for loading and cleansing are critical to many decision situations — every load process has to be assured against inconsistency across different applications. As more and more base data is updated on a day-to-day basis and timeframes for user access are growing as well, loading and error handling is, in many cases, not sophisticated enough to deliver comprehensively.

The Excellence in Business Intelligence is a Mandatory Competitive Advantage

As already mentioned, key challenges these days are no longer just data quality, availability, visualization, and storage issues. Having the necessary resources, the scalability of the systems and the achievable data interpretation and cleaning are, in many cases, necessary today. A variety of tools available for every purpose is giving users access to lots of detailed information. But how comprehensive, meaningful, and useful is this information? The heterogeneous application portfolio delivers redundant and contradictory information from several data sources. Consolidation in terms of time, measure definition, and consistent integration with internal and external data is missing.

To assure competitive ability, it is necessary to focus on the effective information needs of every process participant. Decision makers and knowledge workers need specific and flexible analytical tools that deliver consistent and comparable information. Every department has to rely on a universal logical breakdown structure, agreed-upon key figures, and timeframes. Any information being delivered without adding value to the business process is also consuming time and money in information delivery and retrieval. Valuable internal and external information that is not available to the user can lead to wrong or unsecured decisions and competitive disadvantages in consequence. Therefore, users have to be protected from getting stuck in a knowledge jungle provided by the numerous systems to which they have access.

Considering the individual technical ability of different users and the specialized purposes of information usage, IT has to provide personalized BI components based on a unified information repository. Every knowledge worker must be able to take full advantage of the relevant information by using tailored BI services.

Increasing Complexity of Information Management

IT departments are suffering from the former development. They experience increasing costs and efforts for data storage, data consolidation, aggregation, and knowledge delivery. The described expectations of information recipients have led to complex and vulnerable systems — often under the control of several departments. The key problems on the technical side are:

- Heterogeneous BI applications and solutions are provided with specific and unconsolidated subsets of transactional and aggregated data.

- Changes in business often lead to parallel data collection processes; redundant company breakdown structures have to be aggregated and delivered.
- The improved flexibility of end-user access leads to unpredictable workload and performance issues.
- The timeframes for data administration are shrinking while the number of administrative processes is increasing.
- Background processes such as backup/recovery, extraction/load, aggregation, high availability, and security are becoming increasingly complex and expensive without providing direct business value.

To retain control of BI spending and preserve the maintainability of the data warehouse and BI infrastructure, IT departments have to simplify and optimize the existing environment continuously.

OLAP Implementation Special Issues

Special aspects and issues have to be considered when looking at the implementation of OLAP solutions. In addition to traditional relational database solutions, special technological concepts have been developed for flexible and multidimensional analysis. These technologies support the requirements of flexible data analysis by using optimized storage concepts and sophisticated aggregation strategies. These OLAP data stores are normally called "cubes," because data is analyzed and visualized in three or more dimensions at the same time. Knowledge workers can examine basic and calculated measures using two or more company dimensions, for example, customer hierarchy, product hierarchy or time. In current implementations, the OLAP engine receives requests from a front-end tool, executes these requests, and delivers back the aggregated subset of information to be visualized. OLAP engines have become very powerful in the last few years and enable users to analyze complex company structures and business coherences online. Dimensions are represented in an "historical" or an "actual" view to show, for example, the accounting structure currently valid or the accounting structure valid at the time revenue was realized. These engines have to be configured and maintained carefully, because important issues do arise, such as:

- OLAP engines are using their own, redundant data store and are very sensitive in terms of data structure and quality.

- Usually, many OLAP cubes are implemented and provided for specific needs in parallel. They have to be synchronized and harmonized with the relational base data that reporting solutions are accessing.
- As analytical requests are only partially predictable, the performance is critical and must be monitored continuously.
- The need for more and more complex measures and dimensions leads to difficult and time-consuming maintenance processes.
- Several dimensions need both an "historical" and an "actual" representation. Fulfilling both requirements makes cubes more complex and difficult to use properly.

In addition to these operational issues, the users accessing these cubes need to understand the technology used and the business problem on which they are working. In comparison to reporting solutions, which are normally customized to defined analytical needs, the OLAP user has to personally define his or "business question" and has to understand the capability and restrictions of the tool as well as the measures and dimensions available.

Integration of Internal and External Data Missing

As already mentioned briefly, when looking at current business requirements, the need for valuable external information is increasing. Concise and secured decisions are, in many cases, only possible based on the integration of internal and external information and knowledge. This can be achieved by "modeling" the inside and the outside world in the BI-environment and feeding this outside model with market research data, competitor characteristics, or benchmarking information. In addition to this, knowledge available via Internet, news feeds, or public Web services can be integrated carefully to deliver a comprehensive view of the whole market and identify opportunities and risks early. In time, companies neglecting to identify and integrate these information sources will increasingly fail to identify necessary changes and improvements in their product, marketing, or sales approach.

Reasons for Lack of Success

After summarizing the common business and IT issues, we have to consider the position of BI solutions in the enterprise and basic guidelines for IT solution delivery as well. This gives us important hints on how to set up BI projects correctly.

In enterprises with a history of poor relations between the IT organization and business users, we often identify BI inertia. Users may be suspicious that better BI will open them up to greater management scrutiny, while the IT department may feel threatened that its specialist skills will no longer be needed. The way people think about the value of information and how it is used to shape the business must change.

BI projects often shipwreck because important basic conditions are missing. Some common aspects are:

- missing awareness or lack of interest and motivation among management;
- inappropriate qualification of system developers, system administrators, and system users;
- missing models and methods to visualize, process, and solve decision issues;
- organizational structures that do not fit or are not supported by the decision support infrastructure;
- missing transparency of systems and information flow;
- wrong expectations regarding achievable outcome, performance, or flexibility; and
- missing editorial support for the systems to truly contribute to processes and support decision makers.

Keeping in mind both the issues explained before and these environmental conditions, we are able to derive a successful approach to deliver business oriented and comprehensive Information Management and Business Intelligence solutions.

A Comprehensive and Efficient Approach is Necessary for Success

As we have seen, it is crucial to offer a customized and user-centric set of tools using consistent data from defined sources. A user won't gain the achievable benefits when using a tool that does not reflect his or her technical capabilities. Typically, flexibility, performance, and ease of use have to be improved in relation to the seniority of the user. On the other hand, the user has to be protected from information overload and needs guidance to access all the information and knowledge needed to successfully control and improve the business processes. This can only achieved when IT has a common understanding of the information needs of the enterprise. To reflect these needs and the ongoing development as well, a standardized and unified system architecture has to be set up. Based on the already existing environment, changes in the infrastructure have to be aligned to technical and organizational capabilities, considering the priority of requirements to be fulfilled. A continuous assessment of analytical applications and systems is required to identify erroneous trends early and to anticipate changes in user expectation and processes. Every Information Management initiative must be a joint initiative of IT and business to deliver compliant solutions, use the right technology, and avoid lasting obstacles.

A Generic Approach to Tailoring Information Management and Business Intelligence

Based on many client projects, we developed a generic approach to successfully improve the existing Information Management environment based on the given system architecture and aligned to the process information requirements. Depending on the size of the organization, the quality of existing informational support, and the core processes, one or more initiatives are derived to change the environment and to initialize an ongoing assessment and improvement process for Information Management and Business Intelligence. We call this approach Enterprise Information Management (EIM). *Figure 2* shows the five stages of EIM that are described in detail next.

Figure 2: Five Stages of Enterprise Information Management (EIM)

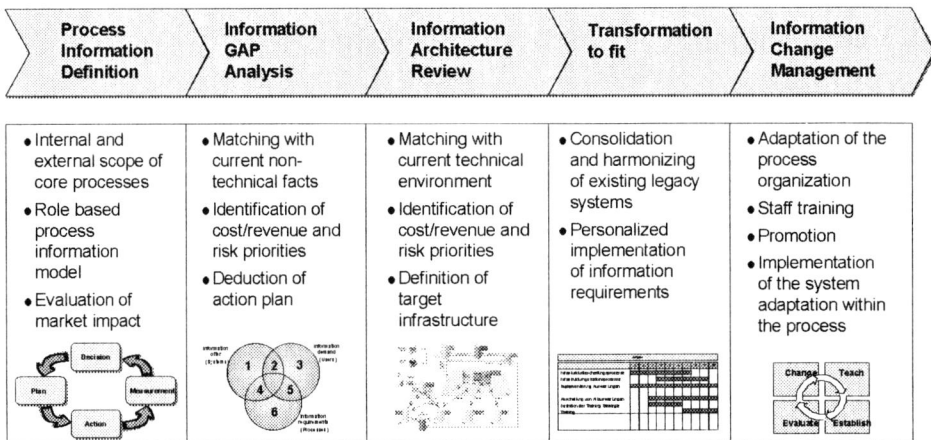

Process Information Definition	Information GAP Analysis	Information Architecture Review	Transformation to fit	Information Change Management
• Internal and external scope of core processes • Role based process information model • Evaluation of market impact	• Matching with current non-technical facts • Identification of cost/revenue and risk priorities • Deduction of action plan	• Matching with current technical environment • Identification of cost/revenue and risk priorities • Definition of target infrastructure	• Consolidation and harmonizing of existing legacy systems • Personalized implementation of information requirements	• Adaptation of the process organization • Staff training • Promotion • Implementation of the system adaptation within the process

Process Information Definition: Identifying the Informational Need of the Enterprise

Companies can only construct and shape a valuable Information Management environment if they are aware of the effective informational and decision needs of their processes. Every core process has to be analyzed to specify internal and external information requirements in terms of measure, time, and context. Company breakdown structures must be defined and unified. The way the processes are reviewed strongly depends on the complexity of the business and the dependencies between processes or business units. Every key process must be described completely. In addition to the identification of relevant measures, the process information definition has to reveal:

- the potential of each process and decision issue to change;
- the value proposition of information for the process to support assessment of systems and benefits case;
- the role model for decision making;
- external information to support and improve decision making for activities; and
- the dimensions of the company's business model and disagreements in terms of measures and dimensions between processes and business units.

Having done this specification, a detailed analysis of the current information situation of the enterprise can then take place.

Information Gap Analysis: Defining Key Fields of Action

After you have identified the internal and external informational needs to operate your processes successfully, the next step is to identify the gaps between the existing informational environment and these requirements. In the best case, the informational demand, offer, and need are completely coherent. In this case, you already have optimized information and BI services that can only be improved in terms of technology usage. In most cases, the demand (represented by user behavior), the real requirements (represented by the processes), and the offer (represented by the systems available) only overlap to a certain extent. *Figure 3* illustrates this situation.

The intersection in the middle of the three circles represents coherent BI and Information Management solutions. All other intersections represent risks for the enterprise and opportunities for improvement. Every situation and points for action to be realized in the transformation stage are described:

Figure 3: Fields of Information Gap Analysis

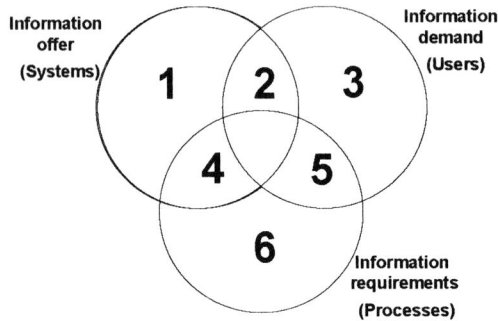

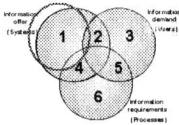

1.   Useless Information Offering

Situation: The information offered by existing Information Management and Business Intelligence systems is not needed in the process nor requested by system users.

Quality:

- Usually these services remain from further projects and initiatives that have not been successful or are not needed anymore.
- Legacy solutions that have been replaced by newer application are still active for some reason.
- Requests defined for a former organizational company structure or by former employees are still fulfilled.

Steps for Action:

- Taking a full inventory of existing applications, reports, classifications, and users.
- Clustering the inventory to identify candidates for portfolio simplification.
- Turning off applications and services with little or no value proposition to the company
- Streamlining existing OLAP models

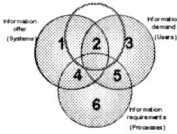

2.   Non-Relevant Serviced Information Requests

Situation: Reports and applications are available and used by employees and
knowledge workers but do not deliver any value to the processes or
business objectives.

Quality:

- The provision of information and the usage of these solutions as well is
wasting time and money.
- Employees are spending their working time on wrong activities.
- This situation is, in some cases, expensive and difficult to change because
system users insist on using the applications with which they are familiar.

Steps for Action:

- Communicating process information needs to all participants of the
process.
- Training of knowledge workers in using the right systems and requesting
the right information.
- Changing decision processes might help to change information usage.
- Turning off applications and services with little or no value proposition to
the company.
- Streamlining existing OLAP models.

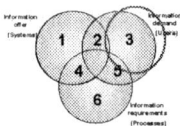

3.   Useless Information Requests

Situation: Users do request and ask for non-relevant information that has not
previously been available.

Quality:

- Problems in decision making and process control are often justified by
missing information.
- It is dangerous and expensive to set up projects based on these requests
that will not deliver any value.
- In most cases, other solutions are necessary that are sometimes already
available or have to be implemented

Steps for Action:
- Training and qualifying employees to understand the processes and decision needs urgently.
- Identifying available existing alternatives first.
- Training for knowledge workers to get used to alternative existing solutions.
- Implementing the systems missing to successfully and correctly support the existing decision problems.

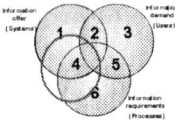

4. Organizational Weakness

Situation: The information needed in the process is provided by existing applications but never used by the user.

Quality:
- Process performance is weak although the systems and information needed are in place.
- If applying to critical process steps, the competitiveness is needlessly endangered.
- As in the preceding cases, qualification of knowledge workers has to be improved.

Steps for Action:
- Improving process execution by training or replacing process participants.
- Changing the processes to define dedicated decision steps to take advantage of the existing information and systems.

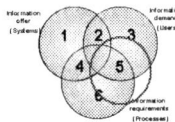

5. Identified Missing Information

Situation: Users are requesting information impartially needed to execute this process, but this information is not derivable based on the existing environment.

Quality:
- Problems in process quality and ability to execute are identified correctly· Systems are not capable of delivering the information or the information is not available in the environment at all.
- The company is at risk to lose competent employees because of their frustration.
- Delivery of missing solutions has instant impact on company performance.

Steps for Action:
- Defining and prioritizing all needs in order to serve the most important ones first.
- Implementing missing solutions to fulfill the objective requirements.

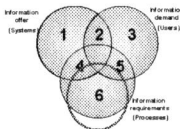

6.   Lack of Competency

Situation: Information needed in the process is neither available nor requested.

Quality:
- Extreme critical situation because the organization is not conscious of missing any relevant information.
- Processes are possibly executed badly or focused on the wrong key indicators.
- Change is necessary but will be costly because systems and users have to be accommodated as well.

Steps for Action:
- Substantially checking and realigning processes and process documentation.
- Using reference models, best practice processes, and external industry sector competency.
- Training and communication.
- Assessing opportunities and risk of change before implementation.

This analysis should be a joint activity of IT and business to ensure a common understanding of the actual situation, quality of problems, technological opportunities, and projects to derive from the findings.

Information Architecture Review: Specifying the Right System Architecture Roadmap

Based on the findings of the gap analysis, the architecture roadmap for Information Management and Business Intelligence has to be optimized. Given a productive operational environment, changes can only done step-by-step considering the impacts on processes, organization, and technology. Having a clear future architecture in mind, change projects can successfully be implemented and prioritized by their value proposition to the business and the technical options that apply to the current environment. From a technical view, the elimination of useless applications, the standardization of existing solutions, and the process-oriented promotion of existing solutions deliver the highest financial and organizational impact for IT operations.

The architecture roadmap defines infrastructure, components, applications, and services to offer in the future. The specification should consider the phases of implementation, maintenance, and further development, as well as following basic guidelines:

- A central data warehouse remains the most powerful concept for extraction, consolidation, and delivery of internal and external data. Every data source should remain under control of a central data management that takes care of consistency, compliance, and data quality.
- Standardized products and applications should be used wherever possible. Companies should avoid custom application and interface development.
- The number of vendors delivering products for the IM and BI portfolio should be minimized, although the various effective needs of the business users will, in most cases, lead to more than one product in use. The vendors should be selected carefully, looking at their products as well as the company's ability.
- Tools should be integrated for the knowledge worker, because, in most cases, the borders between technological solutions (like default reporting and OLAP) do not reflect the way the user perceives his or her work.
- Personalized integration of analytic data with external and internal unstructured information is becoming more and more important. Users should have access to these various sources via an enterprise portal.
- Back-end processes provided for operational systems (like backup/ restore, high availability, system monitoring, and security) apply to informational systems as well and have to be planned thoroughly because of small timeframes and large data volumes.

- Analytic solutions must be integrated into support functions such as user help desk, online-help, e-learning, and company training.

Keeping these aspects in mind a change plan for the architecture roadmap can be defined.

Transformation to Fit: Setting Up the Right Projects

Having analyzed and prioritized the key fields of action and the necessary changes in IT architecture, the improvement of the BI environment can be achieved using a so-called change program covering several projects and initiatives of different type. These initiatives are derived from the findings of the information gap analysis and the architecture roadmap and can be:

- adjusting processes and information to take full advantage of the existing information services;
- training and educating the user and knowledge worker so they can understand the decision needs and take full advantage of BI systems;
- consolidating existing solutions and applications, especially turning off running solutions with little or no value to the processes;
- standardizing interfaces for load processes and information exchange; and
- setting up new applications that simplify and enhance information delivery.

While setting up and implementing these projects, general guidelines should be kept in mind:

- Focus on the value proposition of initiatives. Projects promising measurable benefits and strong improvement for the business should always be first in line.
- Concentrate on short project duration. In contrast to long-running ERP projects, Information Management and BI projects should not run longer than three to six months because decision requirements change fast.
- BI projects are always joint efforts of business and IT. Business users will not adopt new technologies without being involved in the development phase, and IT will not be able to cover the business needs without instant feedback.
- A BI project needs sponsorship of senior management because project benefits are often on a strategic level or spread across several business units and functions.

Information Change Management: Maintaining the BI Environment

As we have already seen, maintaining a BI environment is much more difficult than building one. To stay successful in operating BI solutions, a process of continuous assessment and improvement must be established.

The assessment of information systems has to take into account different quality indicators. In addition to effective value proposition to the business, criteria and figures for the following aspects should be defined and monitored to evaluate system capacity and options for further improvement:

- actuality, correctness, reliability, and availability;
- functionality of applications, visualization, and presentation of information;
- effectiveness of decision support;
- system security;
- overall system spending; and
- usage of applications and system workload.

The organization has to learn continuously to improve applications, educate users, and identify the need for change early. A team representing the company's IT and business departments has to take control of the Information Management improvement process. This committee has to discuss the ongoing internal and external changes leading to new requirements for Information Management. It has to focus on:

- the requirements derived from changing business activities;
- changes in the usage of the systems;
- user satisfaction in using BI applications;
- need for training and development;
- need for system enhancement and scalability;
- review and prioritization of running and planned BI change projects; and
- consideration of opportunities that new technologies provide.

This ongoing monitoring committee helps to continuously improve the environment, avoid obstacles in usage and anticipation of offered solutions, and identify indicators for change early.

NEW FORMS OF APPLICATIONS WILL SUPPORT THIS COMPREHENSIVE BUSINESS INTELLIGENCE APPROACH

As indicated in the market summary, several new forms of BI and Information Management will gain maturity in the next years.

Most of these technologies will support the trend toward integrated Information Management and cross-company solutions. This will lead to increasing collaboration and cooperative Business Intelligence initiatives. It is expected that new technical products will help to overcome existing barriers between technical environments. Because of this, concentration on standardized interfaces is strongly recommended to collaborate with key business partners easily in the future and to take advantage of collaborative Business Intelligence solutions. In addition, we will experience an increasing standardization of external data sources making integration and delivery of external information much easier than before.

Another field of development is the market of packaged BI applications. The main domains for packaged analytical applications are profitability analysis, CRM analytics, Supply Chain Management (SCM), ERP, Corporate Performance Management (CPM), and supplier analytics (Buytendijk, 2002). Vendors increasingly support concepts like CPM. They try to support an enfolding application development based on BI Architecture. These components help implement integrated management components supporting concepts such as Balanced Scorecard, Activity Based Costing, or Economic Value Added. Having a well-defined and centralized infrastructure for Information Management, these solutions can easily be adopted in the BI portfolio in the future. Adopters of this technology have to be careful because sometimes data mart proliferation comes along using complex packaged solutions. When using these applications, the metadata of the BI environment must be highly structured and standardized.

The market for solutions like that is currently still characterized by partnerships, consolidation, and market expansion. Vendors should be selected carefully in the next few years, because many existing standards and components are still subject to change dramatically.

Looking at the IT application portfolio as a whole, the one-way information delivery from operational to analytical applications will increasingly be replaced by closed loop environments. Complex decision-making processes will lead to final results automatically updating operational systems. This will especially apply to CRM solutions and to collaborative production planning.

All these tendencies are helping companies to use BI easier and to support the comprehensive approach of Information Management.

CONCLUSION

In the preceding sections, we discussed the current tendencies and problems in the successful adoption of BI technology. Core solutions like OLAP and reporting have matured, and new concepts supporting complex business questions and cross-company collaboration are developing fast.

To stay successful and take full advantage of these sophisticated technologies, Business Intelligence and Information Management must be understood as a permanently evolving part of the enterprise. Knowledge workers and users have to understand and anticipate this technology and need continuous guidance in terms of training and development. IT organizations have to understand the business requirements and changes and adopt their infrastructure to support these needs.

The valuable contribution of analytical applications to the sustainable success of business processes must be reflected on a strategic level and be integrated in every activity of change. The ability to change is vital to the successful operation of analytical information systems. The same applies to the ability to learn inside the organization.

Many new concepts and technologies, like Corporate Performance Management or collaborative use of IT and Business Intelligence are, as described before, at the beginning of their lifecycle. Only a minor part of these solutions will develop to a stage of maturity. Nevertheless, successful enterprises will have to continuously evaluate, adopt, and integrate these new technologies aligned to the business objectives. Only those company leaders who are aware of Information and Knowledge Management being a significant competitive advantage of the 21st century will be able to keep their enterprises successful. A comprehensive Business Intelligence approach organized and incorporated both by business and IT experts and supported by senior management will achieve this.

REFERENCES

Buytendijk, M. (2002). BI applications experience increased adoption, slowly. Gartner research note, *Gartner Research*, 5, November, M-18-3159.

Conner, D. (2003) Data warehouse failures commonplace, Online Report, 20 January. Retrieved online at NetworkWorldFusion: http://www.nwfusion.com/news/2003/0120dataware.html.

Cutter Consortium (2003). Survey Report. January. Retrieved online at: http://www.cutter.com/press/030106.html.

Data (1999). *Data Inc Magazine*. January 01. Retrieved December 12, 2002, from: http://inc.com/magazine.

Dressner, H. (2002). Sailing in rough waters. Gartner's BI magic quadrant update. Gartner Article, *Gartner Research*, 11 September. IGG-09112002-02.

Dressner, H., Hostmann, B., & Buytendijk, M. (2003). Management update: Gartner's Business Intelligence Magic Quadrants. Gartner Article. Gartner Research, 12 February. IGG-02122003-01.

Gabriel, R. (1998). Strategische Bedeutung der Analytischen Informationssysteme. In P. Chamoni & P. Gluchowski (Eds.), *Analytische Informationssysteme*, (pp. 411-420). Berlin: Springer-Verlag.

Hall, C. (1999). Data warehouse & business intelligence: Survey report. *Cutter Consortium*, March.

Haning, U. (2002). *Knowledge Management & Business Intelligence*. Berlin Heidelberg: Springer-Verlag.

Kimball, R. (1996). *The Data Warehouse Toolkit*. New York: John Wiley & Sons.

Muksch, H. (2000). *Das Datawarehouse-Konzept: Architektur - Datenmodelle – Anwendungen*. Wiesbaden, Germany: Gabler-Verlag.

Pense, N. (n.d.). www.olapreport.com. Detailed Market research and vendor evaluation for business intelligence.

Strange, K. (2002). Eight ways to stop the $40 billion in BI waste. Gartner commentary research note. *Gartner Research*, 21 June. COM-16-8454.

Watson, H., & Haley, B. (1998). Datawarehousing: A framework and survey of current practices. In P. Chamoni & P. Gluchowski (Eds.), *Analytische Informationssysteme*, (pp. 411-420). Berlin: Springer-Verlag.

ENDNOTES

[1]   Definition by Howard Dressner (1989), Gartner Research.

[2]   Watson, H., & Haley, B. J. (1998). Datawarehousing: A framework and survey of current practices. In P. Chamoni & P. Gluchowski (Eds.), *Analytische Informationssysteme* (pp. 411-420). Berlin: Springer-Verlag.

[3]   Cutter Consortium (2003). *Survey Report.* January 2003. Cutter Consortium at: http://www.cutter.com/press/030106.html.

[4]   Conner, D. (2003). *Datawarehouse failures commonplace.* Online report, January 20, 2003. NetworkWorldFusion at: http://www.nwfusion. com/news/2003/0120dataware.html.

[5]   Hall, C. (1999). Datawarehouse & Business Intelligence. Survey Report, March 1999. Cutter Consortium.

[6]   Dressner, Hostmann, Buyitendyk : Gartner's Updated BI Magic Quadrant– Gartner research 12 February 2003 : IGG-02122003-01.

[7]   The Magic Quadrant is copyrighted by Gartner, Inc., and is reused with permission. Gartner's permission to print its Magic Quadrant should not be deemed to be an endorsement of any company or product depicted in the quadrant. The Magic Quadrant is Gartner's opinion and is an analytical representation of a marketplace at and for a specific time period. It measures vendors against Gartner-defined criteria for a marketplace. The positioning of vendors within a Magic Quadrant is based on the complex interplay of many factors. Well-informed vendor selection decisions should rely on more than a Magic Quadrant. Gartner research is intended to be one of many information sources and the reader should not rely solely on the Magic Quadrant for decision-making. Gartner expressly disclaims all warranties, express or implied of fitness of this research for a particular purpose.

[8]   Gabriel, R. (1998). Strategische Bedeutung der Analytischen Informationssysteme. In P. Chamoni & P. Gluchowski (Eds.), *Analytische Informationssysteme* (pp. 411-420). Berlin: Springer-Verlag.

[9]   Data Data, Inc. Magazine. January 01, 1999. Retrieved December 12, 2002: http://inc.com/magazine.

[10] Strange, K. (2002). Eight ways to stop the $40 billion in BI Waste. Gartner commentary research note. Gartner Research, June 21, 2002. COM-16-8454.

[11]   Strange, K. (2002). Eight ways to stop the $40 billion in BI Waste. Gartner commentary research note. Gartner Research, June 21, 2002. COM-16-8454.

[12]   Buytendijk, M. (2002). BI applications experience increased adoption, slowly. Gartner research note. Gartner research, November 5, 2002. M-18-3159.

Chapter V

An Intelligent Knowledge-Based Multi-Agent Architecture for Collaboration (IKMAC) in B2B e-Marketplaces

Rahul Singh, University of North Carolina at Greensboro, USA

Lakshmi Iyer, University of North Carolina at Greensboro, USA

Al Salam, University of North Carolina at Greensboro, USA

ABSTRACT

This chapter presents an Intelligent Knowledge-Based Multi-Agent Architecture for Collaboration (IKMAC) in B2B e-Marketplaces. IKMAC is built upon existing bodies of knowledge in intelligent agents, knowledge management, e-business, XML, and web service standards. This chapter focuses on the translation of data, information, and knowledge into XML documents by software agents, thereby creating the foundation for knowledge representation and exchange by intelligent agents that support collaborative work between business partners. The realization of the proposed architecture is explained through an infomediary-based e-Marketplace prototype in which agents facilitate collaboration by exchanging their knowledge using XML and related sets of standards. Use of such systems will provide collaborating partners with intelligent knowledge management (KM) capabilities for seamless and transparent exchange of dynamic supply and demand information.

INTRODUCTION

This chapter presents an Intelligent Knowledge-Based Multi-Agent Architecture for Collaboration (IKMAC) in B2B e-Marketplaces. IKMAC is built upon existing bodies of knowledge in intelligent agents, knowledge management (KM), e-business, eXtensible Markup Language (XML) and web services standards. IKMAC incorporates a consolidated knowledge repository to store and retrieve knowledge captured in XML documents, to be used and shared by software agents within the multi-agent architecture. The realization of the proposed architecture is explicated through an infomediary-based e-Marketplace example in which agents facilitate collaboration by exchanging their knowledge using XML and related set of standards. This chapter focuses on the translation of data, information, and knowledge into XML documents by software agents, thereby creating the foundation for knowledge representation and exchange by intelligent agents that support collaborative work between business partners.

CONTEXT

Rapid growth in Internet technologies has tremendous impact on business processes in the Digital Economy. As the reliance on electronic information sources grows — fuelled by the growth in the Internet and the global Digital Economy, the relevance and pertinence of information become critical for effective use of scarce resources and time. As businesses discover new ways of using the information-sharing and process-enabling features of the Digital Economy, greater demands are placed on goal-oriented problem-solving activities. The growing complexity in information sources and business processes requires an alliance of human analysis, intuition, and judgment aided by intelligent agent support for the range of information processing tasks. Companies, in the current Digital Economy, are forced by intense competition to develop innovative strategies and solutions to optimize the transfer of goods, information, and services from suppliers to business customers and, ultimately, to consumers. The integrated value chain extends beyond a single company and encompasses all related trading partners, thereby extending the focus of integration outside the organization's walls.

Emerging Internet-based technologies, such as XML and related sets of standards (http://www.w3c.org), ebXML (http://www.ebxml.org), web services, the Semantic Web, and intelligent multi-agent technology provide businesses with great opportunities to not only develop solutions that streamline and integrate business-to-business (B2B) transaction processes, but also to create intelligent electronic marketplaces (e-Marketplaces) throughout their value chain (Singh et al., Forthcoming). There is a significant first-mover advantage that a company may be able to capture if it integrates the emerging Internet-based technologies within a strategic competitive vision for the Digital Economy. Realizing the potential benefits of emergent technologies is dependent on the effective sharing and use of business intelligence and process knowledge among business partners to provide accurate, relevant, and timely information and knowledge. This requires system models to support and enable information integration, knowledge exchange, and improved collaboration among business partners. Such systems must provide collaborating partners with intelligent knowledge management (KM) capabilities for seamless and transparent exchange of dynamic supply and demand information. Implementing and managing such integration over distributed and heterogeneous information platforms, such as the Internet, is a challenging task; yet, realizing this task can have significant benefits for organizations embracing such collaborations.

BACKGROUND

Intelligent Agents

Intelligent agents are *computer systems situated in some environment that are capable of flexible autonomous action in this environment in order to meet its design objectives* (Jennings & Wooldridge, 1998). The terms agents, software agents, and intelligent agents are often used interchangeably in the literature. All agents do not necessarily have to be intelligent. Jennings and Wooldridge observe that agent-based systems are not necessarily intelligent and require that an agent be *flexible* to be considered intelligent. Such flexibility in intelligent agent-based systems requires that the agents should be (Bradshaw, 1997; Jennings & Wooldridge, 1998):

- cognizant of their environment and be *responsive* to changes therein;
- reactive and *proactive* to opportunities in their environment;
- autonomous in goal-directed behavior;
- collaborative in their ability to interact with other agents in exhibiting the goal-oriented behavior; and
- adaptive in their ability to learn with experience.

Agent-based systems may consist of a single agent engaged in autonomous goal-oriented behavior or multiple agents that work together to exhibit granular as well as overall goal-directed behavior. The general multi-agent system is one in which the interoperation of separately developed and self-interested agents provide a service beyond the capability of any single agent model. Such multi-agent systems provide a powerful abstraction that can be used to model systems where multiple entities, exhibiting self-directed behaviors, must coexist in an environment and achieve the system-wide objective of the environment.

Intelligent agents are action-oriented abstractions in electronic systems, entrusted to carry out various generic and specific goal-oriented actions on behalf of users. The agent abstraction manifests itself in the system as a representation of the user and performs necessary tasks on behalf of the user. This role may involve taking directions from the user on a need basis and advising and informing the user of alternatives and consequences (Whinston, 1997). The agent paradigm can support a range of decision-making activities including information retrieval, generation of alternatives, preference-order ranking of options and alternatives, and supporting analysis of the alternative-goal relationships. In this respect, intelligent agents have come a long way from being digital scourers and static filters of information to active partners in information-processing tasks. Such a shift has significant design implications for the abstractions used to model information systems, objects, or agents, and for the architecture of information resources that are available to entities involved in the electronic system. Another implication is that knowledge must be available in formats that are conducive to its representation and manipulation by software agents.

XML and Related Set of Technologies

Since the advent of the Internet, the World Wide Web has become very popular because of the simplicity provided by HTML for its usage and content presentation. HTML provides a fixed set of tags that are used to markup content (information) primarily for consumption by human beings. However,

HTML is very limited in its extensibility and customization of markup tags and description of the data contained in those tags. This is a severe constraint that limits the use of HTML by application software for information sharing in a distributed computing environment where software applications, including software agents, are expected to work with available data, rules, and knowledge without human intervention. The use of XML and its related set of standards, developed by the World Wide Web Consortium (W3C) (http://www.w3c.org), have helped overcome some of these limitations. XML is a meta-language that allows for the creation of languages that can be represented by customized XML tags. For example, a company in the furniture industry may develop customized tags for the representation of content to serve its business domain. By creating custom tags, the company can represent the data in a more meaningful and flexible way than by using HTML. The company may also develop documents that represent business rules using XML that can be shared between people or software agents.

Unambiguous understanding of the content of customized XML tags by interested parties requires description of both the content and structure of XML documents. This description of structures in XML documents is provided by the XML schema, which can be written following the set of standards called XML Schema and/or the Document Type Definition (DTD) language as adopted and standardized by the W3C. The XML schema describes the specific elements, their relationships, and the specific types of data that can be stored in each of these elements. Essentially, an XML schema describes the structure of XML documents and their contents.

XML documents can be parsed and validated by application software provided either the DTD or the XML Schema of the corresponding document is made available. XML parsers written in C, C++ or Java can process and validate XML documents (containing business rules and data) based on XML schemas written based on either the DTD or the XML Schema specification. Application software-appropriate parser utilities are able to read and/or write to XML documents following the W3C standards and specification. This provides the foundation technology, built upon agreed and accepted standard from W3C, for the capture, representation, exchange, and storage of knowledge represented by business rules and related data in XML format that can be potentially used and shared by software agents.

Some recent promising initiatives to develop technologies for what is being called the "Semantic Web" (Berners-Lee, Hendler, & Lassila, 2001) attempt to make the content of the web unambiguously computer-interpretable, thus making it amenable to agent interoperability and automatic reasoning techniques (McIlraith, Tran, & Zeng, 2001). Two important technologies for developing Semantic Web are already in place — XML and the Resource Description Framework (RDF). The W3C developed the RDF as a standard for metadata to add a formal semantics to the Web, defined on top of XML, to provide a data model and syntax convention for representing the semantics of data in standardized interoperable manner (McIlraith et al.). The RDF Working Group also developed RDF Schema (RDFS), an object-oriented type system that can be effectively thought of as a minimal ontology modeling language. Recently, there have been several efforts to build on RDF and RDFS with more AI-inspired knowledge representation languages such as SHOE, DAML-ONT, OIL and DAML+OIL (Fensel, 2000).

Even though these initiatives are extremely promising for agent interoperability and reasoning, they are at their early stages of development. Thus, use of XML standards and related technology can not only automate processes and reduce human interventions, but also unite business partners and supply chains for better collaboration and knowledge transfer. XML provides standardized representations of data structures so data can be processed appropriately by heterogeneous systems without case-by-case programming. This has tremendous benefits for e-commerce applications and supply chain systems that operate across enterprise boundaries. XML-based messages can be retrieved from back-end repositories and fed out through a portal interface allowing for the creation of custom tags that contain data pertaining to specific domains. In this chapter, we focus on the use of more mature and widely used and available standardized technologies, such as XML and DTDs, to represent knowledge. This approach, along with other initiatives, should allow researchers to develop intelligent agent-based systems that are both practical and viable for facilitating collaborative commerce.

Knowledge Management and e-Business

Emerging new business models are causing fundamental changes in how organizations conduct business by replacing control structures with the freedom to manage complexity, and by replacing conflict with cooperation as a means to be economically efficient (Beam, 1998; Davis, 1998; Skyrme, 1997). To achieve such cooperation, organizations require active knowledge management (KM) and knowledge management systems (KMS). A realization of the need for greater collaboration among trading partners is fueling the growth of KM to help identify integrative and interrelated elements to enable collaborations. Operationally, KM is "a process that helps organizations find, select, organize, disseminate, and transfer important information and expertise necessary for activities such as problem solving, dynamic learning, strategic planning and decision making" (Gupta, Iyer, & Aronson, 2000). From an organizational perspective, it is the management of corporate knowledge that can improve a range of organizational performance characteristics by enabling an enterprise to be more "intelligent acting" (Wiig, 1993). The imperatives of KM in an organization are to transform knowledge to add value to the processes and operations of the business, leverage knowledge strategic to business to accelerate growth and innovation, and use knowledge to provide competitive advantage to the business.

Bolloju, Khalifa, and Turban (2002) consider the integration of KMS and Decision-Support Systems (DSS) for improved decision making, claiming that each decision activity creates new knowledge. They propose an approach to integrate decision support and KM that facilitates knowledge conversion through automated knowledge discovery techniques (KDT) for knowledge externalization. This approach utilizes knowledge repositories to store externalized knowledge, and extends KDT to support various types of knowledge conversions. The Knowledge Warehouse (KW) architecture by Nemati, Steiger, Iyer, and Herschel (2002) shows facilities capture and codify knowledge that enhances the retrieval and sharing of knowledge across the organization. The primary goal of the KW architecture is to provide the decision maker with an intelligent analysis platform that enhances the utility and utilization of KM. KM, as a discipline, helps companies focus on identifying knowledge, explicating it in a way that it can be shared in a formal manner, thereby promoting its re-use. Ba, Lang, and Whinston (1997) enumerate the KM principles necessary to achieve intra-organizational knowledge bases as: (1) the use of corporate data to derive and create higher level information and knowledge, and (2) the provision of tools to transform scattered data into meaningful business information. Many organizations are developing KMS designed specifically to facilitate the sharing and integration of knowledge used by organizations for increasing collaboration.

In the current Digital Economy, organizations gain competitive advantage through collaborative commerce (c-Commerce) by sharing information and synchronizing transactions in the collaborative network of value chain partners. c-Commerce includes a broad array of meanings such as collaboration in planning, manufacturing (design and development), inventory management (forecasting and replenishment), and relationship management (Benelli, Gravitt, & Diana, 2001). Sharing information and knowledge between trading partners is a primary requirement for successful collaboration (Bechek & Brea, 2001). In this chapter, c-Commerce refers to enabling collaboration among trading partners by enhancing information and knowledge partnerships in infomediary-enabled e-Marketplaces. To accomplish the level of collaboration required for c-Commerce, businesses need a comprehensive solution to facilitate the sharing of information and knowledge. Just as a common method for publishing data on the web spawned the evolution of e-business, a common means to publish information about business services can make it possible for organizations to quickly discover the right trading partner from the millions online. It will also aid in conducting business once preferred businesses are discovered, and create an industry-wide approach for businesses to quickly and easily integrate systems and business processes with their customers and partners on the Internet, with transparent flows of information about their products and services. The facilitation of such truly successful service-centric computing requires that businesses be easily able to discover each other, to make their needs and capabilities known, and to integrate systems and services using each businesses' preferred technology, web services, and commerce processes.

An organization's ability to establish connectivity, put product or service information online, access and interact with a broad range of customers, process transactions, and fill orders will influence the level of collaboration it can achieve among its business partners. This requires a way to manage information and knowledge that is contained in heterogeneous sources and systems. Knowledge management for c-Commerce involves a strategic commitment to improving the organization's effectiveness, including its internal processes and inter-organizational activities.

Role of Intelligent Agents, XML and KM in Delivering Business Intelligence

The W3C XML specification allows for the creation of customized tags for content modeling in XML documents. These customized tags can be used for creating data-centric content models or for creating rule-based content models. Data-centric content models imply XML documents that have XML tags that contain data, for example, from a database. Such XML documents can be parsed and read by application software for further processing of the data in distributed computing environments. XML documents containing rule-based content models can be used for knowledge representation. XML tags can be created to represent rules and corresponding parameters. Software agents can then parse and read the rules in these XML documents for use in making intelligent decisions.

Prior to making intelligent decisions, the software agents should be able to learn and codify or represent their knowledge in XML. Decision Trees and inductive learning algorithms such as ID3, C4.5 can be used by agents to develop the rule-based decision tree. This learned decision tree can be converted into an XML document with the corresponding use of a DTD. This XML document, containing the learned decision tree, forms the basis for knowledge representation and sharing with other software agents in the community.

COMPONENTS AND ELUCIDATION OF THE IKMAC ARCHITECTURE

As stated earlier, KMS include facilities for knowledge creation, knowledge exchange, storage and retrieval of knowledge in an exchangeable and usable format, and facilities to use the knowledge in decision-making activity. IKMAC is comprised of intelligent agents as the basic abstraction used for knowledge encapsulation and exchange to supporting collaborative activities. The agent abstraction is created using objects as the base class and incorporates additional features as warranted by agent functionality. Knowledge agents also interact with a knowledge repository to actively affirm the accuracy of the decision models used by the knowledge agents and serve as the active component of the decision support system. A domain knowledge object represents information about a specific problem domain in IKMAC. The domain knowledge object contains information about the characteristics of the various domain attributes that are important to the problem domain. The domain knowledge object also contains rules that specify decisions using the domain attributes of the domain knowledge object. Therefore, the domain knowledge object represents a description of the problem context and a description of the rules for making decisions in the problem context. As discussed earlier, there are many benefits to storing this knowledge in XML format, including standardization of semantics, validation ability and "well-formedness," ease of use, re-use and storage, and the ability to exchange complete XML documents in a format that conforms to established standards published by the World Wide Web Consortium (http://www.w3c.org). The domain knowledge object represents the abstraction used for creating, exchanging, and using modular knowledge objects in IKMAC.

IKMAC uses intelligent agents as the mechanism for the encapsulation and exchange of knowledge between agents at the site of knowledge creation and the site of knowledge storage. Intelligent agents are also utilized for the delivery of the knowledge to the user interface to support decision-making activity. Knowledge exchange and delivery in IKMAC is facilitated through the exchange of the domain knowledge objects among intelligent agents.

Figure 1 illustrates the basic building block of IKMAC, where an agent has a composition relationship with the Domain Knowledge object and thereby has access to knowledge in the form of standard XML Document Object Model (DOM) objects. Every agent has the ability to share its knowledge, in the form of the domain knowledge component, by invoking its ShareKnowledge behavior. The Domain Knowledge object contains behaviors to inform its containing agent of the name of the problem domain, share information about the various domain attributes that are pertinent to the specific knowledge context, and share rules about making decisions for their specific problem domain. We use these core components to develop the functionality of IKMAC to learn rules and domain attributes from raw data, create domain specific knowledge, share it with other agents, and apply this knowledge in either solving domain-specific problems or domain-specific collaborative activities with users. Once the attributes and domain rules are captured in the Domain Knowledge object, using standard XML DOM format, they can be exchanged between agents.

Figure 1: Each Agent in IKMAC has Access to a Domain Knowledge Object that Represents the Modular Abstraction of Domain Specific Knowledge

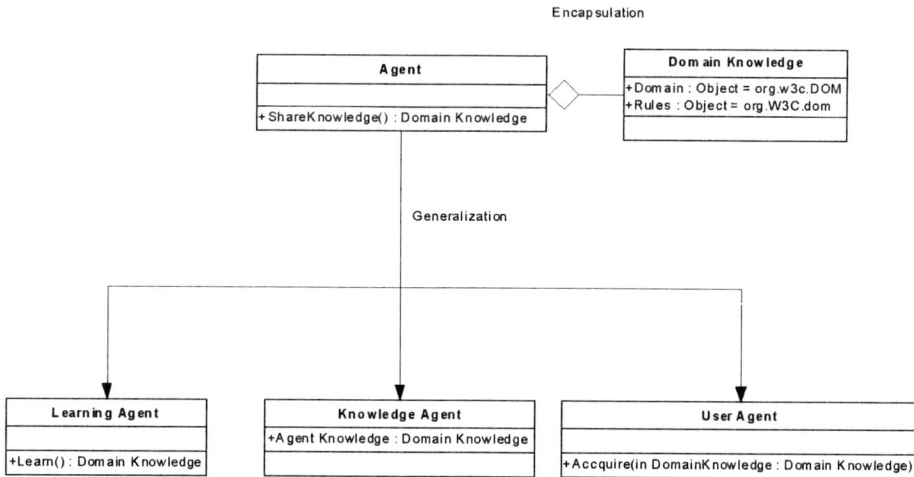

The Learning Agent interacts with a repository of raw data and extracts raw data that are used to generate domain-specific knowledge. The proposed model does not specify the storage representation in order to signify the fact that the data contained in the repository may be of multiple representation formats including flat files, data stored as relational tables that can be extracted using multiple queries into a Record Set, or data represented using XML documents. The process of extracting the data from the repository provides the context and syntactical representation of the information to create the domain attributes that are pertinent to the decision-problem context. The objective of this step is to generate domain-specific knowledge, in the form of domain attribute information, and rules for making decisions in the specific problem context. The system ensures that this knowledge is generated in a format conducive to sharing and use of the information across a distributed and heterogenous platform. We use the domain knowledge object as the modular abstraction for knowledge representation and knowledge exchange facilitation in IKMAC.

Once created, domain knowledge is made available for all agents in the system through sharing the domain knowledge object between the learning agent and the knowledge agent. The knowledge agent manages the knowledge available in the IKMAC knowledge repository and allows other agents to be aware of, request, and receive the domain knowledge in the system. The system utilizes the domain knowledge object as the modular knowledge abstraction for communication of knowledge among the multiple agents of the system. Therefore, when the domain knowledge object is shared with an agent of the system, the agent becomes aware of the problem-context descriptions and the rules that govern decision making for the specific problem context. The knowledge agent is responsible for maintaining the collection of domain knowledge available in the system through its interactions with a knowledge repository. The knowledge agent contains methods to generate rules to support ad hoc queries by the user agent. This is supported through the interactions of the knowledge agent with the knowledge repository. The Knowledge Repository is implemented using set of XML documents that are stored in a repository capable of storing XML documents, such as the Oracle 9i family of information management products (http://www.oracle.com). The knowledge repository allows for easy storage and retrieval of the knowledge contained in a domain knowledge object. Thus, the knowledge is available to all the agents in the system through the activities of the KM behaviors of the knowledge agent object. In this respect, the interactions among the agents in this system are modeled as collaborative interactions, where the agents in the multi-agent community work together to provide decision support and knowledge-based explanations of the decision problem domain to the user.

The users of IKMAC interact with the system through User Agents that are constantly aware of all domain knowledge contexts available to the system through a registry of domain contexts of the domain knowledge objects. This registry is published and managed by the knowledge agent. This allows every user agent, and hence every user, to be aware of the entire problem space covered by the system. The user agent requests and receives the knowledge available for a specific problem domain by making a request to the knowledge agent, at the behest of the user. The knowledge agent, upon receiving this request, shares a domain knowledge object with the user agent, thereby making problem domain information and decision rules available to the user agent. The knowledge agents also service any ad hoc queries that cannot be answered by the user interface agents, such as queries regarding knowledge parameters that are not available to the user interface agents. In such cases, the knowledge agent — with direct access to the knowledge repository — can provide such knowledge to the user agents for the benefit of the user. This information is shared in the form of two W3C-compliant XML document object model (DOM) objects, Domain and Rules as shown in *Figure 1*. These documents represent an enumeration and explanation of the domain attributes that are pertinent to the problem context and the rules for making decisions in the specified problem context. Once the domain knowledge object is available to the user agent, the user agent becomes problem-domain aware and is ready to assist the user through a decision-making process in the specific problem domain.

The above sections provide a complete description of the process of knowledge creation, knowledge representation, knowledge exchange, KM, and the use of the knowledge for collaboration employed by IKMAC. *Figure 2* provides a schematic of this overall process. As shown in *Figure 2*, IKMAC is designed for a distributed platform where the knowledge is available to the agents in the system on an intranet- and an Internet-based platform by enclosing the domain knowledge objects in Simple Object Access Protocol (SOAP) wrappers that enables the knowledge-broker functions of the knowledge agent by making its knowledge available as a web service.

As discussed above, IKMAC consists of intelligent agents that provide support for collaboration to the end-users. All agents in the IKMAC are FIPA-compliant (http://www.fipa.org), in that they communicate using XML DOM objects as the communication medium and extensions of the base language,

Figure 2: An Intelligent Knowledge-Based Multi-Agent Architecture for Collaboration (IKMAC)

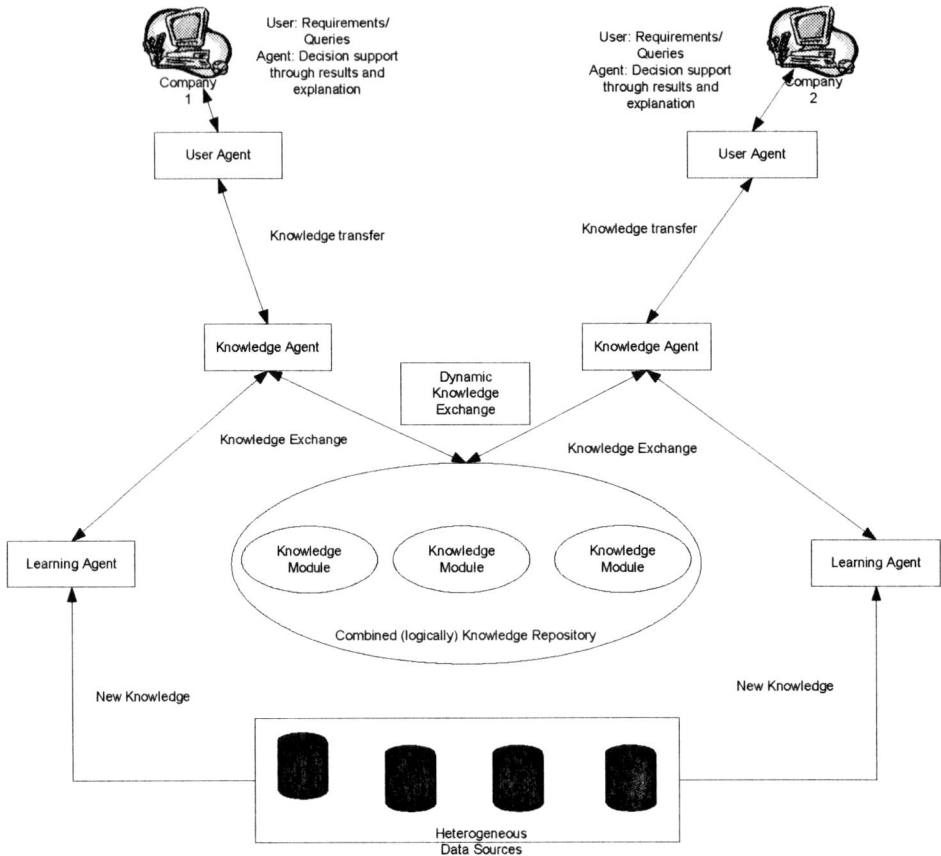

Java, objects. The learning agents create knowledge from the raw data in a data repository. Knowledge agents primarily acquire this knowledge from learning agents and manage this knowledge through a knowledge repository. User agents help in the transfer of knowledge between users and the knowledge agents and assist human decision-making activities. The exchange of knowledge between agents and between users and agents is achieved through sharing of content information using XML. The agents work on a distributed platform and enable the transfer of knowledge by exposing their public methods as web services using SOAP and XML.

The rule-based modular knowledge is captured in XML documents that can be used and shared by agents. Capturing and representing modular knowledge in XML format facilitates their storage in a knowledge repository — a repository that enables storage and retrieval of XML documents. The architecture allows for multiple knowledge modules depending upon the problem domain. The benefits of such knowledge repositories are the historical capture of knowledge modules that are available to agents in the agent community. This ensures that a newly created agent is instantiated with the access to complete current knowledge available to the entire system. This is achieved in IKMAC since agents have captured rule-based knowledge modules and have stored such knowledge modules in XML format in the knowledge repository for the benefit of the entire agent community and the system.

IKMAC can also provide decision support and explanation facility to the end-users where agents are able to explain how they arrived at a particular decision. This has three important benefits:

1.   The end-user is able to understand how the decision was made by the software agent;
2.   The end-user is able to make a clear assessment of the viability of the decision; and
3.   The end-user is able to learn and gain more knowledge about the problem domain by studying the decision paths used by the agent.

Agents are able to explain the rules and parameters that were used in arriving at the stated decision. Non-technical end-users are able to easily understand how a problem was solved through inductive learning and decision tree model-based explanations, as compared to other existing machine learning and problem-solving methods such as neural networks, statistical, and fuzzy logic-based systems (Sung, Chang, & Lee, 1999). The IKMAC architecture can provide collaborative support to internal processes, as well as to processes that interface with external partners. In the either case, the proposed architecture incorporates the W3C web services architecture to use the simple object access protocol (SOAP) and XML. This allows for the synchronous and asynchronous exchange of information and knowledge among the collaborating partners. The incorporation of this architecture creates a flexible means of exposing the services of the agents using the web services architecture by a company to its potential or existing global population of customers and suppliers.

ILLUSTRATIVE BUSINESS EXAMPLE: E-SUPPLY CHAINS AND E-MARKETPLACES

We use the infomediary-based e-Marketplaces (Grover & Teng, 2001) as an example to show how the IKMAC model can facilitate collaboration among business partners. An analysis of the infomediary business model shows that the individual buyers and suppliers seek distinct goal-oriented information capabilities from the infomediary. The process usually begins with buyers and suppliers providing decision parameters through their individual demand or supply functions. This is followed by a discovery activity that is comprised of buyers and suppliers searching for a match of their requirements in the infomediaries. The result of this activity is the discovery of a set of suppliers capable of meeting the buyers' needs. Typically, buyers will then engage in internal decision-making activity to select a supplier from the discovered set that best meets their needs. Such a decision process may be influenced by historical information such as past experiences of buyers' reliability and trustworthiness of the supplier.

The infomediary business model can provide valuable information to this decision process by serving as a knowledge repository of transactional histories for both buyers and suppliers. Once a supplier is identified, the infomediary performs a transaction facilitation role and enables the flow of information between the buyer and supplier that leads to the flow of tangible goods or services between the buyer and the supplier. In order to maintain and enable its services, the infomediary will need to collect and maintain post-transaction information from both the buyer and the supplier. This information is used as knowledge for the discovery process for subsequent transactions. Thus, the infomediary model can serve a larger purpose than facilitation of individual transaction; it can enable collaborative relationships between buyers and suppliers that are founded on trust that ensues from usage-oriented beliefs (Welty & Becerra-Fernandez, 2001). Thus, the infomediary performs the following three critical roles:

1. *Discovery:* of buyers and suppliers that meet each others' requirements;
2. *Facilitation:* of transactions to enable the flow of information and tangible goods and services between the buyers and suppliers in a knowledge-rich environment; and
3. *Support:* of knowledge-intensive decision processes that lead to deep collaborative relationships between partners in the supply chain.

Figure 3: Enablement of Collaboration in a Multi-Agent Infomediary-Based e-Marketplace

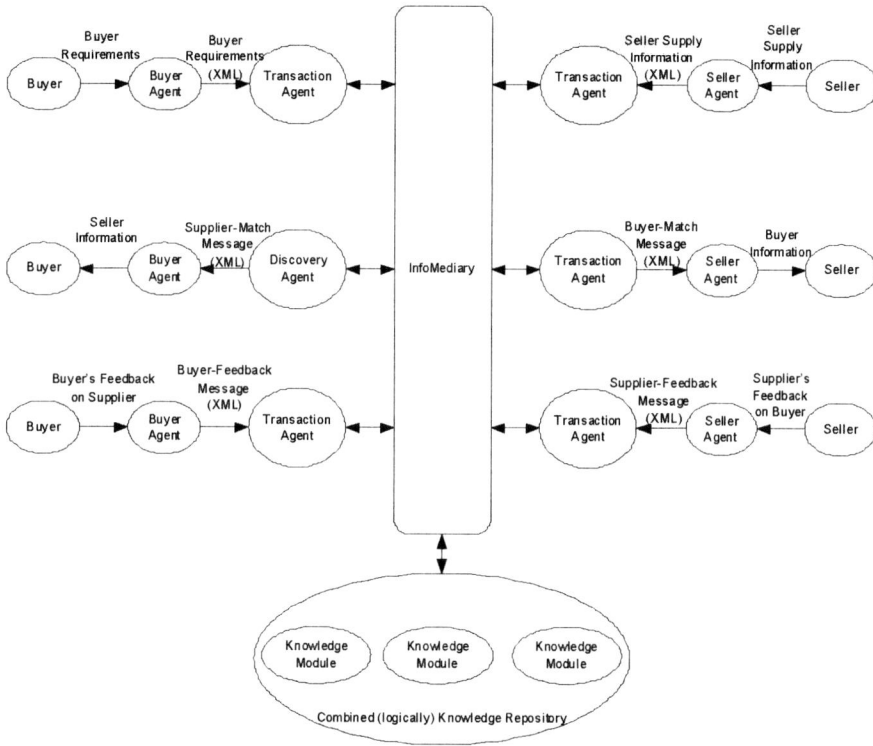

Figure 3 illustrates the enablement of collaboration in a multi-agent infomediary-based e-Marketplace.

In *Figure 3*, a buyer and a seller are represented in the virtual marketplace by a buyer agent and a seller agent, respectively. These agents convert the raw input from buyers and sellers into XML documents and pass it to the infomediary through transaction agents. This is then stored in a combined knowledge repository. As discussed earlier, each agent has the ability to share its knowledge, in the form of the domain-knowledge component, by invoking the ShareKnowledge behavior.

The discovery agents of the infomediary are then responsible for matching buyer requirements with supplier capabilities. The information pertaining to the matching is passed on to the buyer and seller agents by the discovery agent as XML documents. *Figures 5* and *6* shows sample XML documents containing

Figure 4: Infomediaries Communicate to Share Knowledge and Enable
Collaboration

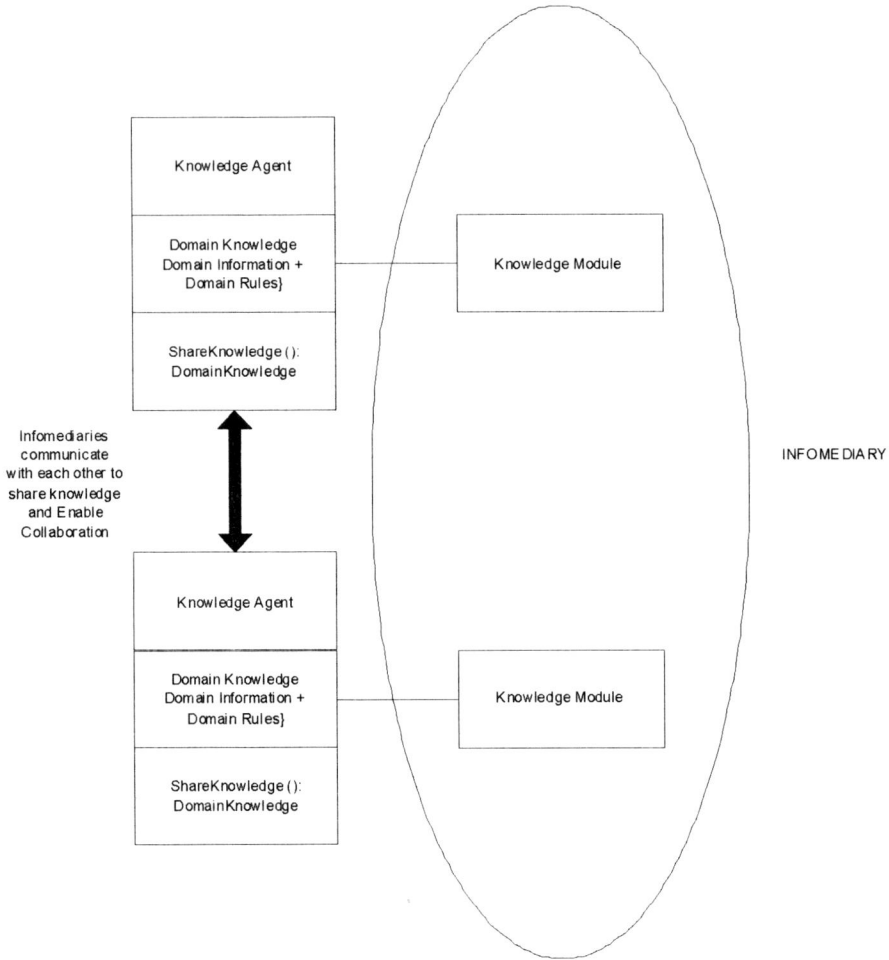

Domain Attributes and Domain Business Rule representation as a basis for
information and knowledge exchange in the multi-agent infomediary-based e-
Marketplace.

The buyer and seller agents can then provide the results to the buyer and
seller in a meaningful format with necessary explanations. Thus, the integration
of multiple infomediaries can facilitate transparency by allowing the exchange
of the much needed real-time information about trading partners in e-Marketplaces. *Figure 7* shows an expanded view of one entity in a multi-agent
infomediary-based model for knowledge sharing.

Figure 5: XML Document Showing Domain Attributes for Information and Knowledge Exchange in the Multi-Agent Infomediary-Based e-Marketplace

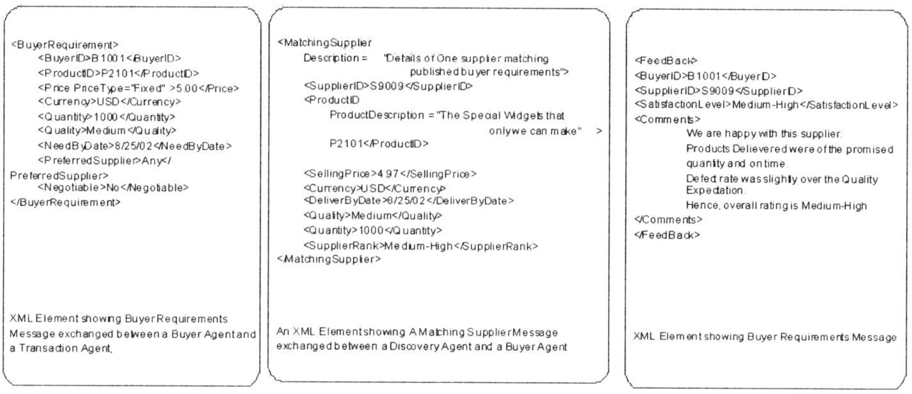

Figure 6: A Sample Buy Decision — Domain Business Rule Representation in XML Format as the Basis for the Knowledge Context for a Business Entity

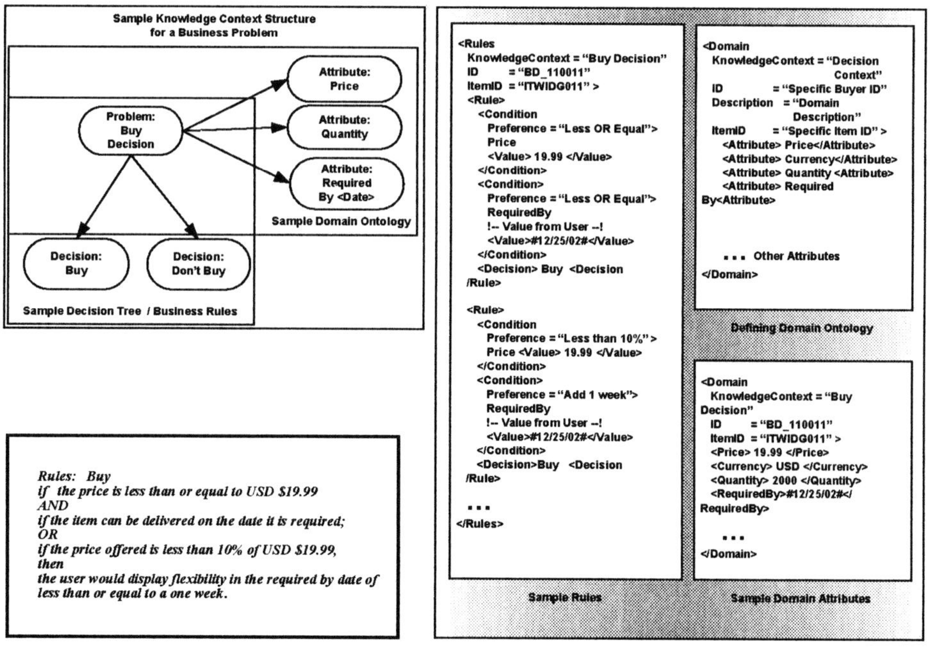

Figure 7: An Expanded View of One Entity in a Model for Knowledge Sharing

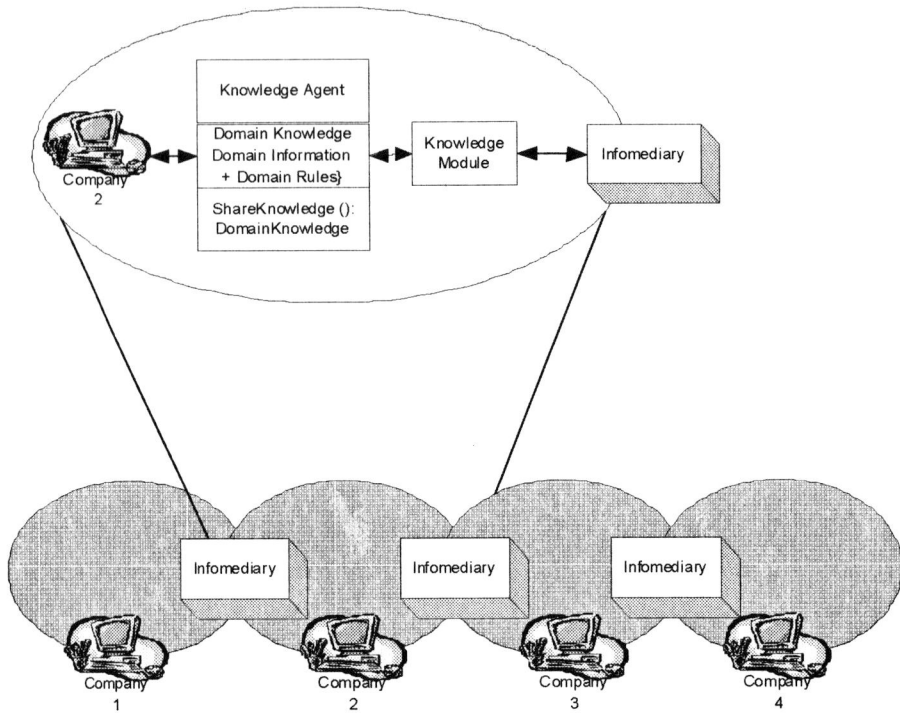

Thus, the use of intelligent agents to monitor developments in multiple infomediary-based e-Marketplaces not only makes the entire supply chain transparent, but also reduces the cognitive demands on human decision makers by providing explanations and managing the information about various facets of the decision-problem domain.

SUMMARY, CONCLUSION, AND FUTURE DIRECTIONS

The example presented here attempts to capture much of the core business processes involved in a typical supply chain network while remaining general enough to allow for further research. We are currently involved in research that extends this core model to processes in various other domains including knowledge-enabled financial decision support through various stages in a financial decision, spanning various organizations collaborating to deliver value to the customer. We believe that the exploration of various business realms to test and refine the architecture presented here is an interesting and useful avenue for future research. IKMAC is built on widely accepted, yet constantly evolving standards, such as XML and its related set of standards and the developing research on intelligent agents and their applications in various facets of business.

Collaborative multi-agent systems are very promising modeling abstractions for collaborative work flows, and research in this area to extend the architecture presented here will be beneficial to the academic and business communities alike. Efforts such as PMML by the data mining group hold much promise for the encoding and exchange of machine learning algorithms to systemize knowledge exchange using standardized, XML-based semantics. Future research in the utility of such models to enable collaborative knowledge exchange is a promising endeavor. Also, the implications that efforts such as the Semantic Web, ebXML, and enhanced web services may have on knowledge-based collaborative architectures such those presented here holds much promise for academics and professionals alike.

Realizing the potential benefits of emergent technologies is dependent on the effective sharing and use of business intelligence and process knowledge among business partners to provide accurate, relevant, and timely information and knowledge. This requires system models to support and enable information integration, knowledge exchange, and improved collaboration among business partners. This chapter presented such a system — IKMAC for knowledge-based and agent-enabled collaboration — to enable collaborative work in B2B e-Marketplaces. IKMAC is built upon the existing bodies of knowledge in intelligent agents, knowledge management, e-business, and XML and web services standards. An integral building block of IKMAC is the translation of data, information, and knowledge into XML documents by software agents, thereby creating the foundation for knowledge representation and exchange by intelligent agents to support collaborative work between business partners. IKMAC incorporates a consolidated knowledge repository to store and retrieve knowledge, captured in XML documents, to be used and shared by software agents within the multi-agent architecture. We show an initial proof of concept that utilizes an infomediary-based e-Marketplace example in which agents facilitate collaboration by exchanging their knowledge using XML and related set of standards.

REFERENCES

Ba, S., Lang, K.R., & Whinston, A.B. (1997). Enterprise decision support using Intranet technology. *Decision Support Systems,* (20)2, 99-134.

Beam, H.H. (1998, August). The infinite resource: Creating and leading the knowledge enterprise. *The Academy of Management Executive,* 12(3).

Bechek, B., & Brea, C. (2001). Deciphering collaborative commerce. *Journal of Business Strategy,* (March/April), 36-38.

Bellini, H., Gravitt, J.P., & Diana, D. (2001). *The birth of collaborative commerce.* Whitepaper, Salomon Smith Barney (June 20).

Berners-Lee, T., Hendler, J., & Lassila, O. (2001). The semantic web. *Scientific American,* (May), 34-43.

Bolloju, N., Khalifa, M. & Turban, E. (2002). Integrating knowledge management into enterprise environments for the next generation decision support. *Decision Support Systems,* 33, 163-176.

Bradshaw, J.M. (ed.). (1997). *Software Agents.* Boston, MA: MIT Press.

Davis, M. (1998, Fall). Knowledge management information strategy. *The Executive's Journal,* 15.

Fensel, D. (2000, November/December). *IEEE Intelligent Systems,* 67.

Grover, V., & Teng, J. (2001, April). E-commerce and the information market. *Communications of the ACM,* 44(4), 79-86.

Gupta, B., Iyer, L., & Aronson, J.E. (2000). Knowledge management: A taxonomy, practices and challenges. *Industrial Management and Data Systems,* 100(1), 17-21.

Jennings, N.R., & Wooldridge, M. (1998). *Agent Technology: Foundations, Applications, and Markets.* London: Springer.

McIlraith, S., Tran, T.C., & Zeng, H. (2001). Mobilizing the semantic web with DAML-enabled web services. *Proceedings of the Semantic Web Workshop,* Hong Kong, China.

Nemati, H.R., Steiger, D., Iyer, L.S., & Herschel, R.T. (2002). Knowledge warehouse: An architectural integration of knowledge management. Decision support, artificial intelligence and data warehousing. *Decision Support Systems,* 33(2), 143-161.

Singh, R., A.F. Salam and L.S. Iyer. (forthcoming). Intelligent Infomediary-base eMarketpla ces: Agents in e-Supply Chains. *Communications of the ACM.*

Skyrme, D.J. (1997). Knowledge management: Oxymoron or dynamic duo? *Managing Information,* 4(7).

Sung, T., Chang, N., & Lee, G. (1999). Dynamics of modeling in data mining: Interpretive approach to bankruptcy prediction. *Journal of Management Information Systems, 16*(1), 63-85.

Welty, B., & Becerra-Fernandez, I. (2001). Managing trust and commitment in collaborative supply chain relationships. *Communications of the ACM, 44*(6), 67-63.

Whinston, A.B. (1997). Intelligent agents as a basis for decision support systems. *Decision Support Systems, 20*(1).

Wiig, K.M. (1993). *Knowledge Management Foundations.* Texas: Schema Press.

Chapter VI

Text Mining in Business Intelligence

Dan Sullivan, The Ballston Group, USA

ABSTRACT

As the demand for more effective Business Intelligence (BI) techniques increases, BI practitioners find they must expand the scope of their data to include unstructured text. To exploit those information resources, techniques such as text mining are essential. This chapter describes three fundamental techniques for text mining in business intelligence: term extraction, information extraction, and link analysis. Term extraction, the most basic technique, identifies key terms and logical entities, such as the names of organizations, locations, dates, and monetary amounts. Information extraction builds on terms extracted from text to identify basic relationships, such as the roles of different companies in a merger or the promotion of a chemical reaction by an enzyme. Link analysis combines multiple relationships to form multistep models of complex processes such as metabolic pathways. The discussion of each technique includes an outline of the basic steps involved, characteristics of appropriate applications, and an overview of its limitations.

INTRODUCTION

Traditionally, business intelligence has focused on analyzing data gathered from transaction processing systems, such as enterprise resource planning (ERP), customer relationship management (CRM), sales force automation (SFA), claims processing, and other structured data sources. Structured data sources implement well-defined, but relatively limited data models. Relational and object-oriented databases are commonly used to implement these models. Somewhat less structured and more flexible are semi-structured data sources, such as XML-based models. Like structured data models, semi-structured models have well-defined structures that are relatively limited in scope but allow more flexibility with the range and ordering of data elements. At the far end of the data structure spectrum is unstructured data. As the name implies, there is no formal schema for such data. Free-form text, audio, and video are the most common forms of unstructured data. (The term "unstructured" is something of a misnomer when referring to text since language is highly structured according to linguistic principles, but the term is widely used nonetheless, and convention will be followed here.) Unstructured data is abundant in most organizations but to date has not been tapped as a source of business intelligence.

Recent advances in computational linguistics as well as Web and enterprise search make the integration of unstructured data into a business intelligence infrastructure feasible and effective. Together, these advances are broadly considered text mining, which is defined as analysis of natural language text to extract key terms, entities, and relationships between those terms and entities. These extracted elements are used for several purposes, including:

- categorizing and classify documents;
- generating summaries of texts;
- providing data for visualization tools for navigating large text databases; and
- mapping multistep relationships between series of entities.

These operations fit well into the domain of business intelligence which fundamentally identifies key business data and aggregates that data into a form suitable for supporting tactical decision making.

Consider the following decision-making task. A sales director for a telecommunications company is planning a new promotion on wireless services and needs information about:

- performance of past promotions;
- general trends in the company's sales;
- new market factors that influence purchasing decisions;
- capacity within the firm's own infrastructure; and
- competitors' past behavior and plans for similar promotions.

A traditional sales data mart populated with information from sales transactions will readily answer questions about past promotions and general trends. An operations data mart would similarly address capacity and infrastructure questions. These, however, are backward-looking measures and, while necessary to the decision-making process, they are not sufficient.

The telecommunications market is highly volatile because of merging technologies (e.g., wireless phone, personal digital assistants, and email devices), the entry of niche re-sellers such as prepaid wireless, and shifts in customer demographics (e.g., the increase in teenage customers. Some of these factors are reflected in traditional business intelligence systems but only after they cross a measurable threshold. To detect and assess the impact of these factors earlier requires analysis of text-based sources, such as internal reports on future markets, competitor advertising and marketing material, industry news, government reports, and other internal and external sources.

The following sections will examine three core text-mining techniques useful to such analysis:

- Term extraction;
- Information extraction; and
- Link analysis.

Term extraction, the most basic technique, identifies key terms and logical entities, such as the names of organizations, locations, dates, and monetary amounts. Information extraction builds on terms extracted from text to identify basic relationships, such as the roles of different companies in a merger or the promotion of a chemical reaction by an enzyme. Link analysis combines multiple relationships to form multistep models of complex processes such as metabolic pathways. Together, these three techniques provide the foundation for integrating text-based business intelligence into existing BI systems.

TERM EXTRACTION

Term extraction is the most basic form of text mining. Like all text-mining techniques, this one maps information from unstructured data to a structured format. The simplest data structure in text mining is the feature vector, a weighted list of words that appear in a text. It provides a representative description, or signature, for the text. For example, consider the following segment from an industry magazine on wireless technology (Dornan, 2000):

A mobile version of fixed wireless, currently used as a fixed line local loop replacement, will soon be an option. Hours before admitting its fraud, WorldCom made a less publicized announcement: It was deploying a data-only version of Europe's 3G system in its fixed spectrum. Though WorldCom may not be the most believable source of information, the vendor that actually makes the system, IPWireless (www.ipwireless.com), says it's still going ahead, starting in Memphis. Sprint (not Sprint PCS) plans to do the same, and is currently running trials to help it decide between IPWireless and Navini (www.navini.com), which has a similar technology.

This can be reduced to an array of terms and weights (see *Figure 1*).

Figure 1

Term	Weight
Mobile	0.2
Fixed wireless	0.3
Fixed line local loop	0.35
WorldCom	0.4
Fraud	0.45
3G System	0.2
IPWireless	0.3
Memphis	0.35
Sprint	0.28
Navini	0.42

The list of terms does not capture the full meaning of the text, but it does identify the key terms mentioned in the article. To identify key terms, text-mining systems perform several operations.

First, commonly used words, known as stop words (e.g., the, and, other), are removed. Second, words are stemmed or reduced to their roots. For example, "phoned" and "phoning" are mapped to "phone." This provides the means to analyze the frequency of root words that bear meaning without syntactic variations. The final step calculates the weight for each remaining term in a document. There are many methods for calculating these weights, but the most commonly used algorithms use a count of the term frequency in a document (the term frequency or *tf factor*) and the frequency of the word across all documents in a collection (the inverse document frequency or *idf factor*) (Baeza-Yates & Ribeiro-Neto, 1999). Large *tf* factors increase the weight of a term, while large *idf* factors lower the weight. The general assumption behind such a scheme is that terms that appear frequently in a document (high *tf* factor) distinguish a document from others unless those terms appear frequently across all texts in the collection (high *idf* factor).

Feature vectors are used for several purposes in text-mining systems. They are used to measure similarity between documents. If the feature vector is considered a line through a multidimensional space, the angle between any two vectors indicates the similarity between the documents. Since the feature vectors contain the most important terms, they can guide the selection of sentences most relevant to a document when creating a summary for the text. Finally, these vectors provide the basis for classifying and clustering documents.

Machine-learning algorithms are widely used in categorizing texts based on feature vectors. Support-vector machines, in particular, are a highly effective class of algorithms for this task (Dumas, Osuna, Platt, & Scholkopf, 1998). To classify documents, a system user identifies example documents for each category (this approach is known as supervised learning). Each document is mapped to a feature vector, and the feature vectors for each category are provided to the machine-learning algorithm which then induces a rule for each category based upon terms and weights. For example, an example rule for categorizing a document in the government regulation category is given in *Figure 2*.

In many applications of text mining, preexisting classification schemes are not available or not appropriate for a particular problem. In those cases, clustering — a form of unsupervised learning — is used to group documents

Figure 2

Term	Operator	Weight	Boolean
Government	>	0.4	AND
Agency	>	0.3	AND
Commission	>	0.33	AND
Regulation	>	0.1	AND
Lobby	>	0.45	

together based upon similarity. This approach is especially useful for initially assessing the contents of a text database and understanding the broad topics covered by that collection.

Term extraction can be applied to a range of text sources and, unlike other text-mining techniques, performance does not degrade with ungrammatical texts.

Many business transaction applications, such as customer relationship management (CRM), clinical records, and insurance claims processing, include structured data, such as numeric measures and coded attributes as well as free-form annotations. CRM systems may track detailed descriptions of customer complaints, doctors may note variations in symptoms or special instructions in a patient's chart, and claims adjusters might add details about an insurance claim that do not fit neatly into the predefined data elements.

Consider a worker's compensation claims system. As with other insurance applications, this would track demographics about claimants, location of the accident, type of accident, etc. It may also include Boolean indicators for common conditions involved in past claims (e.g., slippery floor), but there are practical limitations to the number of such indicators, so free-form text is used for additional details. Narratives could be used to describe activity prior to the accident, unusual environmental conditions, distracting factors, etc. Term extraction could identify key terms in each narrative, for example, turning, bending, twisting prior to the accident; leaks, ambient temperature, wind conditions in the environment conditions notes; and noise, foot traffic and other distracting factors in the final narrative. By mapping the free-form text to a feature vector, the text is modeled in the same attribute/value model used by structured data and thus lends itself to analysis using traditional business intelligence tools such as ad hoc reports, OLAP analysis, and data mining.

IMPROVING UPON TERM EXTRACTION WITH FEATURE EXTRACTION

Term extraction is sufficient in many situations, but categorization and other higher level text-mining operations are improved when feature extraction is employed. Feature extraction is similar to term extraction except that, instead of using just lexical cues such as spaces and punctuation to identify terms, feature extraction uses syntactic properties to identify entities, such as names of businesses, government agencies, dates, monetary amounts, and locations.

A customer email such as:

On Aug. 10, 2003, I purchased a copy of "Proven Portals: Best Practices for Planning, Designing and Developing Enterprise Portals" (Order # 980127302) for $31.95 and still have not received it. The book should have shipped by 08/15/03. Please update me on the status of my order.

contains key pieces of information that can be identified using linguistic cues and knowledge of common formatting rules about dates and monetary amounts. Rather than map to a feature vector, this information is better mapped to an XML representation such as:

```
<email entities>
    <date> Aug 10, 2003 </date>
    <named entity> Proven Portals: Best Practices in Planning, Designing and
Developing Enterprise Portals</named entity>
    <number> 980127302 </number>
    <monetary amount>
        <amount> 31.95 </amount>
        <currency> USD </currency>
    </monetary amount>
    <date> Aug 15, 2003 </ date>
</email entities>
```

Feature extraction techniques provide more detail about semantic attributes than is available with term extraction, but it still lacks important information about relationships between terms. In this example, two dates, one named entity, and one monetary amount are identified but without any indication as to the role of each in the text. For that next level of analysis, one must use information extraction techniques.

Term and feature extraction are best when used for mapping text to simple representation (the term vector) for search, categorization, and clustering operations. Feature extraction, however, is a required building block for information extraction.

INFORMATION EXTRACTION

The next level of complexity in text mining is information extraction. Unlike term extraction which focuses on terms, information extraction focuses on a set of facts that constitute an event, episode, or state. For example, a news story such as the following describes the basic facts about a corporate merger:

Alpha Industries announced today its acquisition of Beta Enterprises for $50 million, USD effective April 1, 2003. The merger depends upon regulatory approval by the Food and Drug Administration (FDA).

Using feature extraction techniques, we could map this story to an XML schema such as:

```
<news-story>
   <named entity> Alpha Industries </named entity>
   <named entity> Beta Enterprises </named entity>
   <monetary amount>
       <amount> 50 million </amount>
       <currency> USD </currency>
   </monetary amount>
   <named entity> Food and Drug Administration (FDA) </named entity>
<news story>
```

Critically missing from this representation is the relationship of the three named entities and the purpose of the monetary amount. Information extraction techniques address this problem by matching patterns of events, episodes, or states to text. Patterns are constructed using entities, terms, punctuation, and special pattern-matching characters. The first step in information extraction is to tag the text with XML markup just as is done in feature extraction. These tags identify entities such as company names and monetary amounts as well as verb phrases such as "merged" or "acquired." After XML tagging (sometimes called chunking), the above story would be:

> *<named entity>Alpha Industries </named entity> <active announce phrase> announced today </active announce phrase> its <active acquire phrase> acquisition of </active acquire phrase> <named entity> Beta Enterprises </named entity> for <monetary amount> <amount> $50 million </amount>, <currency> USD </currency> </monetary amount> effective <date> April 1, 2003 </date>. The merger depends upon <regulation phrase> regulatory approval </regulation phrase> by the <named entity> Food and Drug Administration (FDA) <named entity>.*

A pattern for identifying merger information should at least match the acquiring company, the acquired company, the cost of the acquisition, whether the payment is in cash, stock, or other instruments, and if regulatory approval is required. A simple pattern that would match the above story is:

> <named entity> <active acquires phrase> <named entity> *"for"* <monetary amount> *<regulation phrase>*.

The asterisks match any number of words between entities, such as between the <monetary amount> and <regulation phrase>.

The first named entity matches "<named entity>Alpha Industries </named entity>," the acquire phrase with "<active acquire phrase>" acquisition of "</active acquire phrase>," the second named entity with "<named entity> Beta Enterprises </named entity>," the monetary amount pattern matches with "<monetary amount> <amount> $50 million </amount>, <currency> USD </currency> </monetary amount>," and the regulation pattern matches "<regulation phrase> regulatory approval </regulation phrase>." Since the acquires phrase uses an active form of the verb, the first named entity maps to the acquiring company and the second named entity maps to the acquired. (If the verb were passive, the roles would be reversed.) With this set of matches, one has extracted more information, as represented by the following:

```
<merger story>
    <acquiring company>Alpha Industries </acquiring company>
    <acquired company>Beta Enterprises </acquired company>
    <purchase amount>
        <amount> 50 million </amount>
        <financial instrument> USD </financial instrument>
    </purchase amount>
    <regulation required> yes </regulation required>
</merger story>
```

By applying more sophisticated tagging methods than used in feature extraction, one can identify verb phrases which in turn dictate the roles played by other entities in a sentence. Now, in addition to syntactic attributes (e.g., named entity, date, monetary amount), the analyzed text is labeled with semantic attributes such as acquiring company and purchase amount. These techniques are applicable to a wide range of applications within the realm of business intelligence, including patent analysis, competitive intelligence, and CRM notes analysis. This additional functionality comes, however, at a cost.

First, the preprocessing phase requires more linguistic knowledge than in feature extraction. The preprocessor must identify verbs and pattern-matching rules must embedded knowledge about the placement of entities relative to a verb. For example, the agent of an active verb appears prior to the verb in an English sentence, and the object of the verb, if there is one, follows the verb.

Second, patterns must be developed. The number of patterns grows with the variations in text used to describe an event, episode, or state. Also, as the number of distinct types of information extracted grows, so will the patterns.

Finally, the more sophisticated the textual analysis, the greater the chance of error. Analysts and business intelligence practitioners will need to spend a considerable amount of time testing and tuning information extraction systems to reach acceptable levels of performance.

LINK ANALYSIS

Link analysis is a set of techniques for gaining insight into the relationships between multiple entities having multiple connections, steps, or links. Telecommunications is a typical example of systems that lend themselves to link analysis. Phone calls and network packets start at a given point and move through multiple connections on their way to the final destination. To understand how traffic moves from Server A to Server B over the Internet, we need to understand how routers choose pathways for sending information. In the pharmaceutical industry, scientists study metabolic pathways that can include long sequences of chemical reactions from the time a drug is introduced to the time the desired effect is realized. Link analysis can be used in business intelligence applications to analyze the relationship between entities, facts, and events, such as those derived from term, feature, and information extraction.

Link analysis starts with a large collection of facts or term and entity co-occurrence frequencies. These provide the basic link structure. In the case of term and entity co-occurrence, we have a measure of how frequently two terms appear together that allows us to identify potentially interesting relationships, such as the relationship between A and D in the following set of co-occurrence frequencies. A and B are strongly linked, and B and C are strongly linked, as is C to D, indicating a possible logical connection between A and D.

$$A \rightarrow B \qquad 0.8$$
$$B \rightarrow C \qquad 0.7$$
$$C \rightarrow D \qquad 0.75$$

This term and entity co-occurrence does not identify the type of relationship, for example, A causes B or does C acquire D. Link analysis over facts, however, does provide the additional semantic information missing in the co-occurrence examples. Consider the set of patterns,

A activates B
B inhibits C
D requires C

From these one can conclude that increasing A will cause a reduction in D, because increasing B will, presumably, reduce C, a prerequisite of D.

This type of link analysis is particularly important in bioinformatics and pharmaceuticals. Competitive intelligence in vertical industries, market analysis in financial services, and science and technology management all lend themselves to this type of analysis.

The basic steps in link analysis are as follows. First, define content sources, such as news stories, patent databases, or medical abstracts. Second, preprocess the content and perform basic syntactic and semantic tagging. Third, in the case of information extraction, extract facts, including agents and actions. (The results of this step should be reviewed and edited by a knowledgeable user before proceeding to the next step.) In the case of term or feature co-occurrence, calculate a measure of how frequently the terms appear together.

Applications suited for link analysis can be easily mapped to the node and link structure of directed graphs. Examples include biomedical research, competitive intelligence, and market analysis.

The quality of link analysis depends heavily upon the quality of text analysis and the ability to correctly identify relationships. As with any language-based analysis, standardizing on a single set of terms is challenging, but link analysis applications should map terminology used in source texts to a fixed vocabulary whenever possible.

CONCLUSION

Business intelligence for the Digital Economy demands a wide range of data sources, not just numeric data. Three basic techniques, term and feature extraction, information extraction, and link analysis are providing the foundation for text-related business intelligence techniques. These techniques map key elements of free-form text to structured formats that lend themselves to analytic techniques. Term extraction, with relatively simple linguistic processing requirements, leverages statistical analysis to measure the relevancy of terms which in turn represent concepts in a collection. Information extraction identifies both relevant entities and their relationship. Link analysis is one method for analyzing the relationship between facts derived from information extraction techniques. Unlike traditional business intelligence techniques, these are prone to error, even when programmed correctly. The state of the art in language processing is not sufficient to accurately analyze the range of topics and styles found in the business environment. Even with the current limitations, text-mining techniques can provide valuable insight not readily available from existing, structured data.

REFERENCES

Baeza-Yates, R., & Ribeiro-Neto, B. (1999). *Modern Information Retrieval*. New York: ACM Press.

Dornan, A. (2002). Breaking wireless data free from its cell. *Network Magazine*. September 5. Accessed July 2003 at: http://www.networkmagazine.com/shared/article/showArticle.jhtml?articleId=8703409&classroom=.

Dumais, S., Osuna, E., Platt, J., & Scholkopf, B. (1998, July/August). Using SVMs for text categorization. *IEEE Intelligent Systems*, 21-23.

Chapter VII

Bypassing Legacy Systems Obstacles:
How One Company Built Its Intelligence to Identify and Collect Trade Allowances

James E. Skibo, University of Dallas, USA

ABSTRACT

This chapter describes both the nature of trade allowances and the unique approach taken by one major retailer in overcoming legacy system obstacles in its efforts to identify and collect allowances. Trade allowances have the potential for very substantial returns for retailers and they are often used as a bargaining tool between manufacturers and retailers. Also, the nature of the allowances is that they are rarely ever account-specific and, as a result, are collected by organizations on a first-come, first-served basis. In other words, whichever organization manages to claim the allowance first is generally the organization that will get the funds from manufacturers. As a result, there is only a small body of literature on the subject and virtually no literature that describes the systems used for trade allowance identification and collection. It is *necessary to understand what trade allowances are in order to fully understand the system employed to identify and collect them, and this chapter provides a brief primer on trade allowances. The chapter then describes the unique approach taken by a major retailer to garner a significant amount of income from these allowances. The approach was novel in that it bypassed the traditional approach that would have been to expend the time and resources to reinvigorate or reinvent its many legacy systems. Starting with less than $700,000 in trade allowances in the years preceding 1997, the system developed by the retailer has netted them in excess of $65 million (USD) in 2002.*

INTRODUCTION

This chapter describes a unique niche of business referred to as trade allowances and the systems methodology employed by one retailer to grow that segment of its income. The retailer had some experience in negotiating and obtaining trade allowances and had consistently garnered trade allowance revenues of slightly less than $1 million USD annually versus $35 million in marketing expenses. In the mid-1990 time frame, the retailer began to compare its trade allowance income with industry intelligence that indicated an aggressive approach towards trade allowance revenue should yield significantly higher returns, i.e., in the range of one to three percent of sales. Since the retailer had in excess of $3 billion in annual sales, this equated to a potential revenue stream of $30 to $90 million annually. Obviously with this amount of revenue at stake, the retailer chose to make the identification and collection of trade allowances one of its strategic goals. Because of the success of the retailer's efforts and the amount of money involved, it is not possible to reveal the real name of the retailer in this chapter. To do so would potentially jeopardize its trade allowance revenue; therefore, the retailer will be referred to as Capital Discount.

A unique characteristic of trade allowances is that they are often not specific to one account. Normally, a manufacturer will set aside one percent of its cost of goods for trade allowances, but will not specify which account will receive the allowances. It is possible that the manufacturer will offer some trade allowance support to one account and not to the other, or have criteria that only certain accounts can meet, such as volume-based allowances. Also, trade allowances are often paid on a basis of funds availability. Therefore, the retailer who can file its claims the fastest will have the advantage (Houk & Association of National Advertisers, 1995). The other characteristic of trade allowances is breakage. That is to say that retailers do not claim all of the trade allowance dollars offered or available. In 1999, the latest year for which data are available, it was estimated that more than $38 billion in trade allowances were offered, but less than half, $17 billion, were actually claimed by retailers (Trade One Marketing, Inc., 2003). This does not necessarily mean that claims for the remaining $21 billion were not made; it means that they were either not made or were not honored by the manufacturers, because one of the other characteristics of trade allowance is that they almost always contain criteria that must be met before the claim will be honored. Typically, some sort of proof-of-performance is required that shows that advertising actually took place within the guidelines established by the manufacturer. Therein lies one of the challenges of trade allowances — knowledge of the manufacturer's guidelines.

In their most elementary form, trade allowances are monies provided by manufacturers or service providers to retailers or wholesalers in order to promote their goods and services above those of other manufacturers or service providers. This is why grocery or discount stores will have end fixtures or aisle fixtures stacked with one manufacturer's product; that manufacturer has provided an incentive for the display and, in markets with tight margins, the trade allowance for the display sometimes represents the sole profit the retailer will realize on the sale of the product. Trade allowances also help the retailer pay for weekly sales fliers found in local newspapers, yellow page listings in the phone book, and so on. In the case of wholesalers, trade allowance income permits large as well as smaller local wholesalers to compile massive product catalogs for the industries they serve. These catalogs are typically given away free of charge to potential customers, and the wholesalers must have some subsidy to pay for their production. Combined with its industry knowledge, Capital saw this as an opportunity to make all of its marketing expense-neutral to the company. This chapter describes the journey of Capital Discount from achieving less than $1 million annually to reaching more than $66 million five years later. The objective of this chapter is to detail Capital's journey and its unique application of technology in order to bridge the many legacy systems found within its IT infrastructure. The approach taken may have wider application in other industries facing similar challenges

BACKGROUND

While the concept of trade allowances is almost eighty years old (Agnew, 1926), there is little in the literature that describes, in detail, the systems and methodology used to identify and collect them. With the advent of modern advertising as a formalized approach to marketing products and services, Agnew was the first to describe the fundamental principles of trade allowances and their management. The literature is absent any significant exploration of trade allowances until the 1970s. In that time frame, discount retailers were emerging on the national scene, and there was renewed interest in trade allowances as a method of maximizing revenue for the discounters who operated on small profit margins but high volume. This particular type of retailer also made extensive and costly use of supplements in local newspapers as a means of advertising its low prices. As the more savvy discounters demanded trade allowances, the literature began to detail the new use for trade allowances in the discount sector (Young, 1979; Young, Greyser, & Marketing Science Institute, 1982). The literature tended to detail the use of trade allowances from the manufacturer's perspective, often taking on the role of a "how to" guide for managing effective trade allowance programs (Bullock, 1983; Crimmins & Association of National Advertisers Cooperative Advertising Committee, 1984; Young & Greyser, 1983). In the same time frame, the literature began to document the methodologies of the discount retailers in using trade allowances as one of the many strategic tools for maintaining profit margins in what was becoming a highly crowded and competitive environment (Bayus, Lee, & Rao, 1989; Litvack, 1984). The literature continued to expand to offer integrative approaches that detailed both the manufacturer's and retailer's roles in trade allowance management to include specific actions required of both parties to identify and claim trade allowances (Houk & Association of National Advertisers, 1995; Jørgensen, 1998, 2000; Jørgensen & Zaccour, 1996). For the first time, the literature began to discuss the systems that might be used in a successful trade allowance management program, again, from the perspective of both parties. In many cases, smaller retailers have an advantage in dealing with trade allowances because they have had to rely on them in order to compete with larger better-funded companies. Larger retailers, on the other hand, have done a poor job in identifying and claiming trade allowances. The reason for this is that the process involves some labor-intensive activity outside of the manufacturer's and retailer's normal billing and payment systems. Typically, this involves physically measuring all printed media so that claims can be developed based on not only the square inches of the actual ad, but proration of all headers and gutters as well.

Currently, there is no available software application that can accomplish this accurately. While Quark and Adobe will correctly measure a highlighted square, they cannot aggregate dimensions from multiple images within the same file. As a result, the measurement step is the most labor intensive in the entire trade allowance claim development process, and many large retailers simply do not undertake the steps necessary to develop claims. Pountney's (2002) work has shown some promise for possibly integrating Visual FoxPro, however, this has not been attempted for this application. More interesting might be the integration of both Pountney's work with Riccardi's (2003) suggestion that Web-based tools should be used to manage database applications, including those databases containing graphic content. Because the page images require human thought as to what may or may not be included in the claim for a particular manufacturer, the ultimate solution may reside in a fuzzy logic application that integrates graphic content with subsets of database applications, such as a feed to common platform DB2 databases. Miller (2002) somewhat suggests this but does not actually conclude that this is totally possible. The author of this chapter feels it is possible and desirable, however, it is also possible that the commercial application is so limited as to not provide the return on investment needed to spur development of such an application.

OPERATING ENVIRONMENT

Figure 1 shows the impact of manual processes throughout the trade allowance management process within a typical retailer, and this macro-level process flow also applies to Capital. The number of manufacturers offering trade allowances will vary depending on the market-segment a retailer or wholesaler occupies. Typically, this is in a range of 50 to 100 trade allowance programs for each 1,000 suppliers. In the case of Capital, it has more than 8,000 primary suppliers of retail products and services. Within that population, it has identified approximately 700 trade allowance programs. These vary from simple annual accruals, to highly complex volume-based accruals that span multiple calendar quarters. A sampling of these is illustrated in *Figure 2*. As a further complication, some accruals are based on purchases while others are based on receipts, and some are even based on Point of Sales (POS) sales data. These variations are manufacturer-specific, with no particular relation to product category such as consumable products versus apparel versus hardlines products.

In 1996, the identification and collection function for trade allowances resided within Capital's marketing department. The department had the long-term record of claiming and receiving less than $1 million annually on sales of more than $3 billion. The claims were developed using data imported from a variety of sources within the organization including various DB2 tables with

Figure 1: Macro-Level Trade Allowance Process Flows

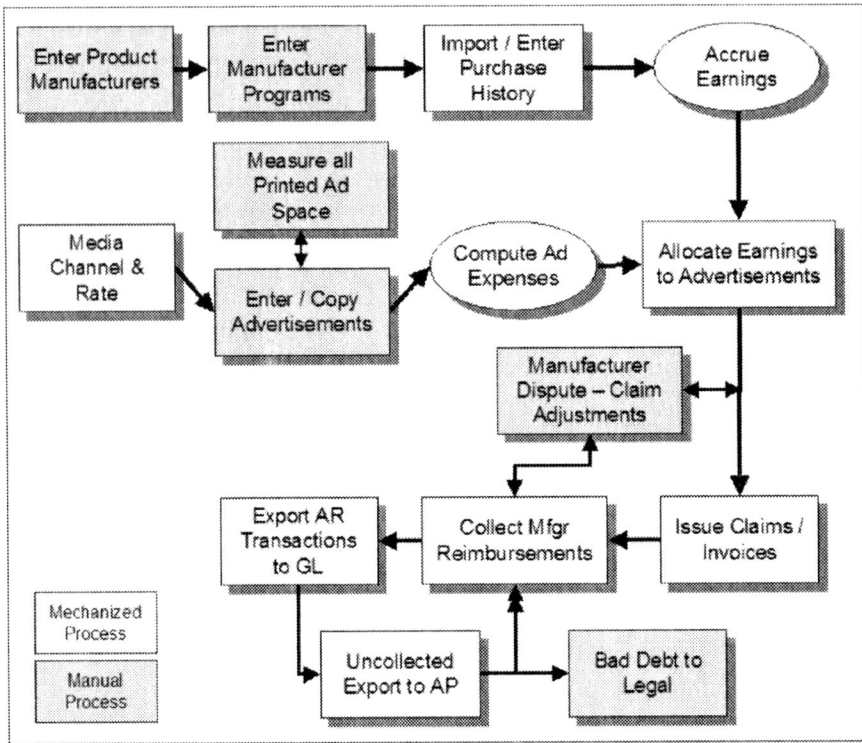

Figure 2: Typical Accrual Programs

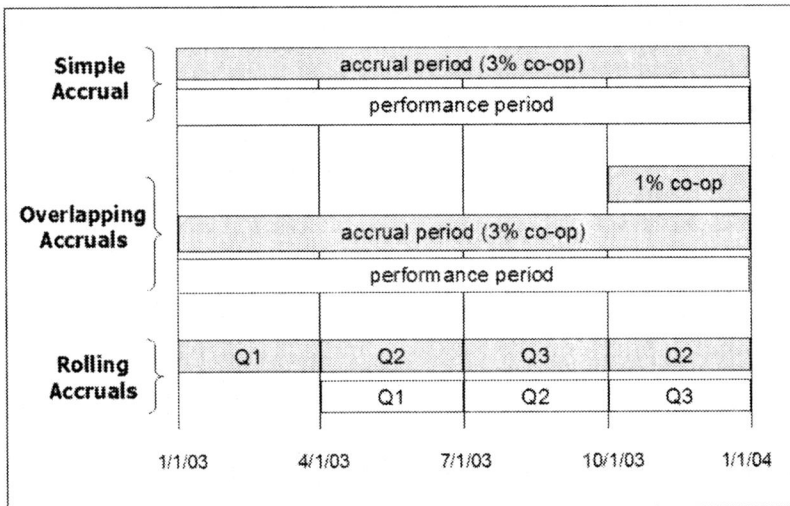

purchasing and receipt data, NCR Teradata Retail Point of Sale (RPOS) unit sale data at store level, Oracle data warehoused organizational financial data, and several mainframe flat files from a variety of 1960s-era programs used to handle receipts by beverage and snack distributors at the local store level. Data from each of these sources is needed to develop trade allowance claims. Note that since trade allowances are normally reimbursed by functions other than the supplier's accounts payable function, invoices for trade allowances are termed "claims" rather than "invoices" in order that the claims will be mail-routed to the supplier's trade allowance disbursement function and not to accounts payable.

The gathering of data was accomplished by a variety of queries and table building, however, it was largely a level of effort for the human resources of the function; that is, nothing mechanical drove the creation of the claims. This had the obviously vulnerability of human error and missed claim opportunities. There were approximately 900 claims developed each year, and the methodology seemed manageable for this approach, albeit vulnerable to error. Claims developed had terms of net 30 days with a grace period of 60 days. As the claims were developed, the department then input the claims data into Capital's accounts receivable system and ran occasional queries to check for aged receivables. As aging beyond 60 days occurred, the group manually moved the claim data to clear the receivable and then added the same data into Capital's accounts payable system so the claim could be deducted from a future invoice payment to the respective supplier. In this manner, the department turn-keyed trade allowances for Capital to also include the receipt and processing of supplier trade allowance payments for the claims.

AR AND AP ENVIRONMENTS

Other anomalies of trade allowance programs are that they rarely fit neatly into either the retailer's or the supplier's mainstream systems. For example, manufacturers rarely will pay trade allowances as part of their accounts payable or accounts receivables functions. Normally, suppliers have a separate function within the organization to handle trade allowance claims. The primary reason for this is because these claims normally require the supplier to validate the claim and supporting documentation such as advertising tear sheets, radio scripts, and other proofs of performance that is submitted with the claim.

The role of most retailers is one of invoice payers as opposed to invoice generators. As such, most retailers do not have an invoicing system because there is no need for its functionality. Where a retailer does have an invoicing system, it is almost always not functional for trade allowances because of the naming convention for claims. In Capital's case, it did have a billing system because it also sold on-account in bulk to several contractors and local municipalities. Capital's system was a highly modified CICS-based application by Walker. Coincidentally, it also used a similar application for its Accounts Payable (AP) functions. Oddly, however, the two systems were not integrated and transactions occurring on the Accounts Receivable (AR) side were not passed to the AP side and vice versa. This is a bit unusual for two common platform systems from the same vendor, but not at all unusual for legacy systems (Brodie & Stonebraker, 1995; Fotiadis & Nikolopoulos, 2000; Ulrich, 2002).

Capital uses an in-house developed legacy MVS-based application that is DB2 driven. The DB2 database contains the items being promoted in any given sales week along with other data such as the pricing, trade allowances, etc., needed for its stores to order in time for the sales event. It is critical at this point to mention that the trade allowance data contained in this system was what was either known to the buyer or what had been negotiated for the specific event. Capital's supplier master file did not — and still does not — contain fields or logic for trade allowances.

PURCHASING SYSTEMS ENVIRONMENT

Capital employs a variety of purchasing systems, some of which are legacy systems dating back to the late 1960s, while its largest is a 2002 state-of-the-art perpetual inventory and sales-driven system. Older legacy systems were used to handle purchasing and receiving of local rack distributor products such as milk, bottled beverages, snack items, and baked goods. There are two distinct systems employed: one for local distributors who will invoice for items as a separate action from delivery, and one to handle local deliveries where the local rack suppliers delivery ticket is the invoice for products delivered. The two separate systems evolved as an adjunct to the pattern of invoicing developed by local suppliers in the 1960s and 1970s. The latter two systems are CICS-based and have no database structure or feeds to external data stores in place. At the opposite end of that spectrum are Capital's in-house developed drop-ship and distribution center replenishment systems. Both have extensive data feeds to subsidiary data stores and are readily accessible by corollary systems.

CATALOG ENVIRONMENT

Capital publishes several small seasonal catalogs throughout the year. Typically, these have a page count of less than 100 pages per catalog, with an average of five items per page. The system to control the catalog operation is an in-house developed legacy system dating from the early 1960s. A replication of the items offered in both the catalog supplements and Capital's weekly sales fliers for its "brick-and-mortar" stores is also contained on Capital's Web site. The Web-based ordering system is operated completely independently of the mainframe catalog system, which is then updated via batch feeds each evening.

TRADE ALLOWANCE SYSTEM

In 1995, Capital's senior management became aware of the revenue potential for trade allowances and established reinventing the function as a top priority for the company. However, one of the challenges for an effective trade allowance claiming system was the need for the accumulation and use of data from virtually all of Capital's key data sources, particularly line item purchasing and receiving history, line item accounts payable detail, and promotional activity and resulting sales detail.

Over the next half year, various COTS packages were explored, but none seemed to match the exact requirements that Capital needed, principally because the packages would have required Capital to build the necessary data feeds in order for the packages to function. Most COTS packages reviewed were priced in the $100 thousand range, and Capital estimated that cost would double when IT man-hours to write the interfaces were included. Also, all of the COTS packages were PC/server based, and none had been successfully implemented in a company the size of Capital. As part of the review, Capital did extensive due diligence to determine the exact data feeds that would be required to implement the COTS packages. As a result, Capital developed a knowledge of what was involved with an effective trade allowance system, and it became clear to Capital that for approximately the same cost of the COTS package, it could internally develop its own system.

One of the key drivers for the decision to develop its own trade allowance system was the volume of transactions Capital envisioned for its system. For example, in order to calculate accruals, the resulting system would routinely need to access over 50 million purchase order line item records and over sixty million invoice detail records. Capital felt this was beyond the current ability of

Figure 3: Functional Interfaces Required

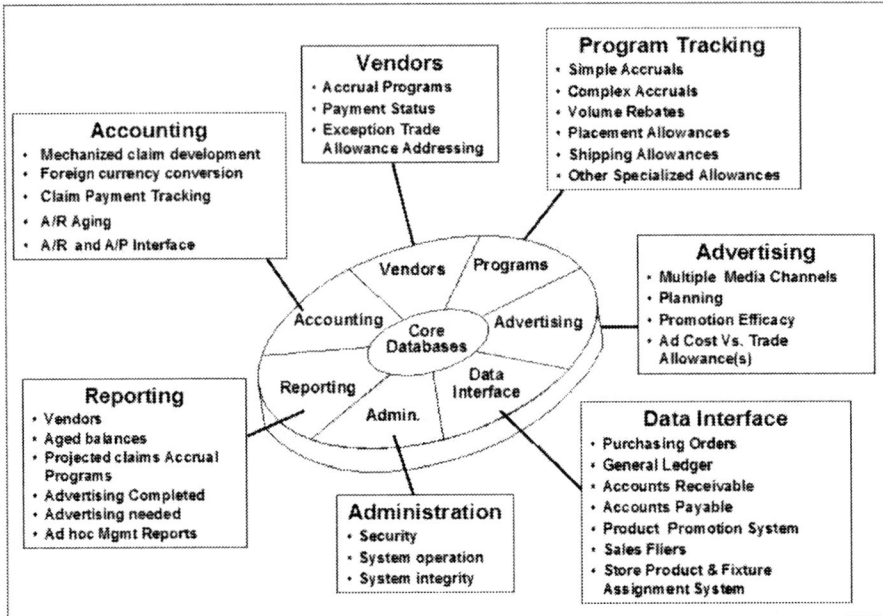

a PC/server application. Other considerations were that the system would have to interface with the general ledger system, AR and AP systems, Purchase Order (PO) write systems, POS sales data, Oracle financial data warehouses, Catalog, and logistics systems. A model of the interfaces is shown in *Figure 3*. In essence, the system required data feeds from virtually every operating system in the company.

Project approval and funding for $200 thousand in IT man-hours was approved in May 1997, and development started in June. Initial steps taken were to migrate the Access database into a SQL server environment. This was purely an interim step to ensure data integrity of the existing trade allowance data. The largest challenge was how to bridge the variety of systems and platforms in operation. Initially, it appeared that Capital's system could be developed with real-time interfaces to all of the programs required. However, the very first program requirement to be accessed was the company's AP system. Direct feeds from the AP system were found to cause an overall slowdown in payment processing CPU time. This approach was therefore abandoned in favor of evening processing with batch feeds from all of the applicable systems. Another significant issue was data retention. In order to identify and collect trade allowances, it is necessary to have detail data for up to five years. Yet Capital discovered that its various systems, designed for other specific functions, had data purge criteria that was discarding the data needed to identify and collect trade allowances. For example, the AP function only needed detail invoice data for 90 days, and, therefore, only maintained summary data after that point; the advertising system retained only the current 12 months' data; and the purchasing systems retained detail data for two years and thereafter only summary data. In all cases, the trade allowance system required five years of data retention. Capital considered modifying all systems to put in place new data retention periods; however, the man-hour time and resources necessary to accomplish the programming were cost and resource prohibitive. As a work-around, Capital leveraged the declining price of storage and bought the stand-alone storage needed to retain five years of data for every one of the systems interfaced. Relatively simple-to-program data feeds were built from all supporting systems, and the necessary data storage became a resident part of the trade allowance system rather than within the discrete systems accessed by its processes. This ensured that the trade allowance system would always have the archival data necessary in case of any future claims dispute. Currently, the system stores five terabytes of data. However, this is not the total amount that will be needed because there are additional trade allowance claims that Capital is exploring, and each type will require additional data stores.

Using the data from multiple systems, the trade allowance system came online in December 1998, 15 months after development was started. Because some data had not been retained by the legacy systems, the new trade allowance system was not able to fully capture the allowances due. However, the startup of the system took an historical view and developed claims for 1996, 1997, and all of 1998, and the initial claims totaled slightly more than $4.5 million. These were only for Capital's weekly sales fliers. Income growth of just this segment of the system has risen to more than $26 million in 2002.

As it became evident that the system was capable of producing more claims than just those for weekly sales fliers, Capital expanded the system in late 1999 to include allowances for store signs that bear brand names and logos and for its catalog supplements. The latter has added $5 million per annum to Capital's revenues. Other areas of revenue have included trade allowances for shipping ($2 million per annum), defective merchandise ($2 million per annum), and price support for sales items ($29 million per annum), as well as several other smaller areas of revenue. Combined, Capital's trade allowance system created claims for more than $66 million in 2002 (*Figure 4*).

Figure 4: Capital's Trade Allowance Revenue, 1990-2002

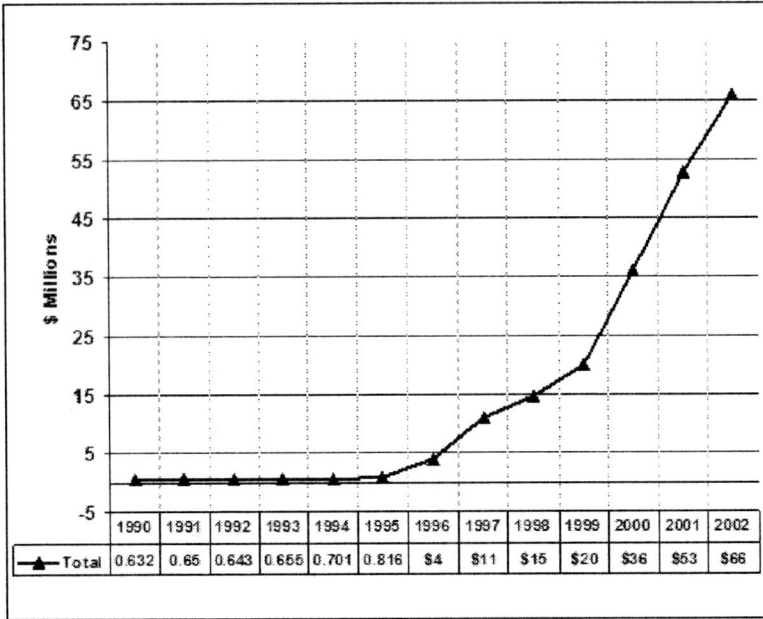

Year	1990	1991	1992	1993	1994	1995	1996	1997	1998	1999	2000	2001	2002
Total	0.632	0.65	0.643	0.655	0.701	0.816	$4	$11	$15	$20	$36	$53	$66

FUTURE TRENDS

An alternative approach to bridging legacy and or dissimilar operating platforms for the identification and collection of trade allowances would certainly be the Internet. While the world of trade allowances remains largely secretive, it would seem both reasonable and possible to exchange retailer or wholesaler specific data via the Internet and facilitate both manufacturer access and insight into claims and the proof-of-performance in an electronic format. The industry still requires actual paper copies for proof-of-performance; however, this is an anachronism in today's environment because virtually all modern printing is accomplished from electronic files.

Therefore, the author would hope to see a broader application of trade allowances along the lines of the figure below (*Figure 5*). In this environment, the extensive manual processes shown in Figure 1 would largely disappear. To put a price tag on this, Capital's manufacturers estimate it costs them approximately $150 to $250 to review and process each claim. Capital is now developing approximately 14,000 claims each year, which means its manufacturers are incurring costs of at least $2.1 million, which could be passed along to Capital or shared with Capital as income if these processes could be

Figure 5: The Ideal Future

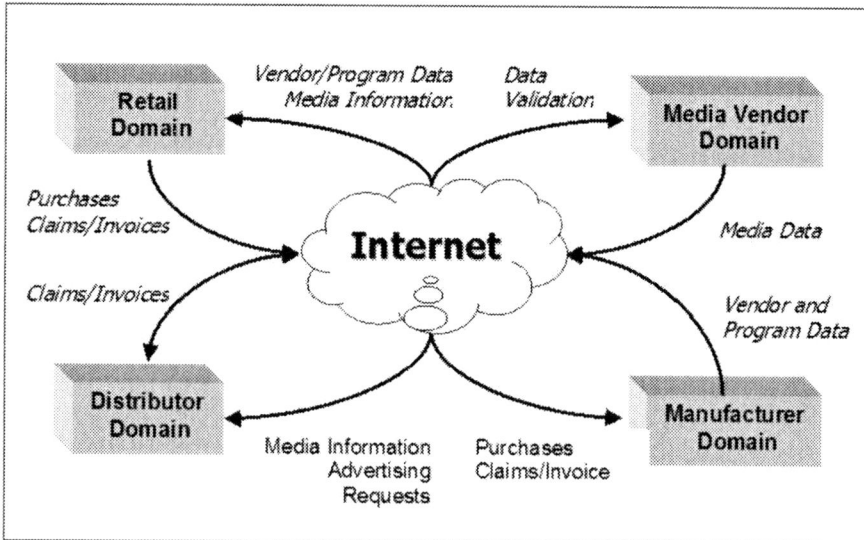

alleviated. Rao (2001) provides an interesting insight for the global sector that seems to be adaptable to trade allowances. Langer (2002) also has proposed similar strategies for e-commerce systems, however those seem uniquely adapted to solving many of the trade allowance problems because they offer client-unique security, and Schwartz, Divitini, Brasethvik and the European Conference on Information Systems (2000) have also integrated this type of knowledge management into an Internet-based solution for organizations. These solutions provide the necessary security of information between retailer and manufacturer, and simultaneously provide data in an electronic format that can be used by management systems for either of parties involved. Additional areas of possible exploration and application would be the use of Artificial Intelligence (AI) to develop measures for printed ads.

CONCLUSION

There is rich terrain for development of follow-on systems for the identification and development of trade allowances. While it is a unique niche in business, these allowances have significant revenue potential. The revenue, however, can only be identified through large-scale data manipulation and state-of-the art technology.

REFERENCES

Agnew, H. (1926). *Cooperative Advertising by Competitors: Promoting a Whole Industry by Combined Efforts in Advertising.* New York, London: Harper & Brothers.

Bayus, B., Lee, H., & Rao, A. (1989). *An Analysis of Collaborative Advertising.* Ithaca, NY: Cornell University Johnson Graduate School of Management.

Brodie, M., & Stonebraker, M. (1995). *Migrating Legacy Systems: Gateways, Interfaces & the Incremental Approach.* San Francisco, CA: Morgan Kaufmann Publishers; IT/Information Technology.

Bullock, E. (1983). *Marketing of Cooperative Advertising.* Hazelwood, MO: Bullock Publishing.

Crimmins, E., & Association of National Advertisers' Cooperative Advertising Committee. (1984). *Cooperative Advertising.* New York: Gene Wolfe & Co.

Fotiadis, D., & Nikolopoulos, S. (2000). *Advances in Informatics.* Singapore, River Edge, NJ: World Scientific.

Houk, B., & Association of National Advertisers. (1995). *Co-Op Advertising.* Lincolnwood, IL: NTC Business Books.

Jørgensen, S. (1998). *Cooperative Advertising in a Dynamic Vertical Marketing Channel.* Montréal: Groupe d'études et de recherche en analyse des décisions.

Jørgensen, S. (2000). *Cooperative Advertising in a Marketing Channel.* Montréal: Groupe d'études et de recherche en analyse des décisions.

Jørgensen, S., & Zaccour, G. (eds.) (1996). Dynamic competitive analysis in marketing. *Proceedings of the International Workshop on Dynamic Competitive Analysis in Marketing,* Montréal, Canada (September 1-2). New York: Springer-Verlag.

Langer, A. (2002). *Applied E-Commerce: Analysis and Engineering for Ecommerce Systems.* New York: John Wiley & Sons.

Litvack, D. (1984). *Effective Off-Pricing and Co-Operative Advertising Strategies: An Experiment.* Ottawa: Faculté d'administration Université d'Ottawa (Faculty of Administration University of Ottawa).

Miller, P. (2002). *Modular Specification and Verification of Object-Oriented Programs.* Berlin, New York: Springer-Verlag.

Pountney, C. (2002). *The Visual FoxPro Report Writer: Pushing it to the Limit and Beyond.* Whitefish Bay, WI: Hentzenwerke Publishing.

Rao, C. (2001). *Globalization and Its Managerial Implications.* Westport, CT: Quorum Books.

Riccardi, G. (2003). *Database Management with Web Site Development Applications*. Boston, MA: Addison Wesley.

Schwartz, D., Divitini, M., Brasethvik, T., & European Conference on Information Systems. (2000). *Internet-Based Organizational Memory and Knowledge Management*. Hershey, PA: Idea Group Publishing.

Trade One Marketing, Inc. (2003). *Available trade allowances, Vol. 2003*. Available online at: http://www.tradeonemktg.com.

Ulrich, W. (2002). *Legacy Systems: Transformation Strategies*. Upper Saddle River, NJ: Prentice Hall.

Young, R. (1979). *Cooperative Advertising, Its Uses and Effectiveness: Some Preliminary Hypotheses*. Cambridge, MA: Marketing Science Institute.

Young, R., & Greyser, S. A. (1983). *Managing Cooperative Advertising: A Strategic Approach*. Lexington, MA: Lexington Books.

Young, R., Greyser, S., & Marketing Science Institute. (1982). *Cooperative Advertising: Practices and Problems*. Cambridge, MA: Marketing Science Institute.

Chapter VIII

Expanding Business Intelligence Power with System Dynamics

Edilberto Casado, Gerens Escuela de Gestión y Economía, Peru

ABSTRACT

This chapter explores the opportunities to expand the forecasting and business understanding capabilities of Business Intelligence (BI) tools with the support of the system dynamics approach. System dynamics tools can enhance the insights provided by BI applications — specifically by using data-mining techniques, through simulation and modeling of real world under a "systems thinking" approach, improving forecasts, and contributing to a better understanding of the business dynamics of any organization. Since there is not enough diffusion and understanding in the business world about system dynamics concepts and advantages, this chapter is intended to motivate further research and the development of better and more powerful applications for BI.

INTRODUCTION

Currently, Business Intelligence (BI) tools make it possible to analyze big amounts of data to get important conclusions about business processes, customer behavior, etc. The main concern is that such conclusions are presented as data correlations following a "straight-line thinking" paradigm (i.e., an outcome is expressed as a function of one or more independent variables); however, many real-world experiences show that this assumption is not always valid.

This chapter explores the opportunities to expand the forecasting and business understanding capabilities of BI tools with the support of the system dynamics approach. System dynamics tools can enhance the insights provided by BI applications — specifically by using data-mining techniques — through simulation and modeling of real world under a "systems thinking" approach, improving forecasts, and contributing to a better understanding of the business dynamics of any organization.

BACKGROUND

Business Intelligence (BI) is a term that has been defined from several perspectives, though all share the same focus. For example, Brackett (1999) defines BI as "a set of concepts, methods, and processes to improve business decisions using information from multiple sources and applying experience and assumptions to develop an accurate understanding of business dynamics."

From a management perspective, BI involves a proactive process of information analysis focused on strategic decision making, and actually it is a critical discipline to gain business insight, as Brackett (1999) also mentions:

> *Business Intelligence involves the integration of core information with relevant contextual information to detect significant events and illuminate cloudy issues. It includes the ability to monitor business trends, to evolve and adapt quickly as situations change and to make intelligent business decisions on uncertain judgments and contradictory information. It relies on exploration and analysis of unrelated information to provide relevant insights, identify trends and discover opportunities.*

As a discipline to empower a "forward-thinking" view of the world, one of the most valuable concepts within BI is the "knowledge discovery in databases" or "data mining." The Gartner Group, as cited by SPSS, Inc. (1997), defines data mining as "the process of discovering meaningful new correlations, patterns, and trends by sifting through large amounts of data stored in repositories, using pattern recognition technologies as well as statistical and mathematical techniques."

Having in mind this definition of data mining, this chapter will be focused on its business applications and its challenges to become a powerful predictive tool.

A QUICK OVERVIEW OF DATA-MINING TECHNIQUES AND ALGORITHMS

We found in the literature a lot of classifications and lists about data-mining techniques and algorithms. However, several authors (Berson & Smith, 1997; Pilot Software's Data Intelligence Group, 1995; Thearling, 2003) agree with the following list of the most commonly used techniques:

1. *Decision Trees:* Decision trees are tree-shaped structures that represent sets of decisions. These decisions generate rules for the classification of a dataset. For the application of this technique, there are two popular methods:
    • *Classification and Regression Trees (CART),* which builds a decision trees based on an "entropy metric" derived from information theory, that is used to determine whether a given split point for a given predictor is better than another.
    • *Chi-Square Automatic Interaction Detection (CHAID),* which is similar to CART, but relies on chi-square tests to choose the optimal splits rather than the entropy metric.
2. *Rule Induction:* Rule induction is another data-mining technique based on the extraction of useful if-then rules from data based on statistical significance.
3. *Nearest Neighbor:* Nearest neighbor is another technique that classifies each record in a dataset based on a combination of the classes of the k record(s) most similar to it in a historical dataset (where $k > 1$). This technique is also known as the *k-nearest neighbor* method.
4. *Neural Networks:* Neural networks are nonlinear predictive models that learn through training and resemble biological neural networks in structure.

5. *Genetic Algorithms:* Genetic algorithms are another technique used in data mining that use processes such as genetic combination, mutation, and natural selection in a design based on the concepts of evolution.

LIMITATIONS OF BI METHODS AND TOOLS FOR PREDICTIVE APPLICATIONS

Statistical Foundation of Data Mining

Most of the current BI methods and tools, such as rule induction, decision trees, neural networks, etc., are extensively used to develop predictive models, and their conceptual foundation are a combination of mathematical, statistical, and artificial intelligence techniques. It is here that we find a source of limitation for a wider set of real-world applications, since statistics works with historical data and there is no full guarantee about predictions based on such data.

As a practical example of the limitations of statistical methods for market behavior prediction, the work by An, Uhm, Kim, and Kwak (2002) is cited here. Regarding an application to forecast automobile demand in Korea, they argue that "statistical methods cannot forecast the present mature market with information gathered in the early developing market period because the characteristics of present market are different from those of the previous market." Also, they argue that "statistical methods cannot forecast short-term auto demand such as monthly demand because it depends on long-term information such as quarterly and yearly sales and short-term demand has an impact on dynamic changes of short-term market."

Explanation of Results

Another limitation of some data-mining methods like neural networks, genetic algorithms, etc., is their inability to provide an adequate explanation of their results. Moxon (1996) argues that "many of the tools employed in data-mining analysis use complex mathematical algorithms that are not easily mapped into human terms."

Regarding neural networks, the Parallel Computer Centre at The Queen's University of Belfast (1997) has cited the following affirmation attributed to Arun Swami of Silicon Graphics:

> *Neural networks have been used successfully for classification but suffer somewhat in that the resulting network is viewed as*

a black box and no explanation of the results is given. This lack of explanation inhibits confidence, acceptance and application of results.

A similar observation is applicable to genetic algorithms.

Thinking Paradigm Under Application of Data-Mining Methods

As a consequence of their statistical foundation, data-mining methods provide information about trends and patterns in the context of a "straight-line thinking" paradigm (i.e., an outcome is expressed as a function of one or more independent variables). For example, to meet company goals or take advantage of new opportunities, business managers make decisions handling a subset of variables under their control and formulating assumptions about the rest of variables outside their control. However, this approach may not always lead to the desired objective; instead, managers could see unexpected results, and therefore could conclude that insights gained through data mining are not valid.

The described situation reflects the application of an open-loop view of the world (i.e., an action is taken based on available information, and this action must lead to a result). Instead, real world is a feedback system made of interacting elements in a closed-loop context, where an action leads to a result that affects current conditions, and the changed conditions become the basis for future action (Forrester, 1991).

SYSTEM DYNAMICS APPROACH

Taking into account the shortcomings described earlier, there is a fundamental need to treat organizations and their surrounding environment as systems and, more specifically, as complex systems (Beinhocker, 1997; Berreby, 1998; Sterman, 2000). Here, an approach known as system dynamics is introduced as a powerful complement for BI methods and tools.

System dynamics was created by Jay W. Forrester, Germeshausen Professor Emeritus of Massachusetts Institute of Technology (MIT), in 1956. The System Dynamics Society (www.systemdynamics.org) defines this approach as "a methodology for studying and managing complex feedback systems, such as one finds in business and other social systems."

The term "business system" relates to the complete set of processes and the structure that sustains organizational operation. However, "social system" is a broader concept that must be understood as "any system where human beings interact." Examples of social systems are a private company, a government agency, a market of goods, a city, a country, etc.

The primary application of system dynamics is modeling complex systems to understand their dynamics (i.e., to learn how system conditions change through time) and influence their behavior. Some extensions of this application are the forecast of demand, as described by Sterman (2000) for the semiconductor market, and by An, Uhm, Kim, and Kwak (2002) for the automobile market in Korea, and the study of alternative futures or scenario planning as described by Forrest (1998).

TOOLS OF SYSTEM DYNAMICS — BASIC CONCEPTS

There are two fundamental tools in system dynamics used to represent the structure and behavior of a system: causal loop diagrams, and stock-and-flow diagrams.

Causal Loop Diagrams

A causal loop diagram is a tool used to represent the feedback structure of a system. It is a closed representation of the sequence of involved causes and effects and also contains an identification of the more important feedback loops within the system (Kirkwood, 1998; Sterman, 2000).

A causal loop diagram is made with variables connected by arrows to denote the cause — effect relationships between them. Each arrow (also known as "causal link") is assigned with a "polarity" to denote the sense of the effect between variables: a positive (+) polarity indicates that the value of the "effect variable" (adjacent to the arrowhead) changes in the same direction as the value change of the "cause variable" (in the opposite extreme of the arrowhead); a negative (-) polarity indicates that the effect variable changes its value in the opposite direction of the value change of the cause variable.

Other elements to include in a causal diagram are the "loop identifiers." These denote the nature of each important loop in the diagram, and they can be either a "reinforcing" or positive loop (a loop that seeks expansion), identified by a plus sign surrounded by a circular arrow; or a "balancing" or negative loop (a loop that seeks stabilization), identified by a minus sign also surrounded by a circular arrow (*Figure 1*).

Figure 1: Causal Loop Diagram and Its Elements

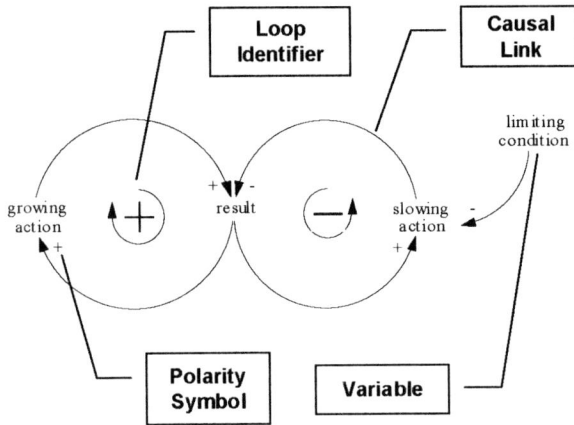

Figure 1 shows the causal loop for the system archetype known as "limits to growth" or "limits to success," which characterizes many organizational growth processes. A system archetype (also known as "generic structure") is common to many systems, and it is a key concept to understanding real-world systems (Senge, 1990).

Stock-and-Flow Diagrams

A stock-and-flow diagram is another way to represent the feedback structure of a system. But, unlike a causal loop diagram, it can include more precise and detailed information about the nature of the system it represents. *Figure 2* shows the following basic elements in a stock-and-flow diagram (Kirkwood, 1998; Sterman, 2000):

- *Stocks* (represented by a rectangle), which characterize the state of the system at a given time.
- *Flows* (represented by a pipe with a valve), which characterize the rates of change in the condition of the system.
- *Sources* (represented by a cloud), which characterize the stocks from which flows are originated outside the boundary of the system.
- *Sinks* (represented by a cloud), which characterize the stocks into which flows are leaving the boundary of the system.
- *Auxiliary variables* (represented by names linked to stocks or flows), which allow the inclusion of functions, constants, and other elements that serve to clarify the diagram.

Figure 2: Stock-and-Flow Diagram and Its Elements

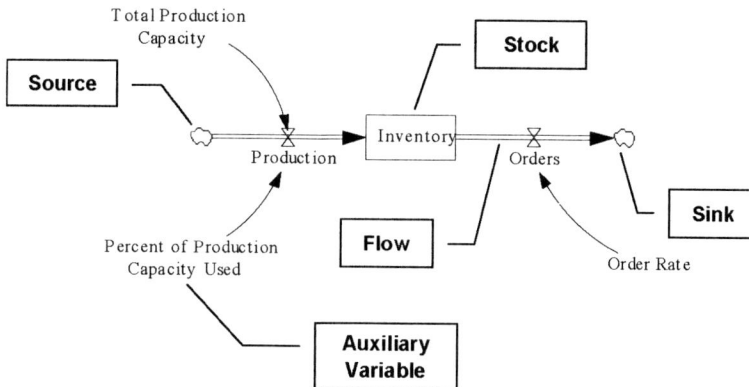

While causal loop diagrams are more oriented to a qualitative description of a system, stock-and-flow diagrams allow mathematical functions to be related to their elements and, therefore, they represent a quantitative description. *Figure 3* shows an example of a set of equations for the diagram of *Figure 2*.

LIMITATIONS OF SYSTEM DYNAMICS

The limitations of system dynamics come from its primary application as modeling tool, and this fact is reflected in the expression "any model is only as good as its assumptions." Sterman (1991, 2000) has cited the following shortcomings of simulation models:

Accuracy of the Decision Rules

Every system dynamics model must be constructed beginning with two processes: the problem articulation or purpose, which must be oriented to solve a specific problem; and the proposal of a dynamic hypothesis, which is a supposition about the behavior of the system to model. The main problem resides in the decision rules under the dynamic hypothesis, which cannot be determined directly from statistical data. Decision rules must be discovered from observation, and this task is limited by the perception of the modeler about the system to be studied.

Soft Variables

Reputation, customer satisfaction, employee motivation, and other soft or intangible variables are fundamental to understanding complex systems. Unfor-

Figure 3: Set of Equations for the Stock-and-Flow Diagram of Figure 2

```
(01)   FINAL TIME = 100
       Units: Month
       The final time for the simulation.

(02)   INITIAL TIME = 0
       Units: Month
       The initial time for the simulation.

(03)   Inventory = INTEG (
          +Production-Orders,
              100)

(04)   Order Rate =
          100
       Units: items/Month

(05)   Orders =
          Order Rate
       Units: items/Month

(06)   Percent of Production Capacity Used =
          0.8
       Units: Dmnl
```

tunately, in most cases, there is no measure of these data, and under this circumstance, these variables are usually discarded from the model. At present, the development of fields such as Intellectual Capital and Knowledge Management is contributing to a better estimation of soft variables; in the meantime, the best approach is to include at least reasonable estimates of such variables rather than ignoring them.

Model Boundary

The model boundary is an important factor that affects its validity. This concept determines which variables will be treated as exogenous (outside the boundary) and which as endogenous (inside the boundary), and what feedbacks will be incorporated. As with decision rules, the definition of the boundary will be limited by the perception of the modeler about the system.

BUSINESS INTELLIGENCE AND SYSTEM DYNAMICS TOOLS WORKING TOGETHER

With the current availability of computer power and software tools, there is a great opportunity to take the best of business intelligence and system dynamics to improve decision-making processes.

This approach involves the creation of a system dynamic model to represent the target system. Later, those relationships without a mathematical expression available (because there is no theory or formula available for them) will be represented by rules or equations obtained from data-mining processes. The advantage of this approach is that, once validated, the system dynamics model is a powerful tool for decision making, since it reflects the nature of the target system and provides better insights about its behavior, without the limitations of BI tools described earlier. In contrast, this approach is affected by the limitations of system dynamics tools, and the direct inclusion of rules or equations into the model could hide important causal relationships that need to be discovered.

AN APPLICATION EXAMPLE

The example described below is about a Customer Relationship Management (CRM) application, where data mining and system dynamics tools are used. A similar approach can be extended for any other business application.

Reddy (2001) talks about three basic processes in CRM: *acquisition* (of new customers), *retention* (of the most profitable customers), and *enhancement* (of the customer relationship). Supporting these processes can be facilitated with a better understanding of customer behavior; however, the existence of many intangible factors (e.g., customer satisfaction, product features, brand awareness, etc.) and the difficulty in measuring them adequately is a challenge for a successful application of CRM.

Figure 4 shows a simplified system dynamics model of a CRM application related to a Brand A, where the processes of customer acquisition and retention are represented. Acquisition is made through sales and marketing or through the phenomena of "word of mouth," and retention is related to a loss of customers rate.

The average customer satisfaction index for Brand A is calculated through surveys and other data (for example, frequency of repeated purchases); then, data-mining tools provide a set of rules or equations that define mathematical relationships between customer satisfaction and acquisition (or loss) of cus-

Figure 4: Simplified System Dynamics Model of a CRM Application

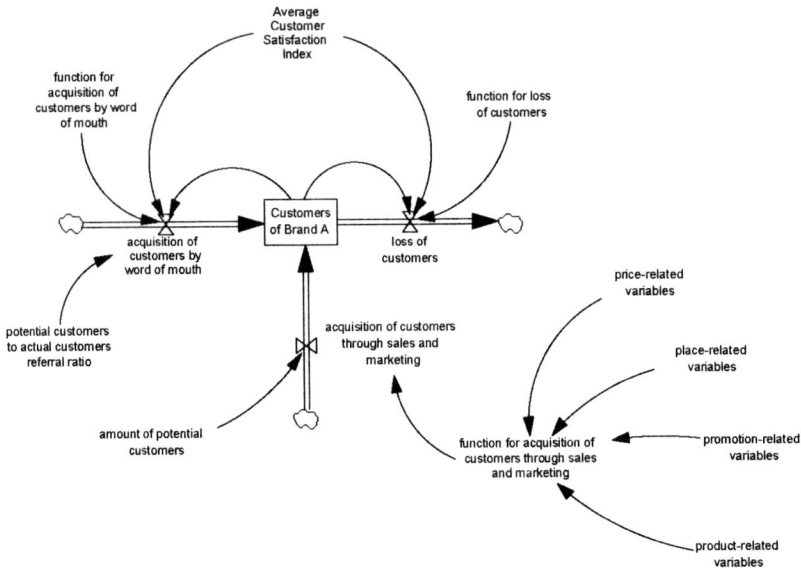

tomers in the form of functions that can be integrated in expressions like the following examples:

*(1) acquisition of customers by word of mouth = customers of brand A * potential customers to actual customers referral ratio * function for acquisition of customers by word of mouth(average customer satisfaction index)*

*(2) loss of customers = customers of brand A * function for loss of customers(average customer satisfaction index)*

In the equations (1) and (2), "customers of Brand A" is the amount of actual customers of Brand A, and "potential customers to actual customers referral ratio" is the estimated proportion of potential customers that could be referred by actual customers. The "function for acquisition of customers by word of mouth" and the "function for loss of customers" are derived from data-mining processes.

In a similar fashion, another function for the acquisition of customers through sales and marketing is obtained incorporating variables related to the well-known components of the "marketing mix": price, product, promotion, and place (Kotler, Armstrong, & Chawla, 2003). As a better understanding of the cause-and-effect relationships of the CRM process is achieved, such function can be reformulated as a new set of stock-and-flow diagrams that include, if needed, a new set of functions obtained via data-mining methods. To clarify these concepts, a simplified example is described.

We suppose that the "function for acquisition of customers through sales and marketing" involves, in addition to other marketing mix-related variables, the amount of money spent on advertising (X) and the amount of stores having Brand A in stock (Y). Through a neural network algorithm, a function of the form $Z = a \cdot X + b \cdot Y + c$ (where a, b, and c are constants) is obtained, and thus we know a mathematical relationship between such variables. However, this expression does not explain conceptually the real effect and impact of X and Y on Z.

To overcome this issue, we could incorporate the principles of an approach known as "Dynamic Brand Value Management" or DBVM (Desmet et al., 1998), which takes into account the factors that influence brand value and also dynamic elements such as time delays and feedback loops. *Figure 5* shows the redesigned model for the CRM application, where a "virtuous

Figure 5: Redesign of the Model in Figure 4 to Incorporate Concepts of the Dynamic Brand Value Management Framework

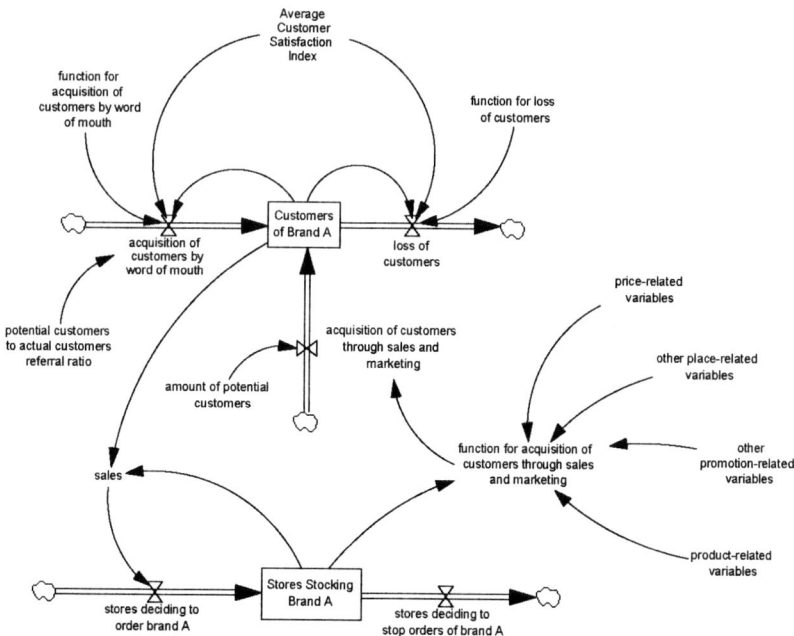

reinforcing loop" is visible: when a product sells well (see variable "sales"), more retailers are motivated to order it (see variable "stores deciding to order Brand A"), and the product sells even better.

As more valid cause-and-effect relationships are added, the model will provide more insights for the CRM processes, and it will be possible to apply the intrinsic knowledge contained here to formulate new strategies when a change in the underlying conditions occur, and when there is not enough available data to mine.

FUTURE TRENDS

The cooperation between BI and system dynamics tools will progress with a framework that facilitates the model creation process and the integration of their respective elements. Oguz (2002), for example, proposes the concept of a "complex analytic layer" in addition to the "data warehouse layer" associated to BI applications. Such "complex layer" will contain two components: a model-based process application, oriented to a proactive data acquisition; and a model-based analysis/statistical analysis, oriented to run complex models, whether linear or nonlinear. This second component would be suitable to include system dynamics tools.

Another way to improve the cooperation between BI and system dynamics tools is the definition of a common methodology to create and evaluate models that incorporate elements from both approaches. A starting point could be a methodology such as that proposed by the "Cross-Industry Standard Process for Data Mining" Consortium (2000), which has analogous elements with the generic methodology to create system dynamics models, as described by Sterman (2000).

CONCLUSION

System dynamics is a powerful complement for business intelligence in general. With a clear vision of the features, advantages, and limitations of these tools, we can expect important improvements in decision making and consequently in organizational performance.

The application of system dynamics implies the need to adopt the "systems thinking" paradigm as a new way to see business dynamics. A gradual process is suggested for this purpose, combining skills development exercises with the support of modeling software, if this is available (Casado, 2002). Another concern is the need to continue to trace the developments in knowledge management and intellectual capital, because it is necessary to improve the quantification and representation of intangible variables to be included in system dynamics models.

In the near future, the increasing rate of adoption of BI tools will equilibrate the advantage of their utilization by an organization with respect to others. At this point, only a clear understanding of the behavior of social systems, beyond discovering only trends and patterns, will bring back competitive advantage in the business world.

REFERENCES

An, S., Uhm, K., Kim, K., & Kwak, S. (2002). System dynamics model for forecasting demand of each automobile type in the Korean automobile market. In *Proceedings of the 20th International Conference of the System Dynamics Society*. Palermo, Italy (July 28-August 1).

Beinhocker, E. (1997). Strategy at the edge of chaos. *The McKinsey Quarterly*. 1st quarter. Retrieved January 3, 2003: http://www.mckinsey quarterly.com/strategy/sted97.asp.

Berreby, D. (1998). Complexity theory: Fact-free science or business tool? *Strategy & Business*. 1st quarter. Retrieved January 3, 2003: http:// www.strategy-business.com/press/article/?art=14737&pg=0.

Berson, A., & Smith, S. (1997). *Data Warehousing, Data Mining & OLAP*. New York: McGraw-Hill.

Brackett, M. (1999, March). Business Intelligence Value Chain. *DM Review*. March. Retrieved January 3, 2003: http://www.dmreview.com/ master.cfm?NavID=198&EdID=115.

Casado, E. (2002). Thinking outside the lines. *Intelligent Enterprise*. June 28. Retrieved January 3, 2003: http://www.iemagazine.com/020628/ 511feat3_1.shtml.

Cross-Industry Standard Process for Data Mining (2000). *CRISP-DM 1.0: Step-by-step data_mining guide*. Retrieved January 3, 2003: http:// www.crisp-dm.org/CRISPWP-0800.pdf.

Desmet, D., Finskud, L., Glucksman, M., Marshall, N., Reyner, M., & Warren, K. (1998). The end of voodoo brand management? *The McKinsey Quarterly, 2nd Quarter*.

Forrester, J. (1991). *System dynamics and the lessons of 35 years*. April 29. Retrieved January 3, 2003: http://sysdyn.mit.edu/sdep/papers/D-4224-4.pdf.

Forrest, J. (1998). System dynamics, alternative futures, and scenario planning. In *Proceedings of the 16th International Conference of the System Dynamics Society,* Quebec, Canada (July 20–23).

Information Discovery, Inc. (1998). A characterization of data mining technologies and processes. *The Journal of Data Warehousing,* January.

Kirkwood, C. (1998). *System dynamics methods: A quick introduction.* College of Business, Arizona State University.

Kotler, P., Armstrong, G., & Chawla, K. (2003). *Principles of Marketing.* 10th edition. Upper Saddle River, NJ: Prentice Hall.

Moxon, B. (1996). Defining data mining. *DBMS Online.* August. Retrieved December 28, 1997: http://www.dbmsmag.com/9608d53.html.

Oguz, M. (2002). Strategic intelligence: Complex analytics Part I – The next step in business intelligence. *DM Review.* April. Retrieved January 3, 2003: http://www.dmreview.com/master.cfm?NavID=198&EdID=5069.

Parallel Computer Centre at The Queen's University of Belfast (1997). *Data mining techniques.* Retrieved December 12, 1997: http://www.pcc.qub.ac.uk/tec/courses/datamining/stu_notes/dm_book_4.html.

Pilot Software's Data Intelligence Group (1995). *An overview of data mining at Dun & Bradstreet.* Retrieved April 28, 2003: http://www.thearling.com/text/wp9501/wp9501.htm.

Reddy, R. (2001). Through a lens smartly. *Intelligent CRM.* March 27. Retrieved January 3, 2003: http://www.intelligentcrm.com/feature/010327/feat1.shtml.

Senge, P. (1990). *The Fifth Discipline: The Art and Practice of the Learning Organization.* New York: Doubleday.

SPSS, Inc. (1997). *What is Data Mining?* Retrieved December 28, 1997: http://www.spss.com/datamine/define.htm.

Sterman, J. (1991). *A skeptic's guide to computer models.* Retrieved January 3, 2003: http://sysdyn.mit.edu/sdep/Roadmaps/RM9/D-4101-1.pdf.

Sterman, J. (2000). *Business Dynamics: Systems Thinking and Modeling for a Complex World.* Boston, MA: Irwin McGraw-Hill.

Thearling, K. (2003). *An introduction to data mining: Discovering hidden value in your data warehouse.* Retrieved April 28, 2003: http://www.thearling.com/text/dmwhite/dmwhite.htm.

Chapter IX

Data Mining and Business Intelligence:
Tools, Technologies, and Applications

Jeffrey Hsu, Fairleigh Dickinson University, USA

ABSTRACT

Most businesses generate, are surrounded by, and are even overwhelmed by data — much of it never used to its full potential for gaining insights into one's own business, customers, competition, and overall business environment. By using a technique known as data mining, it is possible to extract critical and useful patterns, associations, relationships, and, ultimately, useful knowledge from the raw data available to businesses. This chapter explores data mining and its benefits and capabilities as a key tool for obtaining vital business intelligence information. The chapter includes an overview of data mining, followed by its evolution, methods, technologies, applications, and future.

INTRODUCTION

One aspect of our technological society is clear — there is a large amount of data but a shortage of information. Every day, enormous amounts of information are generated from all sectors — business, education, the scientific community, the World Wide Web, or one of many off-line and online data sources readily available. From all of this, which represents a sizable repository of human data and information, it is necessary and desirable to generate worthwhile and usable knowledge. As a result, the field of data mining and knowledge discovery in databases (KDD) has grown in leaps and bounds, and has shown great potential for the future (Han & Kamber, 2001).

Data mining is not a single technique or technology but, rather, a group of related methods and methodologies that are directed towards the finding and automatic extraction of patterns, associations, changes, anomalies, and significant structures from data (Grossman, 1998). Data mining is emerging as a key technology that enables businesses to select, filter, screen, and correlate data automatically. Data mining evokes the image of patterns and meaning in data, hence the term that suggests the mining of "nuggets" of knowledge and insight from a group of data. The findings from these can then be applied to a variety of applications and purposes, including those in marketing, risk analysis and management, fraud detection and management, and customer relationship management (CRM). With the considerable amount of information that is being generated and made available, the effective use of data-mining methods and techniques can help to uncover various trends, patterns, inferences, and other relations from the data, which can then be analyzed and further refined. These can then be studied to bring out meaningful information that can be used to come to important conclusions, improve marketing and CRM efforts, and predict future behavior and trends (Han & Kamber, 2001).

DATA MINING PROCESS

The goal of data mining is to obtain useful knowledge from an analysis of collections of data. Such a task is inherently interactive and iterative. As a result, a typical data-mining system will go through several phases. The phases depicted below start with the raw data and finish with the resulting extracted knowledge that was produced as a result of the following stages:

- *Selection* — Selecting or segmenting the data according to some criteria.
- *Preprocessing* — The data cleansing stage where certain information is removed that is deemed unnecessary and may slow down queries.

- *Transformation* — The data is transformed in that overlays may be added, such as the demographic overlays, and the data is made usable and navigable.
- *Data mining* — This stage is concerned with the extraction of patterns from the data.
- *Interpretation and evaluation* — The patterns identified by the system are interpreted into knowledge that can then be used to support human decision-making, e.g., prediction and classification tasks, summarizing the contents of a database, or explaining observed phenomena (Han & Kamber).

Data mining is a field that is heavily influenced by traditional statistical techniques, and most data-mining methods will reveal a strong foundation of statistical and data analysis methods. Some of the traditional data-mining techniques include classification, clustering, outlier analysis, sequential patterns, time series analysis, prediction, regression, link analysis (associations), and multidimensional methods including online analytical processing (OLAP). These can then be categorized into a series of data-mining techniques, which are classified and illustrated in *Table 1* (Goebel & Le Grunwald, 1999).

In addition, the entire broad field of data mining includes not only a discussion of statistical techniques, but also various related technologies and techniques, including data warehousing, and many software packages and languages that have been developed for the purpose of mining data. Some of these packages and languages include: DBMiner, IBM Intelligent Miner, SAS Enterprise Miner, SGI MineSet, Clementine, MS/SQLServer 2000, DBMiner, BlueMartini, MineIt, DigiMine, and MS OLEDB for Data Mining (Goebel & Le Grunwald, 1999).

Data warehousing complements data mining in that data stored in a data warehouse is organized in such a form as to make it suitable for analysis using data-mining methods. A data warehouse is a central repository for the data that an enterprise's various business systems collect. Typically, a data warehouse is housed on an enterprise server. Data from various online transaction processing (OLTP) applications and other sources are extracted and organized on the data warehouse database for use by analytical applications, user queries, and data-mining operations. Data warehousing focuses on the capture of data from diverse sources for useful analysis and access. A data mart emphasizes the point of view of the end-user or knowledge worker who needs access to specialized, but often local, databases (Delmater & Hancock, 2001; Han & Kamber, 2001).

Table 1: Current Data-Mining Techniques

TECHNIQUE	DESCRIPTION
Predictive modeling	Predict value for a specific data item attribute
Characterization and descriptive data mining	Data distribution, dispersion and exception
Association, correlation, causality analysis (Link Analysis)	Identify relationships between attributes
Classification	Determine to which class a data item belongs
Clustering and outlier analysis	Partition a set into classes, whereby items with similar characteristics are grouped together
Temporal and sequential patterns analysis	Trend and deviation, sequential patterns, periodicity
OLAP (OnLine Analytical Processing)	OLAP tools enable users to analyze different dimensions of multidimensional data. For example, it provides time series and trend analysis views.
Model Visualization	Making discovered knowledge easily understood using charts, plots, histograms, and other visual means
Exploratory Data Analysis (EDA)	Explores a data set without a strong dependence on assumptions or models; goal is to identify patterns in an exploratory manner

FOUNDATIONS/HISTORY OF DATA MINING

It has often been said that to understand where one is going, it is important to know from where one has come. As such, it would be useful to devote some attention to the history of data mining, from the perspective of what technologies have contributed to its birth and development, and also how data-mining technologies and systems can be categorized and classified.

The origins of data mining can be thought of as having come from three areas of learning and research: statistics, machine learning, and artificial intelligence (AI). The first foundation of data mining is in statistics. Statistics is the foundation of most technologies on which data mining is built. Many of the classic areas of statistics, such as regression analysis, standard distributions, standard deviation and variance, discriminant analysis, and cluster analysis are the very building blocks from which the more advanced statistical techniques of data mining are based (Delmater & Hancock, 2001; Fayyad, Piatesky-Shapiro, & Smith, 1996; Han & Kamber, 2001).

Another major area of influence is AI. This area, which derives its power from heuristics rather than statistics, attempts to apply human-thought-like processing to statistical problems. Because AI needs significant computer processing power, it did not become a reality until the 1980s, when more powerful computers began to be offered at affordable prices. There were a number of important AI-based applications, such as query optimization modules for Relational Database Management Systems (RDBMS) and others, and AI was an area of much research interest (Delmater & Hancock, 2001; Fayyad, Piatesky-Shapiro, & Smith, 1996; Han & Kamber, 2001).

Finally, there is machine learning, which can be thought of as a combination of statistics and artificial intelligence. While AI did not enjoy much commercial success, many AI techniques were largely adapted for use in machine learning. Machine learning could be considered a next step in the evolution of AI, because its strength lies in blending AI heuristics with advanced statistical analyses. Some of the capabilities that were implemented into machine learning included the ability to have a computer program learn about the data it is studying, i.e., a program can make different kinds of decisions based on the characteristics of the studied data. For instance, based on the data set being analyzed, basic statistics are used for fundamental problems, and more advanced AI heuristics and algorithms are used to examine more complex data (Delmater & Hancock, 2001; Fayyad, Piatesky-Shapiro, & Smith, 1996; Han & Kamber, 2001).

Data mining, in many ways, is the application of machine learning techniques to business applications. Probably best described as a combination of historical and recent developments in statistics, AI, and machine learning, its purpose is to study data and find the hidden trends or patterns within it. Data mining is finding increasing acceptance in both the scientific and business communities, meeting the need to analyze large amounts of data and discover trends that would not be found using other, more traditional means (Delmater

& Hancock, 2001; Fayyad, Piatesky-Shapiro, & Smith, 1996; Han & Kamber, 2001). Other areas that have influenced the field of data mining include developments in database systems, visualization techniques and technologies, and advanced techniques including neural networks.

Databases have evolved from flat files to sophisticated repositories of information, with complex forms of storing, arranging, and retrieving data. The evolution of database technologies from relational databases to more intricate forms such as data warehouses and data marts, have helped to make data mining a reality. Developments in visualization have also been an influence in developing certain areas of data mining. In particular, visual and spatial data mining have come of age due to the work being done in those areas. Many of the applications for which data mining is being used employ advanced artificial intelligence and related technologies, including such areas as neural networks, pattern recognition, information retrieval, and advanced statistical analyses. From this discussion of the theoretical and computer science origins of data mining, it would be useful to now look at a classification of data-mining systems that can provide some insight into how data-mining systems and technologies have evolved (Delmater & Hancock, 2001; Fayyad, Piatesky-Shapiro, & Smith, 1996; Han & Kamber, 2001).

FOUR GENERATIONS OF DATA MINING TECHNOLOGIES/SYSTEMS

According to Grossman (1998), data-mining systems can be broken down into four main "generations," showing the evolution of systems from rudimentary and complex to more advanced ones. First generation systems are designed to handle small data sets on vector-based data. Second generation data-mining systems can mine data from databases and data warehouses, while third generation data-mining systems can mine data from intranets and extranets. Fourth generation data mining systems can mine data from mobile, embedded, and ubiquitous computing devices.

First Generation Systems

The first generation of data-mining systems support a single algorithm or a small collection of algorithms that are designed to mine vector-valued (numerical, often used to represent three-dimensional image) data. These are the most basic and simplest of the data-mining systems that have been developed and used.

Second Generation Systems

A second-generation system is characterized by supporting high-performance interfaces to databases and data warehouses, as well as increased scalability and functionality. The objective of second generation systems is to mine larger data and more complex data sets, support the use of multiple algorithms, and be able to work with higher dimension data sets. Data-mining schema and data-mining query languages (DMQL) are supported.

Third Generation Systems

Third-generation data-mining systems are able to mine the distributed and heterogeneous data found on intranets and extranets, and also to integrate efficiently with various kinds of systems. This may include support for multiple predictive models and the meta-data required to work with these. Third generation data-mining and predictive-modeling systems are different from search engines in that they provide a means for discovering patterns, associations, changes, and anomalies in networked data rather than simply finding requested data.

Fourth Generation Systems

Fourth-generation data-mining systems are able to mine data generated by embedded, mobile, and ubiquitous computing devices. This is one of the new frontiers of data mining that is only recently being investigated as a viable possibility.

From the viewpoint of current research, it appears that most of the work that has been done in data mining so far has been in the second and third generations, and work is progressing towards the challenges of the fourth. The characteristics of the various generations are described and summarized in *Table 2* (Grossman, 1998).

THE PRESENT AND THE FUTURE

What is the future of data mining? Certainly, the field has made great strides in past years, and many industry analysts and experts in the area feel that its future will be bright. There is definite growth in the area of data mining. Many industry analysts and research firms have projected a bright future for the entire data mining/KDD area and its related area of customer relationship management (CRM). According to IDC, spending in the area of business intelligence,

Table 2: Evolution of Data Mining

Generation	Distinguishing Characteristics	Supported Algorithms	Systems Supported	Systems Models Supported	Type of Data
First	Stand alone application	Supports one or more algorithms	Stand alone systems	Single machine	Vector data
Second	Integration together with databases and data warehouses	Multiple algorithms	Data management systems, including database and data warehouses systems	Local area networks and related system models	Objects, text and continuous media
Third	Includes predictive modeling	Multiple algorithms supported	Data management & predictive modeling	Network computing; intranets and extranets	Includes semi-structured data and web-based data
Fourth	Includes mobile & ubiquitous data	Multiple algorithms supported	Data management predictive modeling & mobile systems	Mobile and ubiquitous computing	Ubiquitous data

which encompasses data mining, is estimated to increase from $3.6 billion in 2000 to $11.9 billion in 2005. The growth in the CRM Analytic application market is expected to approach 54.1% per year through 2003. In addition, data-mining projects are expected to grow by more than 300% by the year 2002. By 2003, more than 90% of consumer-based industries with e-commerce orientation will utilize some kind of data-mining models.

As mentioned previously, the field of data mining is very broad, and there are many methods and technologies that have become dominant in the field. Not only have there been developments in the "traditional" areas of data mining, but there are other areas that have been identified as being especially important as future trends in the field.

MAJOR TRENDS IN TECHNOLOGIES AND METHODS

There are a number of data-mining trends is in terms of technologies and methodologies that are currently being developed. These trends include methods for analyzing more complex forms of data, as well as specific techniques and methods, followed by application areas that have gained research and commercial interest.

The trends that focus on data mining from complex types of data include Web mining, text mining, distributed data mining, hypertext/hypermedia mining, ubiquitous data mining, as well as multimedia, visual, spatial, and time series/sequential data mining. These are examined in detail in the upcoming sections.

The techniques and methods that are highlighted include constraint-based and phenomenal data mining. In addition, two of the areas that have become extremely important include bioinformatics and DNA analysis, and the work being done in support of customer relationship management (CRM).

WEB MINING

Web mining is one of the most promising areas in data mining, because the Internet and World Wide Web are dynamic sources of information. Web mining is the extraction of interesting and potentially useful patterns and implicit information from artifacts or activity related to the World Wide Web (Etzioni, 1996). The main tasks that comprise Web mining include retrieving Web documents, selection and processing of Web information, pattern discovery in sites and across sites, and analysis of the patterns found (Garofalis, 1999; Han, Zaiane, Chee, & Chiang, 2000; Kosala & Blockeel, 2000).

Web mining can be categorized into three separate areas: Web Content Mining, Web Structure Mining, and Web Usage Mining. Web content mining is the process of extracting knowledge from the content of documents or their descriptions. This includes the mining of Web text documents, which is a form of resource discovery based on the indexing of concepts, sometimes using agent-based technology. Web structure mining is the process of inferring knowledge from the links and organization in the World Wide Web. Finally, Web usage mining, also known as Web Log Mining, is the process of extracting interesting patterns in Web access logs and other Web usage information (Borges & Levene, 1999; Kosala & Blockeel, 2000; Madria, 1999).

Web mining is closely related to both information retrieval (IR) and information extraction (IE). Web mining is sometimes regarded as an intelligent form of information retrieval, and IE is associated with the extraction of information from Web documents (Pazienza, 1997).

Aside from the three types mentioned above, there are different approaches to handling these problems, including those with emphasis on databases and the use of intelligent software agents.

Web Content Mining is concerned with the discovery of new information and knowledge from Web-based data, documents, and pages. Because the

Web contains so many different kinds of information, including text, graphics, audio, video, and hypertext links, the mining of Web content is closely related to the field of hypermedia and multimedia data mining. However in this case, the focus is on information that is found mainly on the World Wide Web.

Web content mining is a process that goes beyond the task of extracting keywords. Some approaches have involved restructuring the document content in a representation that could be better used by machines. One approach is to use wrappers to map documents to some data model.

According to Kosala and Blockeel (2000), there are two main approaches to Web content mining: an Information Retrieval view and a database view. The Information Retrieval view is designed to work with both unstructured (free text such as news stories) or semistructured documents (with both HTML and hyperlinked data), and attempts to identify patterns and models based on an analysis of the documents, using such techniques as clustering, classification, finding text patterns, and extraction rules. There are a number of studies that have been conducted in these and related areas, such as clustering, categorization, computational linguistics, exploratory analysis, and text patterns. Many of these studies are closely related to, and employ the techniques of text mining (Billsus & Pazzani, 1999; Frank, Paynter, Witten, Gutwin, & Nevill-Manning, 1998; Nahm & Mooney, 2000). The other main approach, which is to content mine semi structured documents, uses many of the same techniques used for unstructured documents, but with the added complexity and challenge of analyzing documents containing a variety of media elements. For this area, it is frequently desired to take on a database view, with the Web site being analyzed as the "database." Here, hypertext documents are the main information that is to be analyzed, and the goal is to transform the data found in the Web site to a form in which better management and querying of the information is enabled (Crimmins, 1999, Shavlik & Elassi-Rad, 1998).

Some of the applications from this kind of Web content mining include the discovery of a schema for Web databases and of building structural summaries of data. There are also applications that focus on the design of languages that provide better querying of databases that contain Web-based data. Researchers have developed many Web-oriented query languages that attempt to extend standard database query languages such as SQL to collect data from the Web. WebLog is a logic-based query language for restructuring extracted information from Web information sources. WebSQL provides a framework that supports a large class of data-restructuring operations. In addition, WebSQL combines structured queries, based on the organization of hypertext documents, and content queries, based on information retrieval techniques.

The TSIMMIS system (Chawathe et al., 1994) extracts data from heterogeneous and semi structured information sources and correlates them to generate an integrated database representation of the extracted information (Han, Fu, Wang, Koperski, & Zaiane, 1996; Maarek & Ben Shaul, 1996; Meldelzon, Mihaila, & Milo, 1996; Merialdo, Atzeni, & Mecca, 1997).

Others focus on the building and management of multilevel or multilayered databases. This suggests a multilevel database approach to organizing Web-based information. The main idea behind this method is that the lowest level of the database contains primitive semi structured information stored in various Web repositories, such as hypertext documents. At the higher level(s), meta data or generalizations are extracted from lower levels and organized in structured collections such as relational or object-oriented databases. As an example of this, the ARANEUS system extracts relevant information from hypertext documents and integrates these into higher level derived Web hypertexts that are generalized as "database views." Kholsa, Kuhn, and Soparkar (1996) and King and Novak (1996) have done research in this area.

Web Structure Mining has as its goal mining knowledge from the structure of Web sites rather than looking at the text and data on the pages themselves. More specifically, it attempts to examine the structures that exist between documents on a Web site, such as the hyperlinks and other linkages. For instance, links pointing to a document indicate the popularity of the document, while links coming out of a document indicate the richness or perhaps the variety of topics covered in the document. The PageRank (Brin & Page, 1998) and CLEVER (Chakrabarti et al., 1999) methods take advantage of this information conveyed by the links to find pertinent Web pages. Counters of hyperlinks, into and out of documents, retrace the structure of the Web artifacts summarized.

The concept of examining the structure of Web sites in order to gain additional insight and knowledge is closely related to the areas of social network and citation analysis. The idea is to model the linkages and structures of the Web using the concepts of social network analysis. There are also a number of algorithms that have been employed to model the structure of the Web, and have been put to practical use in determining the relevance of Web sites and pages. Other uses for these include the categorization of Web pages and the identification of "communities" existing on the Web. Some of these include PageRank and HITS (Pirolli, Pitkow, & Rao, 1996; Spertus, 1997).

Web Usage Mining is yet another major area in the broad spectrum of Web mining. Rather than looking at the content pages or the underlying structure, Web usage mining is focused on Web-user behavior or, more specifically, modeling and predicting how a user will use and interact with the Web. In general, this form of mining examines secondary data, or the data that is derived from the interaction of users (Chen, Park, & Yu, 1996).

For instance, Web servers record and accumulate data about user interactions whenever requests for resources are received. Analyzing the Web access logs of different Web sites can enable a better understanding of user behavior and the Web structure, thereby improving the design of this collection of resources. The sources of Web usage data could be divided into three main categories: client level, server level, and proxy level. Client-level data is typically data collected by the Web browser itself running on a client machine, or by Java applets or Javascript programs running off the browser. This is in contrast to server-level data, which is probably the more widely used of these three data sources. Server-level data is data gathered from Web servers, including server logs, as well as logs that record cookie data and query data. Finally, proxy-level data, which is in the form of proxy traces, can provide information on the browsing habits of users sharing the same proxy server (Srivastava, Cooley, Deshpande, & Tan, 2000).

There are two main thrusts in Web usage mining: General Access Pattern Tracking and Customized Usage Tracking. General access pattern tracking analyzes the Web logs in order to better understand access patterns and trends. These analyses can shed light on the structure and grouping of resource providers. Applying data-mining techniques to access logs can unveil interesting access patterns that can be used to restructure sites more effectively, pinpoint advertising better, and target ads to specific users.

Customized usage tracking analyzes individual trends. Its purpose is to customize Web sites to users. The information displayed, the depth of the site structure, and the format of the resources can all be dynamically customized for each user over time, based on their patterns of access. It is important to point out that the success of such applications depends on what and how much valid and reliable knowledge one can discover from usage logs and other sources. It may be useful to incorporate information not only from Web servers, but also from customized scripts written for certain sites (Kosala & Blockeel, 2000).

In general, the mining of Web usage data can be divided into two main approaches: analyzing the log data directly, or, alternately, mapping the data into relational tables. In the first case, some special preprocessing is required, and in the second, it is necessary to adapt and encode the information into a form that can be entered into the database. In either case, it is important to ensure the accuracy and definition of users and sessions given the influence of caching and proxy servers (Kosala & Blockeel, 2000).

In the case of Web usage applications, they can also be categorized into impersonalized and personalized. In the first case, the goal is to examine general user navigational patterns, so that it is possible to understand how users go about moving through and using the site. The other case looks more from the perspective of individual users and what would be their preferences and needs, so as to start towards developing a profile for that user. As a result, webmasters and site designers, with this knowledge in hand, can better structure and tailor their site to the needs of users, personalize the site for certain types of users, and learn more about the characteristics of the site's users.

Srivastava, Cooley, Deshpande, and Tan (2000) have produced a taxonomy of different Web-mining applications and have categorized them into the following types:

- *Personalization.* The goal here is to produce a more "individualized" experience for a Web visitor, which includes making recommendations about other pages to visit based on the pages he/she has visited previously. In order to be able to personalize recommended pages, part of the analysis is to cluster those users who have similar access patterns and then develop a group of possible recommended pages to visit.
- *System Improvement.* Performance and speed have always been an important factor when it comes to computing systems, and through Web usage data it is possible to improve system performance by creating policies and using such methods as load balancing, Web caching, and network transmission. The role of security is also important, and an analysis of usage patterns can be used to detect illegal intrusion and other security problems.
- *Site Modification.* It is also possible to modify aspects of a site based on user patterns and behavior. After a detailed analysis of a user's activities on a site, it is possible to make design changes and structural modifications to the site to enhance the user's satisfaction and the site's usability. In one interesting study, the structure of a Web site was changed, automatically, based on patterns analyzed from usage logs. This adaptive Web site project was described by Perkowitz and Etzioni (1998, 1999).
- *Business Intelligence.* Another important application of Web usage mining is the ability to mine for marketing intelligence information. Buchner and Mulvenna (1998) used a data hypercube to consolidate Web usage data together with marketing data in order to obtain insights with regards to e-commerce. They identified certain areas in the customer relationship

life cycle that were supported by analyses of Web usage information: customer attraction and retention, cross sales, and departure of customers. A number of commercial products are on the market that aid in collecting and analyzing Web log data for business intelligence purposes.

- *Usage Characterization.* There is a close relationship between data mining of Web usage data and Web usage characterization research. Usage characterization is focused more on such topics as interactions with the browser interface, navigational strategies, the occurrence of certain types of activities, and models of Web usage. Studies in this area include Arlitt and Williamson (1997), Catledge and Pitkow (1995), and Doorenbos, Etzioni, and Weld (1996).

Three major components of the Web usage mining process include preprocessing, pattern discovery, and pattern analysis. The preprocessing component adapts the data to a form that is more suitable for pattern analysis and Web usage mining. This involves taking raw log data and converting it into usable (but as of yet not analyzed) information. In the case of Web usage data, it would be necessary to take the raw log information and start by identifying users, followed by the identification of the users' sessions. Often it is important to have not only the Web server log data, but also data on the content of the pages being accessed, so that it is easier to determine the exact kind of content to which the links point (Perkowitz & Etzioni, 1995; Srivastava, Cooley, Deshpande, & Tan, 2000).

Pattern discovery includes such analyses as clustering, classification, sequential pattern analysis, descriptive statistics, and dependency modeling. While most of these should be familiar to those who understand statistical and analysis methods, a couple may be new to some. Sequential pattern analysis attempts to identify patterns that form a sequence; for example, certain types of data items in session data may be followed by certain other specific kinds of data. An analysis of this data can provide insight into the patterns present in the Web visits of certain kinds of customers, and would make it easier to target advertising and other promotions to the customers who would most appreciate them. Dependency modeling attempts to determine if there are any dependencies between the variables in the Web usage data. This could help to identify, for example, if there were different stages that a customer would go through while using an e-commerce site (such as browsing, product search, purchase) on the way to becoming a regular customer.

Pattern analysis has as its objective the filtering out of rules and patterns that are deemed "uninteresting" and, therefore, will be excluded from further analysis. This step is necessary to avoid excessive time and effort spent on patterns that may not yield productive results.

Yet another area that has been gaining interest is agent-based approaches. Agents are intelligent software components that "crawl through" the Net and collect useful information, much like the virus-like worm moves through systems wreaking havoc. Generally, agent-based Web-mining systems can be placed into three main categories: information categorization and filtering, intelligent search agents, and personal agents.

- *Information Filtering/Categorization* agents try to automatically retrieve, filter, and categorize discovered information by using various information retrieval techniques. Agents that can be classified into this category include HyPursuit (Weiss et al., 1996) and Bookmark Organizer (BO). HyPursuit clusters together hierarchies of hypertext documents, and structures an information space by using semantic information embedded in link structures as well as document content. The BO system uses both hierarchical clustering methods and user interaction techniques to organize a collection of Web documents based on conceptual information.
- *Intelligent Search Agents* search the Internet for relevant information and use characteristics of a particular domain to organize and interpret the discovered information. Some of the better known include ParaSite and FAQ-Finder. These agents rely either on domain-specific information about particular types of documents or on models of the information sources to retrieve and interpret documents. Other agents, such as ShopBot and Internet Learning Agent (ILA), attempt to interact with and learn the structure of unfamiliar information sources. ShopBot retrieves product information from a variety of vendor sites using only general information about the product domain. ILA, on the other hand, learns models of various information sources and translates these into its own internal concept hierarchy.
- *Personalized Web Agents* try to obtain or learn user preferences and discover Web information sources that correspond to these preferences, and possibly those of other individuals with similar interests, using collaborative filtering. Systems in this class include Netperceptions, WebWatcher (Armstrong, Freitag, Joachims, & Mitchell, 1995), and Syskill and Webert (Pazzani, Muramatsu, & Billsus, 1996).

As a related area, it would be useful to examine knowledge discovery from discussion groups and online chats. In fact, online discussions could be a good way to discover knowledge, since many people who are active in online chatting are usually experts in some fields. Nevertheless, some researchers have done fairly well in this area. The Butterfly system at MIT is a conversation-finding agent that aims to help Internet Relay Chat (IRC) users find desired groups. It uses a natural language query language and a highly interactive user interface.

One study on Yenta (Foner, 1997) used a privacy-safe referral mechanism to discover clusters of interest among people on the Internet, and built user profiles by examining users' email and Usenet messages. Resnick discussed how to tackle the Internet information within large groups (1994). Another development is IBM's Sankha. It is a browsing tool for online chat that demonstrates a new online clustering algorithm to detect new topics in newgroups. The idea behind Sankha is based on another pioneering project by IBM called Quest (Agarwal et al., 1996).

TEXT DATA MINING

The possibilities for data mining from textual information are largely untapped, making it a fertile area of future research. Text expresses a vast, rich range of information, but in its original, raw form is difficult to analyze or mine automatically. As such, there has been comparatively little work in text data mining (TDM) to date, and most researchers who have worked with or talked about it have either associated it with information access or have not analyzed text directly to discover previously unknown information.

In this section, text data mining is compared and contrasted with associated areas including information access and computational linguistics. Then, examples are given of current text data mining efforts.

TDM has relatively fewer research projects and commercial products compared with other data mining areas. As expected, text data mining is a natural extension of traditional data mining (DM), as well as information archeology (Brachman et al., 1993). While most standard data-mining applications tend to be automated discovery of trends and patterns across large databases and datasets, in the case of text mining, the goal is to look for pattern and trends, like nuggets of data in large amounts of text (Hearst, 1999).

Benefits of TDM

It is important to differentiate between TDM and information access (or information retrieval, as it is better known). The goal of information access is to help users find documents that satisfy their information needs (Baeza-Yates & Ribeiro-Neto, 1999). The goal is one of homing in on what is currently of interest to the user. However, text mining focuses on how to use a body of textual information as a large knowledge base from which one can extract new, never-before encountered information (Craven et al., 1998). However, the results of certain types of text processing can yield *tools* that indirectly *aid* in the information access process. Examples include text clustering to create thematic overviews of text collections (Rennison, 1994; Wise et al., 1995), automatically generating term associations to aid in query expansion (Voorhees, 1994; Xu & Croft, 1996), and using co-citation analysis to find general topics within a collection or identify central Web pages (Hearst, 1999; Kleinberg 1998; Larson, 1996).

Aside from providing tools to aid in the standard information access process, text data mining can contribute by providing systems supplemented with tools for exploratory data analysis. One example of this is in projects such as LINDI. The LINDI project investigated how researchers can use large text collections in the discovery of new important information, and how to build software systems to help support this process. The LINDI interface provides a facility for users to build and so reuse sequences of query operations via a drag-and-drop interface. These allow the user to repeat the same sequence of actions for different queries. This system will allow maintenance of several different types of history, including history of commands issued, history of strategies employed, and history of hypotheses tested (Hearst, 1999).

The user interface provides a mechanism for recording and modifying sequences of actions. These include facilities that refer to metadata structure, allowing, for example, query terms to be expanded by terms one level above or below them in a subject hierarchy. Thus, the emphasis of this system is to help automate the tedious parts of the text manipulation process and to combine text analysis with human-guided decision making.

One area that is closely related to TDM is corpus-based computational linguistics. This field is concerned with computing statistics over large text collections in order to discover useful patterns. These patterns are used to develop algorithms for various sub-problems within natural language processing, such as part-of-speech tagging, word sense disambiguation, and bilingual dictionary creation. However, these tend to serve the specific needs of computational linguistics and are not applicable to a broader audience (Hearst, 1999).

Text Categorization

Some researchers have suggested that text categorization should be considered TDM. Text categorization is a condensation of the specific content of a document into one (or more) of a set of predefined labels. It does not discover new information; rather, it summarizes something that is already known. However, there are two recent areas of inquiry that make use of text categorization and seem to be more related to text mining. One area uses text category labels to find "unexpected patterns" among text articles (Dagan, Feldman, & Hirsh, 1996; Feldman, Klosgen, & Zilberstein, 1997). The main goal is to compare distributions of category assignments within subsets of the document collection.

Another effort is that of the DARPA Topic Detection and Tracking initiative. This effort included the Online New Event Detection, the input to which is a stream of news stories in chronological order, and whose output is a yes/no decision for each story, indicating whether the story is the first reference to a newly occurring event (Hearst, 1999).

Text Data Mining: Exploratory Applications of TDM

Another way to view text data mining is as a process of exploratory data analysis (Tukey, 1977), that leads to the discovery of heretofore unknown information or to answers to questions for which the answer is not currently known. Two examples of these are studies done on medical text literature and social impact TDM.

Medical Text Literature TDM

Swanson has examined how chains of causal implication within the medical literature can lead to hypotheses for causes of rare diseases, some of which have received supporting experimental evidence (Swanson & Smalheiser, 1997). This approach has been only partially automated. There is, of course, a potential for combinatorial explosion of potentially valid links. Beeferman (1998) has developed a flexible interface and analysis tool for exploring certain kinds of chains of links among lexical relations within WordNet. However, sophisticated new algorithms are needed for helping in the pruning process, since a good pruning algorithm will want to take into account various kinds of semantic constraints. This may be an interesting area of investigation for computational linguists (Hearst, 1999).

Social Impact TDM

A study was conducted to determine the effects of publicly financed research on industrial advances (Narin, Hamilton, & Olivastro, 1997). The authors found that the technology industry relies more heavily than ever on government-sponsored research results. The authors explored relationships among patent text and the published research literature. A mix of operations (article retrieval, extraction, classification, computation of statistics, etc.) was required to conduct complex analyses over large text collections (Hearst, 1999).

Methods of TDM

Some of the major methods of text data mining include feature extraction, clustering, and categorization. Feature extraction, which is the mining of text within a document, attempts to find significant and important vocabulary from within a natural language text document. This involves the use of techniques including pattern matching and heuristics that are focused on lexical and part-of-speech information. An effective feature extraction system is able not only to take out relevant terms and words, but also to do some more advanced processing, including the ability to overcome ambiguity of variants—in other words, mistaking words that are spelled the same. For instance, a system would ideally be able to distinguish between the same word, if it is used as the name of a city or as a part of a person's name.

From the document-level analysis, it is possible to examine collections of documents. The methods used to do this include clustering and classification. Clustering is the process of grouping documents with similar contents into dynamically generated clusters. This is in contrast to text categorization, where the process is a bit more involved. Here, samples of documents fitting into predetermined "themes" or "categories" are fed into a "trainer," which in turn generates a categorization schema. When the documents to be analyzed are then fed into the categorizer, which incorporates the schema previously produced, it will then assign documents to different categories based on the taxonomy previously provided. These features are incorporated into programs such as IBM's Intelligent Miner for Text (Dorre, Gerstl, & Seiffert, 1999).

DISTRIBUTED/COLLECTIVE DATA MINING

One area of data mining that is attracting a good amount of attention is that of distributed and collective data mining. Much of the data mining that is being done currently focuses on a database or data warehouse of information that is physically located in one place. However, the situation arises where information may be located in different places, in different physical locations. This is known generally as distributed data mining (DDM). Therefore, the goal is to effectively mine distributed data that is located in heterogeneous sites. Examples of this include biological information located in different databases, data that comes from the databases of two different firms, or analysis of data from different branches of a corporation, the combining of which would be an expensive and time-consuming process.

Distributed data mining (DDM) is used to offer a different approach to traditional approaches analysis, by using a combination of localized data analysis, together with a "global data model." In more specific terms, this is specified as:

- performing local data analysis for generating partial data models, and
- combining the local data models from different data sites in order to develop the global model.

This global model combines the results of the separate analyses. Often the global model produced may become incorrect or ambiguous, especially if the data in different locations has different features or characteristics. This problem is especially critical when the data in distributed sites is heterogeneous rather than homogeneous. These heterogeneous data sets are known as vertically partitioned datasets.

An approach proposed by Kargupta et al. (2000) speaks of the collective data mining (CDM) approach, which provides a better approach to vertically partitioned datasets, using the notion of orthonormal basis functions, and computes the basis coefficients to generate the global model of the data.

UBIQUITOUS DATA MINING (UDM)

The advent of laptops, palmtops, cell phones, and wearable computers is making ubiquitous access to large quantity of data possible. Advanced analysis of data for extracting useful knowledge is the next natural step in the world of ubiquitous computing. Accessing and analyzing data from a ubiquitous computing device offer many challenges. For example, UDM introduces additional costs due to communication, computation, security, and other factors. So, one of the objectives of UDM is to mine data while minimizing the cost of ubiquitous presence.

Human-computer interaction is another challenging aspect of UDM. Visualizing patterns like classifiers, clusters, associations, and others in portable devices is usually difficult. The small display areas offer serious challenges to interactive data-mining environments. Data management in a mobile environment is also a challenging issue. Moreover, the sociological and psychological aspects of the integration between data-mining technology and our lifestyle are yet to be explored. The key issues to consider, according to Kargupta and Joshi (2001), include:

- theories of UDM,
- advanced algorithms for mobile and distributed applications,
- data management issues,
- mark-up languages and other data representation techniques,
- integration with database applications for mobile environments,
- architectural issues (architecture, control, security, and communication issues),
- specialized mobile devices for UDMs,
- software agents and UDM (agent-based approaches in UDM, agent interaction — cooperation, collaboration, negotiation, organizational behavior),
- applications of UDM (application in business, science, engineering, medicine, and other disciplines),
- location management issues in UDM, and
- technology for Web-based applications of UDM.

HYPERTEXT AND HYPERMEDIA DATA MINING

Hypertext and hypermedia data mining can be characterized as mining data that includes text, hyperlinks, text markups, and various other forms of hypermedia information. As such, it is closely related to both Web mining, and multimedia mining, which are covered separately in this section but which, in reality, are quite close in terms of content and applications. While the World Wide Web is substantially composed of hypertext and hypermedia elements, there are other kinds of hypertext/hypermedia data sources that are not found on the Web. Examples of these include the information found in online catalogues, digital libraries, online information databases, and the like. In addition to the traditional forms of hypertext and hypermedia, together with the associated hyperlink structures, there are also inter-document structures that exist on the Web, such as the directories employed by such services as Yahoo! (www.yahoo.com) or the Open Directory project (http://dmoz.org) These taxonomies of topics and subtopics are linked together to form a large network or hierarchical tree of topics and associated links and pages.

Some of the important data-mining techniques used for hypertext and hypermedia data mining include classification (supervised learning), clustering (unsupervised learning), semi structured learning, and social network analysis.

In the case of classification, or supervised learning, the process starts off by reviewing training data in which items are marked as being part of a certain class or group. This data is the basis from which the algorithm is trained. One application of classification is in the area of Web topic directories, which can group similar-sounding or spelled terms into appropriate categories so that searches will not bring up inappropriate sites and pages. The use of classification can also result in searches that are not only based on keywords, but also on category and classification attributes. Methods used for classification include naive Bayes classification, parameter smoothing, dependence modeling, and maximum entropy (Chakrabarti, 2000).

Unsupervised learning, or clustering, differs from classification in that classification involves the use of training data; clustering is concerned with the creation of hierarchies of documents based on similarity, and organizes the documents based on that hierarchy. Intuitively, this would result in more similar documents being placed on the leaf levels of the hierarchy, with less similar sets of document areas being placed higher up, closer to the root of the tree. Techniques that have been used for unsupervised learning include k-means clustering, agglomerative clustering, random projections, and latent semantic indexing.

Semi supervised learning and social network analysis are other methods that are important to hypermedia-based data mining. Semi supervised learning is the case where there are both labeled and unlabeled documents, and there is a need to learn from both types of documents. Social network analysis is also applicable because the Web is considered a social network, which examines networks formed through collaborative association, whether between friends, academics doing research or serving on committees, or between papers through references and citations. Graph distances and various aspects of connectivity come into play when working in the area of social networks (Larson, 1996; Mizruchi, Mariolis, Schwartz, & Mintz, 1986). Other research conducted in the area of hypertext data mining include work on distributed hypertext resource discovery (Chakrabarti, van den Berg, & Dom, 1999).

VISUAL DATA MINING

Visual data mining is a collection of interactive methods that support exploration of data sets by dynamically adjusting parameters to see how they affect the information being presented. This emerging area of explorative and intelligent data analysis and mining is based on the integration of concepts from computer graphics, visualization metaphors and methods, information and scientific data visualization, visual perception, cognitive psychology, diagrammatic reasoning, visual data formatting, and 3D collaborative virtual environments for information visualization. It offers a powerful means of analysis that can assist in uncovering patterns and trends that are likely to be missed with other nonvisual methods. Visual data-mining techniques offer the luxury of being able to make observations without preconception. Research and developments in the methods and techniques for visual data mining have helped to identify many of the research directions in the field, including:

- visual methods for data analysis;
- general visual data-mining process models;
- visual reasoning and uncertainty management in data mining;
- complexity, efficiency, and scalability of information visualization in data mining;
- multimedia support for visual reasoning in data mining;
- visualization schemata and formal visual representation of metaphors;
- visual explanations;
- algorithmic animation methods for visual data mining;
- perceptual and cognitive aspects of information visualization in data mining;
- interactivity in visual data mining;
- representation of discovered knowledge;
- incorporation of domain knowledge in visual reasoning;
- virtual environments for data visualization and exploration;
- visual analysis of large databases;

- collaborative visual data exploration and model building;
- metrics for evaluation of visual data-mining methods;
- generic system architectures and prototypes for visual data mining; and
- methods for visualizing semantic content.

Pictures and diagrams are also often used, mostly for psychological reasons — harnessing our ability to reason "visually" with the elements of a diagram in order to assist our more purely logical or analytical thought processes. Thus, a visual-reasoning approach to the area of data mining and machine learning promises to overcome some of the difficulties experienced in the comprehension of the information encoded in data sets and the models derived by other quantitative data mining methods (Han & Kamber, 2001).

MULTIMEDIA DATA MINING

Multimedia Data Mining is the mining and analysis of various types of data, including images, video, audio, and animation. The idea of mining data that contain different kinds of information is the main objective of multimedia data mining (Zaiane, Han, Li, & Hou, 1998). Because multimedia data mining incorporates the areas of text mining and hypertext/hypermedia mining, these fields are closely related. Much of the information describing these other areas also applies to multimedia data mining. This field is also rather new, but holds much promise for the future.

Multimedia information, because of its nature as a large collection of multimedia objects, must be represented differently from conventional forms of data. One approach is to create a multimedia data cube that can be used to convert multimedia-type data into a form that is suited to analysis using one of the main data-mining techniques but taking into account the unique character-istics of the data. This may include the use of measures and dimensions for texture, shape, color, and related attributes. In essence, it is possible to create a multidimensional spatial database. Among the types of analyses that can be conducted on multimedia databases are associations, clustering, classification, and similarity search.

Another developing area in multimedia data mining is that of audio data mining (mining music). The idea is basically to use audio signals to indicate the patterns of data or to represent the features of data mining results. The basic advantage of audio data mining is that while using a technique such as visual data mining may disclose interesting patterns from observing graphical displays, it does require users to concentrate on watching patterns, which can become monotonous. But when representing data as a stream of audio, it is possible to transform patterns into sound and music and listen to pitches, rhythms, tune, and melody in order to identify anything interesting or unusual. Its is possible not only to summarize melodies, based on the approximate patterns that repeatedly occur in the segment, but also to summarize style, based on tone, tempo, or the major musical instruments played (Han & Kamber, 2001; Zaiane, Han, & Zhu, 2000).

SPATIAL AND GEOGRAPHIC DATA MINING

The data types that come to mind when the term data mining is mentioned involve data as we know it — statistical, generally numerical data of varying kinds. However, it is also important to consider information that is of an entirely different kind — spatial and geographic data that contain information about astronomical data, natural resources, or even orbiting satellites and spacecraft that transmit images of earth from out in space. Much of this data is image-oriented and can represent a great deal of information if properly analyzed and mined (Miller & Han, 2001).

A definition of spatial data mining is as follows: "the extraction of implicit knowledge, spatial relationships, or other patterns not explicitly stored in spatial databases." Some of the components of spatial data that differentiate it from other kinds include distance and topological information, which can be indexed using multidimensional structures, and required special spatial data access methods, together with spatial knowledge representation and data access methods, along with the ability to handle geometric calculations.

Analyzing spatial and geographic data include such tasks as understanding and browsing spatial data, uncovering relationships between spatial data items (and also between non-spatial and spatial items), and also using spatial databases and spatial knowledge bases for analysis purposes. The applications of these would be useful in such fields as remote sensing, medical imaging, navigation, and other related fields.

Some of the techniques and data structures that are used when analyzing spatial and related types of data include the use of spatial warehouses, spatial data cubes, and spatial OLAP. Spatial data warehouses can be defined as those that are subject-oriented, integrated, nonvolatile, and time-variant (Han, Kamber, & Tung, 2000). Some of the challenges in constructing a spatial data warehouse include the difficulties of integration of data from heterogeneous sources and applying the use of online analytical processing, which is not only relatively fast, but also offers some forms of flexibility.

In general, spatial data cubes, which are components of spatial data warehouses, are designed with three types of dimensions and two types of measures. The three types of dimensions include the nonspatial dimension (data that is nonspatial in nature), the spatial to nonspatial dimension (primitive level is spatial but higher level generalization is nonspatial), and the spatial-to-spatial dimension (both primitive and higher levels are all spatial). In terms of measures, there are both numerical (numbers only) and spatial (pointers to spatial object) measures used in spatial data cubes (Stefanovic, Han, & Koperski, 2000; Zhou, Truffet, & Han, 1999).

Aside from the implemention of data warehouses for spatial data, there is also the issue of analyses that can be done on the data, such as association analysis, clustering methods, and the mining of raster databases There have been a number of studies conducted on spatial data mining (Bedard, Merrett, & Han, 2001; Han, Kamber, & Tung, 1998; Han, Koperski, & Stefanovic, 1997; Han, Stefanovic, & Koperski, 1998; Koperski, Adikary, & Han, 1996; Koperski & Han, 1995; Koperski, Han, & Marchisio, 1999; Koperski, Han, & Stefanovic, 1998; Tung, Hou, & Han, 2001).

TIME SERIES/SEQUENCE DATA MINING

Another important area in data mining centers on the mining of time-series and sequence-based data. Simply put, this involves the mining of a sequence of data, which can either be referenced by time (time-series, such as stock market and production process data) or is simply a sequence of data that is ordered in a sequence. In general, one aspect of mining time-series data focuses on the goal of identifying movements or components that exist within the data (trend analysis). These can include long-term or trend movements, seasonal variations, cyclical variations, and random movements (Han & Kamber, 2001).

Other techniques that can be used on these kinds of data include similarity search, sequential-pattern mining, and periodicity analysis. *Similarity search* is concerned with the identification of a pattern sequence that is close or similar to a given pattern, and this form of analysis can be broken down into two subtypes: whole sequence matching and subsequence matching. Whole sequence matching attempts to find all sequences that bear a likeness to each other, while subsequence matching attempts to find those patterns that are similar to a specified, given sequence.

Sequential-pattern mining has as its focus the identification of sequences that occur frequently in a time series or sequence of data. This is particularly useful in the analysis of customers, where certain buying patterns could be identified, for example, what might be the likely follow-up purchase to purchasing a certain electronics item or computer.

Periodicity analysis attempts to analyze the data from the perspective of identifying patterns that repeat or recur in a time series. This form of data-mining analysis can be categorized as being full periodic, partial periodic, or cyclic periodic. In general, full periodic is the situation where all of the data points in time contribute to the behavior of the series. This is in contrast to partial periodicity, where only certain points in time contribute to series behavior. Finally, cyclical periodicity relates to sets of events that occur periodically (Han, Dong, & Yin, 1999; Han & Kamber, 2001; Han, Pei et al., 2000; Kim, Lam, & Han, 2000; Pei, Han, Pinto et al., 2001; Pei, Tung, & Han, 2001).

DATA MINING METHODS AND TECHNIQUES

Constraint-Based Data Mining

Many of the data mining techniques that currently exist are very useful but lack the benefit of any guidance or user control. One method of implementing some form of human involvement into data mining is in the form of constraint-based data mining. This form of data mining incorporates the use of constraints that guide the process. Frequently, this is combined with the benefits of multidimensional mining to add greater power to the process (Han, Lakshamanan, & Ng, 1999).

There are several categories of constraints that can be used, each of which has its own characteristics and purpose. These are:

- *Knowledge-type constraints.* This type of constraint specifies the "type of knowledge" that is to be mined and is typically specified at the beginning of any data-mining query. Some of the types of constraints that can be used include clustering, association, and classification.
- *Data constraints.* This constraint identifies the data that is to be used in the specific data-mining query. Since constraint-based mining is ideally

conducted within the framework of an ad hoc, query-driven system, data constraints can be specified in a form similar to that of a SQL query.

- *Dimension/level constraints.* Because much of the information being mined is in the form of a database or multidimensional data warehouse, it is possible to specify constraints that specify the levels or dimensions to be included in the current query.
- *Interestingness constraints.* It would also be useful to determine what ranges of a particular variable or measure are considered to be particularly interesting and should be included in the query.
- *Rule constraints.* It is also important to specify the specific rules that should be applied and used for a particular data mining query or application.

One application of the constraint-based approach is in the Online Analytical Mining Architecture (OLAM) developed by Han, Lakshamanan, and Ng (1999), which is designed to support the multidimensional and constraint-based mining of databases and data warehouses.

In short, constraint-based data mining is one of the developing areas that allows for the use of guiding constraints that should make for better data mining. A number of studies have been conducted in this area: Cheung, Hwang, Fu, and Han (2000), Lakshaman, Ng, Han, and Pang (1999), Lu, Feng, and Han (2001), Pei and Han (2000), Pei, Han, and Lakshaman (2001), Pei, Han, and Mao (2000), Tung, Han, Lakshaman, and Ng (2001), Wang, He, and Han (2000), and Wang, Zhou, and Han (2000).

PHENOMENAL DATA MINING

Phenomenal data mining is not a term for a data-mining project that went extremely well. Rather, it focuses on the relationships between data and the phenomena that are inferred from the data (McCarthy, 2000). One example of this is that by using receipts from cash supermarket purchases, it is possible to identify various aspects of the customers who are making these purchases. Some of these phenomena could include age, income, ethnicity, and purchasing habits.

One aspect of phenomenal data mining, and in particular the goal to infer phenomena from data, is the need to have access to some facts about the relations between these data and their related phenomena. These could be included the program that examines data for phenomena or also could be placed in a kind of knowledge base or database that can be drawn upon when doing the data mining. Part of the challenge in creating such a knowledge base involves the coding of common sense into a database, which has proved to be a difficult problem so far (Lyons & Tseytin, 1998).

DATA MINING APPLICATION AREAS

There are many different applications areas that exist for data mining and, in general, one of the trends in the field is to develop more focused solutions for various application areas. By doing this, it is possible to expand the use of power data-mining technologies to many new industries and applications. Currently, data mining is used in industries as diverse as retail, finance, telecommunications, banking, human resources, insurance, sports, marketing, and biotechnology (Kohavi & Sohami, 2000). There is a broad spectrum of applications that can take advantage of data mining. These include marketing, corporate risk analysis, fraud detection, and even such areas as sports and astronomy.

Marketing (Market Analysis, Management)

Based on data collected from customers, which can include credit card transactions, loyalty cards, discount coupons, customer complaint calls, and surveys, it is possible to do the following analyses:

- Target marketing: Finding clusters of "model" customers who share the same characteristics: interest, income level, spending habits, etc.
- Determining customer purchasing patterns over time.
- Cross-market analysis, which includes associations/co-relations between product sales.
- Customer profiling, where data mining can tell a vendor what types of customers buy what products (using clustering or classification), and also identify customer requirements (identifying the best products for different customers and what factors will attract new customers).
- Multidimensional summary reports and statistical summary information on customers.

Corporate Analysis and Risk Management

From a financial perspective, it is possible to do many useful analyses, including financial planning and asset evaluation, cash-flow analysis and prediction, cross-sectional and time-series analysis (financial-ratio, trend analysis, etc.), and competitive analysis on competitors and market directions (competitive intelligence, CI). Another possible analysis could group customers into classes and develop class-based pricing procedures.

Fraud Detection and Management

Because data mining is concerned with locating patterns within a set of data, it is possible to find "patterns that don't fit," possibly indicating fraud or other criminal activity. The areas in which this has been used include health care, retail, credit card services, telecommunications (phone card fraud), and others.

Some of the methods used historical data to build models of fraudulent behavior and data mining to help identify similar instances. In the auto insurance industry, data mining has been used to detect people who staged accidents to fraudulently collect on insurance. The detection of suspicious money transactions (U.S. Treasury's Financial Crimes Enforcement Network), and also medical insurance fraud (detection of professional patients, fraudulent claims) are also examples where data mining was successfully used. Another major area is telephone fraud, where models are created of "normal" telephone call activity in order to detect patterns that deviate from the expected norm.

Sports and Stars

In the sports arena, IBM Advanced Scout was used by the New York Knicks and Miami Heat teams to analyze NBA game statistics (shots blocked, assists, and fouls) to gain competitive advantage. Data mining has also been credited with helping to find quasars and other astronomical discoveries.

While there are obviously many application areas, there are two that are exceedingly important and have gained attention as key areas: e-commerce/web personalization, and bioinformatics and customer relationship management (CRM).

DATA MINING FOR E-COMMERCE/ WEB PERSONALIZATION

E-Commerce

The intense competition among Internet-based businesses to acquire new customers and retain existing ones has made Web personalization a significant part of e-commerce (Mobasher, Dai, Luo, Sun, & Zhu, 2000). In today's highly competitive e-commerce environment, the success of a Web site often depends on the site's ability to retain visitors and turn casual browsers into potential customers. Automatic personalization and recommender system technologies have become critical tools in this arena because they help tailor the site's interaction with a visitor to his or her needs and interests (Nakagawa, Luo, Mobasher, & Dai, 2001). The current challenge in electronic commerce is to develop ways of gaining deep understanding into the behavior of customers based on data which is, at least in part, anonymous (Mobasher, Dai, Luo, Sun, & Zhu).

While most of the research in personalization is directed toward e-commerce functions, personalization concepts can be applied to any Web browsing activity. Mobasher, one of the most recognized researchers on this topic, defines Web personalization as any action that tailors the Web experience to a particular user, or set of users (Mobasher, Cooley, & Srivastava, 2000). Web personalization can be described as any action that makes the Web experience of a user personalized to the user's taste or preferences. The experience can be something as casual as browsing the Web or as significant (economically) as trading stocks or purchasing a car. The actions can range from simply making the presentation more pleasing to an individual to anticipating the needs of the user and providing the right information, or performing a set of routine bookkeeping functions automatically (Mobasher, 1999).

User preferences may be obtained explicitly or by passive observation of users over time as they interact with the system (Mobasher, 1999).

The target audience of a personalized experience is the group of visitors whose members will all see the same content. Traditional Web sites deliver the same content regardless of the visitor's identity — their target is the whole population of the Web. Personal portal sites, such as MyYahoo! and MyMSN, allow users to build a personalized view of their content — the target here is the individual visitor. Personalization involves an application that computes a result, thereby actively modifying the end-user interaction. A main goal of personalization is to deliver some piece of content (for example, an ad, product, or piece of information) that the end-user finds so interesting that the session lasts at least one more click. The more times the end-user clicks, the longer the average session lasts; longer session lengths imply happier end-users, and happier end-users help achieve business goals (Rosenberg, 2001). The ultimate objectives are to own a piece of the customer's mindshare and to provide customized services to each customer according to his or her personal preferences — whether expressed or inferred. All this must be done while protecting the customers' privacy and giving them a sense of power and control over the information they provide (Charlet, 1998).

The bursting of the so-called "IT bubble" has put vastly increased pressure on Internet companies to make a profit quickly. Imagine if in a "brick and mortar" store it were possible to observe which products a customer picks up and examines and which ones he or she just passes by. With that information, it would be possible for the store to make valuable marketing recommendations. In the online world, such data can be collected. Personalization techniques are generally seen as the true differentiator between "brick and mortar" businesses and the online world and a key to the continued growth and success of the Internet. This same ability may also serve as a limitation in the future as the public becomes more concerned about personal privacy and the ethics of sites that collect personal information (Drogan & Hsu, 2003).

Web Personalization: Personalization and Customization

Personalization and Customization seem to be very similar terms. While the techniques do have similarities, it should be noted that there are some generally recognized differences. Customization involves end-users telling the Web site exactly what they want, such as what colors or fonts they like, the cities for which they want to know the weather report, or the sports teams for which they want the latest scores and information. With customization, the end-user is actively engaged in telling the content-serving platform what to do; the settings remain static until the end-user reengages and changes the user interface (Rosenberg, 2001).

Examples of customization include sites such as Yahoo! and MSN that allow users to explicitly create their own home pages with content that is meaningful to them. This technology is relatively simple to implement, as there is very little computation involved. It is simply a matter of arranging a Web page based on explicit instructions from a user. Such technology is generally used as a basis for setting up a "portal" site.

Personalization is content that is specific to the end-user based on implied interest during the current and previous sessions. An example of personalization use is Amazon.com. Amazon's technology observes users purchasing and browsing behavior and uses that information to make recommendations. The technology is cognitive because it "learns" what visitors to a site want by "observing" their behavior. It has the ability to adapt over time, based on changes in a site's content or inventory, as well as changes in the marketplace. Because it observes end-users' behavior, personalization has the ability to follow trends and fads (Rosenberg, 2001; Drogan & Hsu, 2003).

Musician's Friend

Musician's Friend (www.musiciansfriend.com), which is a subsidiary of Guitar Center, Inc., is part of the world's largest direct marketer of music gear. Musician's Friend features more than 24,000 products in its mail-order catalogs and on its Web site. Products offered include guitars, keyboards, amplifiers, percussion instruments, as well as recording, mixing, lighting, and DJ gear. In 1999, Musician's Friend realized that both its e-commerce and catalog sales were underperforming. It realized that it had vast amounts of customer and product data, but was not leveraging this information in any intelligent or productive way. The company sought a solution to increase its e-commerce and catalog revenues through better understanding of its customer and product data interactions and the ability to leverage this knowledge to generate greater demand. To meet its objectives, Musician's Friend decided to implement Web personalization technology. The company felt it could personalize the shopper's experience and at the same time gain a better understanding of the vast and complex relationships between products, customers, and promotions. Successful implementation would result in more customers, more customer loyalty and increased revenue.

Musician's Friend decided to implement Net Perceptions technology (www.netperceptions.com). This technology did more than make recommendations based simply on the shopper's preferences for the Web site. It used preference information and combined it with knowledge about product relationships, profit margins, overstock conditions, and more.

Musician's Friend also leveraged personalization technology to help its catalog business. The merchandising staff quickly noticed that the same technology could help it to determine which of the many thousands of products available on the Web site to feature in its catalog promotions.

The results were impressive. In 2000, catalog sales increased by 32% while Internet sales increased by 170%. According to Eric Meadows, Director of Internet for the company, "We have been able to implement several enhancements to our site as a direct result of the Net Perceptions solution, including using data on the items customers return to refine and increase the effectiveness of the additional product suggestions the site recommends" (www.netperceptions.com). Net Perceptions' personalization solutions helped Musician's Friend generate a substantial increase on items per order year-over-year—in other words, intelligently generating greater customer demand (Drogan & Hsu, 2003).

J.Crew

J.Crew is one of the clothing industry's most recognized retailers, with hundreds of clothiers around the world and a catalog on thousands of doorsteps with every new season. J.Crew is a merchandising-driven company, which means its goal is to get the customer exactly what he or she wants as easily as possible.

Dave Towers, Vice President of e-Commerce Operations explains: "As a multichannel retailer, our business is divided between our retail stores, our catalog, and our growing business on the Internet." J.Crew understood the operational cost reductions that could be achieved by migrating customers from the print catalog to www.j.crew.com. To accommodate all of its Internet customers, J.Crew built an e-commerce infrastructure that consistently supports about 7,000 simultaneous users and generates up to $100,000 per hour of revenue during peak times.

J.Crew realized early on that personalization technology would be a critical area of focus if it was to succeed in e-commerce. As Mr. Towers put it, "A lot of our business is driven by our ability to present the right apparel to the right customer, whether it's pants, shirts or sweaters, and then up-sell the complementary items that round out a customer's purchase." J.Crew's personalization technology has allowed it to refine the commerce experience for Internet shoppers.

J.Crew has definitely taken notice of the advantages that personalization technology has brought to its e-commerce site. The expanded capabilities delivered by personalization have given J.Crew a notable increase in up-sells or units per transaction (UPTs), thanks to the ability to cross-sell items based on customers' actions on the site. Towers explains:

> *We can present a customer buying a shirt with a nice pair of pants that go with it, and present that recommendation at the right moment in the transaction. The combination of scenarios and personalization enable us to know more about a customer's preferences and spending habits and allows us to make implicit yet effective recommendations.*

Clearly, J.Crew is the type of e-commerce site that can directly benefit from personalization technology. With its business model and the right technology implantation, J.Crew is one company that has been able to make very effective and profitable use of the Internet (Drogan & Hsu, 2003).

Half.com

Half.com (www.half.com), which is an eBay company, offers consumers a fixed price, online marketplace to buy and sell new, overstocked and used products at discount prices. Unlike auctions, where the selling price is based on bidding, the seller sets the price for items at the time the item is listed. The site currently lists a wide variety of merchandise, including books, CDs, movies, video games, computers, consumer electronics, sporting goods, and trading cards.

Half.com determined that to increase customer satisfaction as well as company profits, personalization technology would have to be implemented. It was decided that product recommendations would be presented at numerous locations on the site, including the product detail, add-to-wish list, add-to-cart, and thank you pages. In fact, each point of promotion would include three to five personalized product recommendations. In addition, the site would generate personalized, targeted emails. For example, Half.com would send a personalized email to its customers with product recommendations that are relevant based on prior purchases. In addition, it would send personalized emails to attempt to reactivate customers who had not made a purchase in more than six months.

Half.com decided to try out Net Perceptions technology (www.net perceptions.com) to meet these needs. As a proof of concept, Net Perceptions and Half.com performed a 15-week effectiveness study of Net Perceptions' recommendation technology to see if a positive business benefit could be demonstrated to justify the cost of the product and the implementation. For the study, visitors were randomly split into groups upon entering the Half.com site. Eighty percent of the visitors were placed in a test group and the remaining 20% were placed into a control group. The test group received the recommendations, and the control group did not. The results of this test showed Half.com the business benefits of personalization technology. The highlights were:

- Normalized sales were 5.2% greater in the test group than the control group.
- Visitor to buyer conversion was 3.8% greater in the test group.
- Average spending per account per day was 1.1% greater in the test group.
- For the email campaign, 7% of the personalized emails generated a site visit compared to 5% of the non-personalized.
- When personalized emails were sent to inactive customers (not made a

purchase in six months), 28% of them proceeded to the site and actually made a purchase.

DATA MINING FOR BIOINFORMATICS

Bioinformatics is the science of storing, extracting, organizing, analyzing, interpreting, and utilizing information from biological sequences and molecules. It has been mainly fueled by advances in DNA sequencing and mapping techniques. The Human Genome Project has resulted in an exponentially growing database of genetic sequences. Knowledge Discovery and Data mining (KDD) techniques are playing an increasingly important role in the analysis and discovery of sequence, structure, and functional patterns or models from large sequence databases. High performance techniques are also becoming central to this task (Drogan & Hsu, 2003; Han, Jamil et al., 2001; Han & Kamber, 2001).

Bioinformatics provides opportunities for developing novel mining methods. Some of the grand challenges in bioinformatics include protein structure prediction, homology search, multiple alignment and phylogeny construction, genomic sequence analysis, gene finding and gene mapping, as well as applications in gene expression data analysis, drug discovery in pharmaceutical industry, etc. In protein structure prediction, one is interested in determining the secondary, tertiary, and quaternary structure of proteins, given their amino acid sequence. Homology search aims at detecting increasingly distant homologues, i.e., proteins related by evolution from a common ancestor. Multiple alignment and phylogenetic tree construction are interrelated problems. Multiple alignment aims at aligning a whole set of sequences to determine which subsequences are conserved. This works best when a phylogenetic tree of related proteins is available. Gene finding aims at locating the genes in a DNA sequence. Finally, in gene mapping the task is to identify potential gene loci for a particular disease, typically based on genetic marker data from patients and controls.

As a consequence of the large amount of data produced in the field of molecular biology, most of the current bioinformatics projects deal with structural and functional aspects of genes and proteins. Many of these projects are related to the Human Genome Project. The data produced by thousands of research teams all over the world are collected and organized in databases specialized for particular subjects; examples include GDB, SWISS-PROT, GenBank, and PDB. In the project's next step, computational tools are needed to analyze the collected data in the most efficient manner. For example, bioinformaticists are working on the prediction of the biological functions of genes and proteins based on structural data (Chalifa-Caspi, Prilusky, & Lancet, 1998).

In recent years, many new databases storing biological information have appeared. While this is a positive development, many scientists complain that it gets increasingly difficult to find useful information in the resulting labyrinth of data. This may largely be due to the fact that the information gets more and more scattered over an increasing number of heterogeneous resources. One solution would be to integrate the scattered information in new types of Web resources. The principal benefit is that these databases should enable the user to quickly obtain an idea about the current knowledge that has been gathered about a particular subject. For instance, the Chromosome 17 Database stores all available information about Human Chromosome 17, including all the genes, markers, and other genomic features. In the near future, this integration concept will be expanded to the whole human genome.

Another example of integration is the GeneCards encyclopedia (Rebhan, Chalifa-Caspi, Prilusky, & Lancet, 1997). This resource contains data about human genes, their products, and the diseases in which they are involved. What's special about it is that it contains only selected information that has been automatically extracted from a variety of heterogeneous databases, similar to data mining. In addition, this resource offers advanced user navigation guidance that leads the user rapidly to the desired information.

Since data mining offers the ability to discover patterns and relationships from large amounts of data, it seems ideally suited to use in the analysis of DNA. This is because DNA is essentially a sequence or chain of four main components called nucleotides. A group of several hundred nucleotides in a certain sequence is called a gene, and there are about 100,000 genes that make up the human genome. Aside from the task of integrating databases of biological information noted above, another important application is the use of comparison and similarity search on DNA sequences. This is useful in the study of genetics-linked diseases, as it would be possible to compare and contrast the gene sequences of normal and diseased tissues and attempt to determine what sequences are found in the diseased but not in the normal tissues. The analyses on biological data sequences will be different from those for numerical data, of course.

In addition, since diseases may not be caused by one gene but by a group of genes interacting together, it would be possible to use a form of association analysis to examine the relationships and interactions between various genes that are associated with a certain genetic disease or condition. Another application might be to use a path analysis to study the genes that come into play during different stages of a disease, and so gain some insight into which genes are key during what time in the course of the disease. This may enable the targeting of drugs to treat conditions existing during the various stages of a disease.

Yet another use of data mining and related technologies is in the display of genes and biological structures using advanced visualization techniques. This allows scientists to better understand the further study and analysis of genetic information in a way that may bring out new insights and discoveries than using more traditional forms of data display and analysis.

There are a number of projects that are being conducted in this area, whether on the areas discussed above, or on the analysis of micro-array data and related topics. Among the centers doing research in this area are the European Bioinformatics Institute (EBI) in Cambridge, UK, and the Weizmann Institute of Science in Israel.

DATA MINING FOR CUSTOMER RELATIONSHIP MANAGEMENT (CRM)

Another of the key application areas is the field of customer relationship management (CRM), which can be defined as "the process of finding, reaching, selling, satisfying, and retaining customers" (Delmater & Hancock, 2001).

The use of data mining to support CRM is more of an application area rather than a new technology, but it does show the effective use of data mining for a practical application set. In fact, the use of data mining is helpful in all stages of the customer relationship process, from finding and reaching customers, to selling appropriate products and services to them, and then both satisfying and retaining customers.

In terms of finding customers and generating leads, data mining can be used to produce profiles of the customers who are likely to use a firm's products and services, and also to help look for prospects. If consistent patterns of customers or prospects are identified, it makes it easier to take the appropriate actions and make appropriate decisions. From there, it is possible to better understand the customers and suggest the most effective ways of reaching them. Do they respond better to various forms of advertising, promotions, or other marketing programs?

In terms of selling, the use of data mining research can suggest and identify such useful approaches as setting up online shopping or selling customized products to a certain customer profile. What are the buying habits of a certain segment of customers? Finally, customer service can be enhanced by examining patterns of customer purchases, finding customer needs which have not been fulfilled, and routing of customer inquiries effectively.

Customer retention is another issue that can be analyzed using data mining. Of the customers that a firm currently has, what percentage will eventually leave and go to another provider? What are the reasons for leaving or the character-istics of customers who are likely to leave? With this information, there is an opportunity to address these issues and perhaps increase retention of these customers (Dyche, 2001; Greenberg, 2001; Hancock & Delmater, 2001; Swift, 2000).

OTHER DATA MINING METHODS

In the preceding sections, many different kinds of developing and cutting-edge technologies, methods, and applications were discussed. However, aside from these specific new ideas and trends, there are a number of other issues which should be mentioned.

- *Integrated Data Mining Systems.* The integration of various techniques is one future research area and trend that involves the combination or two or more techniques for analysis of a certain set of data. To date, a majority of the systems in use have only used a single method or a small set of methods, but certain data mining problems may require the use of multiple, integrated techniques in order to come up with a useful result (Goebel & LeGruenwald, 1999).
- *Data Mining of Dynamic Data.* Much of the data being mined today are those that are static and fixed; in other words, they are, in a sense, a snapshot of the data on a certain date and time. However, data, especially business-oriented data, is constantly dynamic and changing, and with the current systems being used, results are obtained on one set of data and — if the data changes — the entire process is repeated on this new set of data. This is more time- and resource-consuming than it needs to be, so refinements to current systems should be made to account for and manage rapid changes in data. Instead of running a complete set of analyses on dynamic data over and over, it would be desirable not only to enhance systems to allow for updating of models based on changes of data, but also to develop strategies that would allow for better handling of dynamic data.

- *Invisible Data Mining.* The concept of invisible data mining is to make data mining as unobtrusive and transparent as possible, hence the term invisible.
- *End-User Data Mining.* Many of the data-mining tools and methods available are complex to use, not only in the techniques and theories involved, but also in terms of the complexity of using many of the available

Table 3: Data Mining Methods

Trend	Description
Web Content Mining	Mine the content of web pages and sites
Web Structure Mining	Mine the structure of websites
Web Usage Mining	Mine the patterns of web usage
Text Data Mining	Mine textual documents and information
Distributed/Collective Data Mining	Mining distributed data which is located in heterogeneous sites
Ubiquitous Data Mining (UDM)	Mine the data used on handheld devices, portable computers, pagers, mobile devices
Hypertext/Hypermedia Data Mining	Mine varied data including text, hyperlinks, and text markups
Visual Data Mining	Mine information from visual data presentations
Multimedia Data Mining	Mining data which includes multimedia elements including audio, video, images, and animation
Spatial/Geographic Data Mining	Data mining using geographic and spatial data
Time Series/Sequence Data Mining	Mining data which is in the form of a time series or data sequence
Constraint-Based Data Mining	Data mining which features the use of user-defined constraints
Phenomenal Data Mining	Mine for phenomena existing within data
Bioinformatics Data Mining	Application area which mines for patterns and sequences in biological data, such as DNA sequences
CRM Data Mining	Application area which is directed towards mining for information which will enable a firm to better serve its customers
Integrated Data Mining Systems	Integration of different techniques, methods, and algorithms
Invisible Data Mining	Embedding data mining into applications so as to make them transparent and invisible
Mining of Dynamic Data	Mining data which changes frequently
End-User Data Mining	Creating data mining systems and software which are usable by professional end users

data-mining software packages. Many of these are designed to be used by experts and scientists well versed in advanced analytical techniques, rather than end-users such as marketing professionals, managers, and engineers. Professional end-users, who actually could benefit a great deal from the power of various data-mining analyses, cannot due to the complexity of the process; they really would be helped by the development of simpler, easier to use tools and packages with straightforward procedures, intuitive user interfaces, and better usability overall. In other words, designing systems that can be more easily used by non-experts would help to improve the level of use in the business and scientific communities and increase the awareness and development of this highly promising field.

REFERENCES

Agrawal, R., Arning, A., Bollinger T., Mehta, M., Shafer, J., & Srikant, R. (1996). The Quest Data Mining System. In *Proceedings of the 2nd International Conference on Knowledge Discovery in Databases and Data Mining*, Portland, Oregon (August).

Arlitt, M., & Williamson, C. (1997). Internet Web servers: Workload characterization and performance implications. *IEEE/ACM Transactions on Networking*, 5, 5.

Armstrong, R., Freitag, D., Joachims, T., & Mitchell, T. (1995). Webwatcher: A learning apprentice for the World Wide Web. In *Proceedings of AAAI Spring Symposium on Information Gathering from Heterogeneous, Distributed Environments,* Stanford, California (March).

Baeza-Yates, R., & Ribeiro-Neto, B. (1999). *Modern Information Retrieval.* Boston, MA; Addison-Wesley Longman.

Bedard, T., & Han, J. (2001). Fundamentals of geospatial data warehousing for geographic knowledge discovery. In H. Miller & J. Han (Eds.), *Geographic Data Mining and Knowledge Discovery.* London: Taylor and Francis.

Beeferman, D. (1998). Lexical discovery with an enriched semantic network. In *Proceedings of the ACL/COLING Workshop on Applications of WordNet in Natural Language Processing Systems,* (pp. 358-364).

Billsus, D., & Pazzani, M. (1999). A hybrid user model for news story classification. In *Proceedings of the Seventh International Conference on User Modeling,* Banff, Canada (June 20-24).

Borges, J., & Leveen, M. (1999). Data mining of user navigation patterns. In *Proceedings of WebKDD '99*, New York, NY.

Brachman, R., Selfridge, P., Terveen, L., Altman, B., Borgida, A., Halper, F., Kirk, T., Lazar, A., McGuinness, D., & Resnick, L. A. (1993). Integrated support for data archaeology. *International Journal of Intelligent and Cooperative Information Systems*, 2(2), 159-185.

Brin, S., &. Page, L. (1998). The anatomy of a large scale hypertextual Web search engine. *Seventh International World Wide Web Conference*, Brisbane, Australia.

Buchner, A., & Mulvenna, M. (1998). Discovering marketing intelligence through online analytical Web usage mining. *SIGMOD Record*, 27, 4.

Catledge, L., & Pitkow, J. (1995). Characterizing browsing behaviors on the World Wide Web. *Computer Networks and ISDN Systems*, 27, 6.

Chakrabarti, van den Berg, & Dom (1999). Distributed hypertext resource discovery through examples. *Proceedings of the 25th VLDB (International Conference on Very Large Data Bases)*, Edinburgh, Scotland.

Chakrabarti, S. (2000, January). Data mining for hypertext. *SIGKDD Explorations*, 1(2).

Chakrabarti, S., Dom, Gibson, Kleinberg, Kumar, Raghavan, Rajagopolan, & Tomkins (1999). Mining the link structure of the World Wide Web. *IEEE Computer*, 32, 8.

Chalifa-Caspi, V., Prilusky, J., & Lancet, D. (1998). *The unified database*. Weizmann Institute of Science, Bioinformatics Unit and Genome Center, Rehovot, Israel.

Charlet, J.-C. (1998). *Firefly networks*. Standford University OIT-22A. March.

Chawathe, S., Garcia-Molina, H., Hammer, J., Irland, K., Papakonstantinou, Y., Ulman, J., & Widom, J. (1994). The TSIMMIS project: Integration of heterogeneous information sources. In *Proceedings of the IPSJ Conference*, Tokyo.

Chen, M., Park, J., & Yu, P. (1996). Data mining for path traversal patterns in a Web environment. In *Proceedings of the 16th International Conference on Distributed Computing Systems*, (pp. 385-392).

Cheung, D., Hwang, C., Fu, A., & Han, J. (2000). Efficient rule-based attributed-oriented induction for data mining. *Journal of Intelligent Information Systems*, 15(2), 175-200.

Craven, M., DiPasquo, D., Freitag, D., McCallum, A., Mitchell, T., Nigam, K., & Slattery, S. (1998). Learning to extract symbolic knowledge from the World Wide Web. In *Proceedings of AAAI*.

Crimmins et al. (1999). Information discovery on the Internet. *IEEE Intelligent Systems*, 14, 4.

Dagan, I., Feldman, R., & Hirsh, H. (1996). Keyword-based browsing and analysis of large document sets. In *Proceedings of the Fifth Annual Symposium on Document Analysis and Information Retrieval (SDAIR)*, Las Vegas, Nevada.

Delmater, R., & Hancock, M. (2001). *Data Mining Explained*. Burlington, MA: Digital Press.

Doorenbos, R., Etzioni, O., & Weld, D. (1996). *A scalable comparison shopping agent for the World Wide Web*. Technical Report 96-01-03, University of Washington, Dept. of Computer Science and Engineering.

Dorre, J., Gerstl, P., & Seiffert, R. (1999). Text mining: Finding nuggets in mountains of textual data. *KDD-99 Proceedings*, San Diego, California.

Drogan, M. & Hsu, J. (2003). Extracting riches from the Web. *Proceedings of SCI2003, 7th World Multiconference on Systems, Cybernetics, and Informatics,* (pp, 214-219).

Dyche, J. (2001). *The CRM Handbook*. Reading, MA: Addison-Wesley.

Etzioni, O. (1996). The World Wide Web: Quagmire or gold mine. *Communications of the ACM*, 39, 11.

Fayyad, U., Piatesky-Shapiro, G., & Smyth, P. (1996). From data mining to knowledge discovery: An overview. In U.M. Fayyad, G. Piatesky-Shapiro, P. Smyth, & R. Uthurusamy (Eds.), *Advances in Knowledge Discovery and Data Mining*. Cambridge, MA: MIT Press.

Feldman, R., Klosgen, W., & Zilberstein, A. (1997). Visualization techniques to explore data mining results for document collections. In *Proceedings of the Third Annual Conference on Knowledge Discovery and Data Mining (KDD)*, Newport Beach, CA.

Foner, L. (1997). Yenta: A multi-agent, referral-based matchmaking system. In *Proceedings of the First International Conference on Autonomous Agents (Agents '97)*, Marina del Rey, California (February).

Frank, E., Paynter, G., Witten, Gutwin, I., & Nevill-Manning, C. (1998). Domain-specific keyphrase extraction. In *Proceedings of 16th Joint Conference on AI*.

Garofalis, M. (1999). Data mining and the Web. *Workshop on Web Information and Data Management*, Workshop in Data Mining WIDM'99, (pp. 43-47).

Goebel & Le Grunwald (1999). A survey of data mining and knowledge discovery software tools. *SIGKDD Explorations*, 1, 1.

Greenberg, P. (2001). *CRM at the Speed of Light*. New York: McGraw-Hill.

Grossman, R. (1998). Supporting the data mining process with next generation data mining systems. *Enterprise Systems*, (August).

Han, J., & Fu, Y. (1999). Discovery of multiple-level association rules from large databases. *IEEE Transactions on Knowledge and Data Engineering*, 11(5), 798-805.

Han, J., & Kamber, M. (2001). *Data Mining: Concepts and Techniques*. San Francisco, CA: Morgan Kaufmann.

Han, J., Dong, G., & Yin, Y. (1999). Efficient mining of partial periodic patterns in time series database. In *Proceedings of International Conference on Data Engineering ICDE '99*, Sydney, Australia (March).

Han, J., Fu, Y., Wang, W., Koperski, K., & Zaiane, O. (1996). Dmql: A data mining query language for relational databases. In *SIGMOD '96 Workshop on Research Issues in Data Mining and Knowledge Discovery (DMKD '96)*, Montreal, Canada.

Han, J., Kamber, M., & Tung, A. (2001). Spatial clustering methods in data mining: A survey. In H. Miller & J. Han (Eds.), *Geographic Data Mining and Knowledge Discovery*. London: Taylor and Francis.

Han, J., Koperski, K., & Stefanovic, N. (1997). GeoMiner: A system prototype for spatial data mining. In *Proceedings SIGMOD '97*, Tucson, Arizona.

Han, J., Lakshmanan, V., & Ng, R. (1999). Constraint-based, multidimensional data mining. *COMPUTER (Special issue on Data Mining)*, 32(8), 46-50.

Han, J., Lu, Chen, Liao, & Pei (2001). DNA-Miner: A system prototype for mining DNA sequences. In *Proceedings of 2001 ACM-SIGMOD*, Santa Barbara, CA (May).

Han, J., Pei, J., & Yin, Y. (2000). Mining frequent patterns without candidate generation. In *Proceedings of 2000 ACM-SIGMOD International. Conference. on Management of Data (SIGMOD '00)*, Dallas, TX, May.

Han, J., Pei, J., Mortazavi-Asl, B., Chen, Q., Dayal, U., & Hsu, M. (2000). FreeSpan: Frequent pattern-projected sequential pattern mining. In *Proceedings KDD '00*, Boston, Massachusetts (August).

Han, J., Stefanovic, N., & Koperski, K. (1998). Selective materialization: An efficient method for spatial data cube construction. In *Proceedings Pacific-Asia Conference in Knowledge Discovery and Data Mining, PAKDD '98*, Melbourne, Australia.

Han, J., Zaiane, O., Chee, S., & Chiang, J. (2000). Towards online analytical mining of the Internet for e-commerce. In W. Kou & Y. Yesha (Eds.), *Electronic Commerce Technology Trends: Challenges and Opportunities*, (pp. 169-198). IBM Press.

Hearst, M.A. (1999). Untangling text data mining. *Proceedings of ACL '99: The 37th Annual Meeting of the Association for Computational Linguistics*, University of Maryland (June 20-26).

Kargupta, H. et al. (2000). Collective data mining. In H. Karhgupta & Chan (Eds.), *Advances in Distributed Data Mining*. Cambridge, MA: MIT Press.

Kargupta, H. & Joshi, A. (2001). Data mining to go: Ubiquitous KDD for mobile and distributed environments. Presentation, *KDD-2001*, San Francisco, CA (August).

Kholsa, I., Kuhn, B., & Soparkar, N. (1996). Database search using information mining. In *Proceedings of the 1996 ACM-SIGMOD International Conference on Management of Data*.

Kim, E., Lam, J.M., & Han, J. (2000). AIM: Approximate intelligent matching for time series data. In *Proceedings of the 2000 International Conferences on Data Warehouse and Knowledge Discovery* (DaWaK'00), Greenwich, UK, (September).

King, R., & Novak, M. (1996). Supporting information infrastructure for distributed, heterogeneous knowledge discovery. In *Proceedings of SIGMOD 96 Workshop on Research Issues on Data Mining and Knowledge Discovery*, Montreal, Canada.

Kleinberg, J. (1998). Authoritative sources in a hyperlinked environment. In *Proceedings of the 9th ACM-SIAM Symposium on Discrete Algorithms*.

Kohavi, R., & Sahami, M. (2000). Data Mining into vertical solutions. *SIGKDD Explorations*, 1(2), 55058.

Koperski, K., & Han, J. (1995). Discovery of spatial association rules in geographic information databases. *Proceedings SSD '95*, Portland, Maine.

Koperski, K., Adhikary, J., & Han, J. (1996). Spatial data mining: Progress and challenges. *SIGMOD '96 Workshop on Research Issues in Data Mining and Knowledge Discovery* DMKD'96, Montreal, Canada.

Koperski, K., Han, J., & Marchisio, K. (1999). Mining spatial and image data through progressive refinement methods. *European Journal of GIS and Spatial Analysis*, 9(4), 425-440.

Koperski, K., Han, J., & Stefanovic, N. (1998). An efficient two-step method for classification of spatial data. *International Symposium on Spatial Data Handling SDH '98*, Vancouver, Canada.

Kosala, R., & Blockeel, H. (2000, July). Web mining research: A survey. *SIGKDD Explorations*, 2(1), 1-15.

Lakshmanan, L., Ng, R., Han, J., & Pang, A. (1999). Optimization of constrained frequent set queries with 2-variable constraints. In *Proceedings SIGMOD '99*, Philadelphia, Pennsylvania (June).

Lakshmanan, L., Sadri, F., & Subramanian, I. (1996). A declarative language for querying and restructuring the Web. In *Proceedings 6th International Workshop on Research Issues in Data Engineering: Interoperability of Nontraditional Database Systems (RIDE-NDS '96)*.

Larson, R. (1996). Bibliometrics of the World Wide Web: An exploratory analysis of the intellectual structure of cyberspace. In *ASIS '96: Proceedings of the 1996 Annual ASIS Meeting*.

Lu, H., Feng, L., & Han, J. (2001). Beyond intra-transaction association analysis: Mining multi-dimensional inter-transaction association rules. *ACM Transactions on Information Systems*.

Lyons, D., & Tseytin, G. (1998). Phenomenal data mining and link analysis. In Jensen & Goldberg (Eds.), *Proceedings of Artificial Intelligence and Link Analysis Fall Symposium*.

Maarek, Y., & Ben Shaul, I. (1996). Automatically organizing bookmarks per content. In *Proceedings of the 5th International World Wide Web Conference* (May 6-10), Paris, France.

Madria et al. (1999). Research issues in data mining. In *Proceedings of Data Warehousing and Knowledge Discovery*, DaWaK '99.

McCarthy, J. (2000). Phenomenal data mining, *SIGKDD Explorations*, 1(2), 24-29.

Mendelzon, A., Mihaila, G., & Milo, T. (1996). Querying the World Wide Web. *Proceedings of Conference on Parallel and Distributed Information Systems PDIS '96*, Miami, Florida.

Merialdo P., Atzeni, P., & Mecca, G. (1997). Semistructured and structured data in the Web: Going back and forth. In *Proceedings of the Workshop on the Management of Semistructured Data* (in conjunction with *ACM SIGMOD*).

Miller, H., & Han, J. (eds.) (2001). *Geographic Data Mining and Knowledge Discovery*. London: Taylor and Francis.

Mizruchi, M., Mariolis, P., Schwartz, M., & Mintz, B. (1986). Techniques for disaggregating centrality scores in social networks. In N. Tuma (Ed.), *Sociological Methodology*. San Francisco, CA: Jossey-Bass.

Mobasher, B. (1999). *WebPersonalizer: A Server-Side Recommender System Based on Web Usage Mining*. DePaul University. Technical Report TR-01-004. March.

Mobasher, Cooley, & Srivastava (2000). Automatic personalization based on Web usage mining. *Communications of the ACM*, August.

Mobasher, Dai, Luo, Sun, & Zhu (2000). *Integrating Web usage and content mining for more effective personalization*. Depaul University. January.

Nahm, U., & Mooney, R. (2000). A mutually beneficial integration of data mining and information extraction. In *Proceedings of the Seventeenth National Conference on AI (AAAI-00)*.

Nakagawa, Luo, Mobasher, & Dai (2001). Improving the effectiveness of collaborative filtering on anonymous web usage data. *Proceedings of the IJCAI 2001 Workshop on Intelligent Techniques for Web Personalization (ITWPO1)*, Seattle, Washington, USA.

Narin, F., Hamilton, K., & Olivastro, D. (1997). The increasing linkage between us technology and public science. *Research Policy*, 26(3), 317-330.

Pazienza, M. (1997). Information extraction: A multidisciplinary approach to an emerging information technology. In *Proceedings of International Summer School on Information Extraction SCIE-97*, Frascati, Rome.

Pazienza, M. (1999). Information extraction. In *Proceedings of International Summer School on Information Extraction SCIE-99*, Frascati, Rome.

Pazzani, M., Muramatsu, M., & Billsus, D. (1996). Syskill & Webert: Identifying interesting web sites. In *Proceedings of AAAI Spring Symposium on Machine Learning in Information Access*, Portland, Oregon.

Pei, J., & Han, J. (2000). Can we push more constraints into frequent pattern mining? In *Proceedings of KDD '00*, Boston, Massachusetts (August).

Pei, J., Han, J., & Lakshmanan, L. (2001). Mining frequent item sets with convertible constraints. In *Proceedings of 2001 International Conference on Data Engineering (ICDE '01)*, Heidelberg, Germany (April).

Pei, J., Han, J., & Mao, R. (2000). CLOSET: An efficient algorithm of mining frequent closed itemsets for association rules. In *Proceedings of DMKD '00*, Dallas, Texas (May).

Pei, J., Han, J., Pinto, H., Chen, Q., Dayal, U., & Hsu, M. (2001). PrefixSpan: Mining sequential patterns efficiently by prefix-projected pattern growth. In *Proceedings of 2001 International. Conference on Data Engineering (ICDE '01)*, Heidelberg, Germany (April).

Pei, J., Tung, A., & Han, J. (2001). Fault-tolerant frequent pattern mining: Problems and challenges. In *Proceedings of 2001 ACM-SIGMOD*, Santa Barbara, California (May).

Perkowitz, M., & Etzioni, O. (1995). Category translation: Learning to understand information on the Internet. In *Proceedings of 15th International Joint Conference on AI*, Montreal, Canada (pp. 930-936).

Perkowitz, M. & Etzioni, O. (1998). Adaptive Web sites: Automatically synthesizing Web pages. In *Proceedings* of *Fifteenth National Conference on AI*.

Perkowitz, M., & Etzioni, O. (1999). Adaptive Web Sites: Conceptual cluster mining. In *Proceedings of the 16th Joint National Conference on AI*.

Pirolli, P., Pitkow, J., & Rao, R. (1996). Silk from a sow's ear: Extracting usable structures from the Web. In *Proceedings from the 1996 Conference on Human Factors in Computing Systems (CHI-96)*, Vancouver, British Columbia, Canada.

Rebhan, M., Chalifa-Caspi, V., Prilusky, J., & Lancet, D. (n.d.). GeneCards: Encyclopedia for genes, proteins and diseases. Weizmann Institute of Science, Bioinformatics Unit and Genome Center Rehovot, Israel.

Rennison, E. (1994). Galaxy of news: An approach to visualizing and understanding expansive news landscapes. In *Proceedings of UIST 94, ACM Symposium on User Interface Software and Technology*, (pp. 3-12). New York.

Resnick, I., Suchak, B. & Riedl, J. (1994). GroupLens: An Open Architecture for Collaborative Filtering of Netnews. *Proceedings of ACM 1994. Conference on Computer Supported Cooperative Work*. Chapel Hill, NC (pp. 175-186).

Rosenberg, M. (2001). The personalization story. *ITWorld.com*, May.

Shavlik, J., & Eliassi-Rad, T. (1999). Intelligent agents for web-based tasks. In *Working Notes of the AAAI/ICML-98 Workshop on Learning for Text Categorization*, Madison Wisconsin.

Spertus, E. (1997). ParaSite: Mining structural information on the Web. In *Proceedings of the 6th International World Wide Web Conference*, Santa Clara, California (April).

Srivastava, J., Cooley, R., Deshpande, M., & Tan, P. (2000). Web usage mining. *SIGKDD Explorations*, 1(2), 12-23.

Stefanovic, N., Han, J., & Koperski, K. (2000). Object-based selective materialization for efficient implementation of spatial data cubes. *IEEE Transactions on Knowledge and Data Engineering*, 12(6), 938-958.

Swanson, D., & Smalheiser, N. (1997). An interactive system for finding complementary literatures: A stimulus to scientific discovery. *Artificial Intelligence*, 91, 183-203.

Swift, R.S. (2000). *Accelerating Customer Relationships: Using CRM and Relationship Technologies.* Englewood Cliffs, NJ: Prentice-Hall.

Tukey, J. (1977). *Exploratory Data Analysis.* Reading, MA: Addison-Wesley.

Tung, K., Han, J., Lakshmanan, L., & Ng, R. (2001). Constraint-based clustering in large databases. In *Proceedings of 2001 International Conference on Database Theory (ICDT'01)*, London, UK (January).

Tung, K., Hou, J., & Han, J. (2001). Spatial clustering in the presence of obstacles. In *Proceedings of 2001 International Conference on Data Engineering (ICDE'01)*, Heidelberg, Germany (April 2001).

Voorhees, E. (1994). Query expansion using lexical-semantic relations. In *Proceedings of the 17th Annual International ACM/SIGIR Conference*, (pp. 61-69). Dublin, Ireland.

Wang, K., He, Y., & Han, J. (2000). Mining frequent itemsets using support constraints. In *Proceedings of 2000 International Conference on Very Large Data Bases* (VLDB'00), Cairo, Egypt (September, pp. 43-52).

Wang, K., Zhou, S., & Han, J. (2000). Pushing support constraints into association mining. *International Conference on Very Large Data Bases.* VLDB'00, Cairo, Egypt (September).

Weiss, R., Velez, B., Sheldon, M., Namprempre, C., Szilagyi, P., Duda, A., & Gifford, D. (1996). HyPursuit: A hierarchical network search engine that exploits content-link hypertext clustering. In *Hypertext'96: The Seventh ACM Conference on Hypertext.*

Wise, J., Thomas, J., Pennock, K., Lantrip, D., Pottier, M., & Schur, A. (1995). Visualizing the non-visual: Spatial analysis and interaction with information from text documents. In *Proceedings of the Information Visualization Symposium 95*, (pp. 51-58). IEEE Computer Society Press.

Xu, J., & Croft, W. (1996). Query expansion using local and global document analysis. In *Proceedings of the 19th Annual International ACM SIGIR Conference on Research and Development in Information Retrieval*, (pp. 4-11). Zurich.

Zaiane, O., Han, J., & Zhu, H. (2000). Mining recurrent items in multimedia with progressive resolution refinement. In *Proceedings of International Conference on Data Engineering ICDE'00*, San Diego, California (March).

Zaiane, O., Han, J., Li, Z., & Hou, J. (1998). Mining multimedia data. In *Proceedings of Meeting Of Minds CASCON '98*, Toronto, Canada (November).

Zhou, X., Truffet, D., & Han, J. (1999). Efficient polygon amalgamation methods for spatial OLAP and spatial data mining. *Sixth International Symposium on Spatial Databases*, SSD'99, Hong Kong.

Chapter X

Management Factors for Strategic BI Success

Somya Chaudhary, Bellsouth Telecommunications Inc., USA

ABSTRACT

This chapter focuses on the factors necessary for strategic Business Intelligence (BI) success from a managerial point of view. BI results from the various information and human knowledge source systems, as well as the holistic view of the business processes within an organization. However, for the BI process to be synergetic within an organization, the management of the organization should be responsible for providing an environment that is conducive to yielding optimum BI generation and utilization. The goal should be to maximize the resources and minimize the inefficiencies that are systematic within an organization. Open lines of communication, with shared goals and objectives, and organization-wide standards are crucial for overall success. The factors for BI success are all interrelated and non-sequential. However, each needs to be executed and communicated with complete diligence on part of the management for overall strategic success. Lastly, to accommodate a healthy and ethical BI environment, the corporate philosophy and work methodologies may warrant necessary modification.

INTRODUCTION

From a management perspective, the definition of Business Intelligence (BI) is the transcription of corporate data into information that sustains an optimum decision-making environment. In basic terms, BI should enable strategic thinking and action within an organization. It makes necessary information available to all levels of an organization, from senior management to the "worker bee." The well-designed BI system utilizes technical as well as nontechnical infrastructures of an organization (Moss, 2003). And how the information is shared within an organization is a contributing factor to the overall success of an organization. Shared corporate philosophy and goals at all levels are a must today. Additionally, the workers require much more information, knowledge, and context. The interdisciplinary teams and work environment require common ground for organizational success (Tapscott, 2003).

However, "through to 2004, more than half of Global 2000 enterprises will fail to properly use BI, losing market share to those that do (0.8 probability)" (Dresner et al., 2002, p.10). Bill Gates, the most successful businessman of our times has been quoted as saying, "How you manage information determines whether you win or lose" (Wu, 2003). Information is the one asset of an organization that is often as unique as the organization itself; managing it is like managing the lifeline to the overall success or failure.

Despite having hoards of information within any given organizations, most organizations of today still fail to see the value of a cohesive BI system. The leaders of these organizations think they know all the answers and can continue to function as they have historically. The wake-up call comes when stiff competition is staring them straight in the face. On the other hand, there are some organizations that know they face competition but lack the know-how to come up with a good tackle plan. In both cases, the reason is the lack of a holistic view of the business, its various functions, and knowledge mines, which results in degraded organizational performance. It's therefore imperative to design BI systems that improve and sustain an organization's ability to make good strategic decisions.

Despite the myriad management styles, corporate philosophies, and individual personalities that exist within the management echelons, there are some basic factors — the fundamentals — that enable strategic BI success to prevail and conquer within any organization. They are:

- Cohesive Corporate Strategy;
- Well-defined IT Infrastructure;

- Business Process of BI within an Organization;
- BI Accountability; and
- Execution on BI.

This chapter is a discussion of the above-listed factors, on achieving optimum BI within an organization. These factors are not an end to themselves but, rather, they are starting point(s) of an iterative process to success.

COHESIVE CORPORATE STRATEGY

All processes within an organization need to be aligned with the overall corporate strategy. That is, all the rank-and-file employees in all departments should understand the corporate strategy and also be able to see how they contribute to the overall corporate goals and objectives. The development of BI, in terms of both key metrics and knowledge sources within the corporation, should never lose sight of the big picture.

However, quite often there is a lack of understanding of the corporate strategy. This may be due to the "divide and conquer" philosophy that many organizations have knowingly or unknowingly adopted. This is where each department is handed down its piece of the pie — corporate goals and objectives. Each department's rank-and-file only gets to know their little piece — departmental goals and objectives. There is no background for them to build upon or tie to other departments. Any interaction between and among departments is often on the premise of "you mind your business, and I'll mind mine." This leads to the department's goals and objectives being "the end" for its-rank and-file employees, rather than "the means to the end" — the corporate goals and objectives.

For example, one national home products retailer has all rank-and-file employees spend their first week on the job at one of its stores. The employees may be assigned tasks such as taking product inventory or serving at customer service. The goal of this exercise is to get them to appreciate the corporate strategy that makes the retailer the leader in the marketplace. This practice makes the corporate frontline strategy a tangible experience.

Michael Porter (1985) states:

Every firm is a collection of activities that are performed to design, produce, market, deliver and support its product. A firm's value chain and the way it performs individual activities are a reflection of its history, its strategy, its approach to implementing its strategy and the underlying economics of the activities themselves.

One easy technique that organizations can employ in translating corporate strategies to every day tasks for its rank-and-file is the organization chart. In any organization, there is always a fully developed formal structure outlining each employee's job and responsibility, i.e., the very basic organizational chart. There is a hierarchy of authority and responsibility, and with each tier in the hierarchy, some power of decision making. The corporate strategy can similarly be broken down and transcribed in terms of authority and responsibility down the echelons of the organization. Additionally, the title that each employee holds should be meaningful and relate directly to the tasks he or she needs to perform.

It's prudent for an organization to communicate the entire corporate strategy to all departments, delineating each department's role, down to each individual employee. The work objectives of individuals may span multiple parts and levels of the organization, enabling faster response to changes in the business environment and customer demands (Tapscott, 2003). To be flexible and adopt to external and internal environmental demands, all rank-and-file employees must understand that if they are not directly serving the external customer, then they should be serving someone who is; that is, serving the internal customers within an organization. On a psychological level, gaining an understanding of the impact of one's department or function on the corporate goals and objectives also serves as a highly rated motivational factor.

WELL-DEFINED IT INFRASTRUCTURE

With all the technological advances made during the last couple decades, BI has evolved to become a powerful tool for corporate success. And today's environment of tight purse strings and tough competition calls for prudent IT strategies. However, IT systems can only be as successful as their contribution to the overall corporate strategy. Stodder (2002) states that a survey conducted by Intelligent Enterprise and Ilog found that although 78% of the CEOs polled believed that they understood the value of IT to their organizations, only 27% of the CIOs and CTOs agreed with that statement. This can be interpreted as an example where the corporate strategy was not fully communicated to the implementers/owners of the IT systems, resulting in myriad IT systems being developed and maintained by the IT organization and the various departments.

There are a number of ways an organization ends up with multiple IT systems. One of them is the traditional IT deployment methodology. This occurs when a large project is divided into deliverables, focusing on delivering first to the most important department and then the next most important, etc. Due to unforeseen circumstances, the project may never be completed in its entirety, and some departments may not receive any benefits from the project. But as these departments were introduced to the benefits of having a certain IT system and did buy into the process, they hoped to get the benefits of such a system. Or there may be an instance where an individual department may not carry enough weight to get IT to deploy or support a system that it deems as being absolutely important. Eventually, these departments will venture out to get their own IT systems to manage themselves. Departments with such IT systems — that are self-owned and managed — hold them with a lot of pride and prejudice. This too adds to the IT system chaos.

Eventually, these multiple IT systems within an organization act as the departmental "Turfdoms." These are databases silos, which often house the same data. However, the data is used differently and may also be referred to differently. The measures and metrics, information, i.e., the BI reported, are understood differently. For example, the upper management may find itself in situations where it has no explanation or understanding of why two departments' monthly sales numbers are so different. They should both be counting product units sold, right? Sounds simple. But then why don't the numbers sync up between the two departmental reports? The answer may be equally simple too. The sales department counts and reports all products sold, regardless of returns, while the finance department recasts its counts of products sold, based on the 90 day return policy. This simple explanation is not always apparent and results in a number reconciliation hunt.

Figure 1 shows a Customer Hierarchy of a hypothetical company, the XYZ Corporation.

Given this scenario, for each product/service that ABC Corp. procures from XYZ Corp., an account is established. The sales division of XYZ Corp. sees each account as an individual customer. However, Marketing takes into consideration the dynamics of the region/location of a customer and considers the individual Atlanta and Orlando offices, etc., as customers. The Sales and Marketing Departments of XYZ Corp. can each righteously argue that its customer level is correct and maintain separate databases with their respective

Figure 1: Customer Hierarchy for the XYZ Corporation

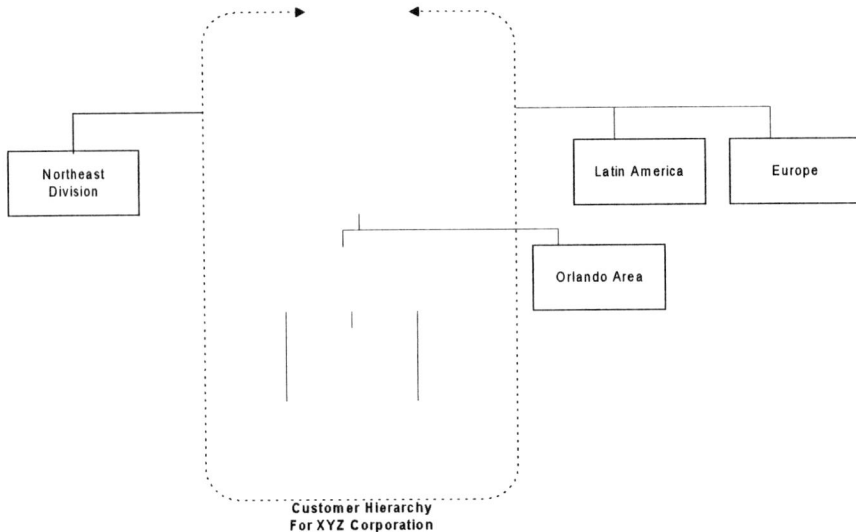

versions of customer data. Even when data is shared between the two databases, without having a data element to tie the two different levels together, the discrepancies between the business metrics of the Sales and Marketing Departments cannot be resolved.

The problem of disjointed IT systems is also the result of vendors who hype their products as a one-stop shop, serving the needs of the entire organization. Empirical evidence proves quite the contrary. Folger (2002) states that through 2005/2006, most large organizations will need three to six vendors for complete coverage. Additionally, Folger states that ITOs should choose standards in three categories: enterprise reporting, ad hoc query and analysis, and online analytic processing (OLAP) servers.

The only way to overcome the problems of disjointed and multiple IT systems and departmental IT "turfs" is to have an overall corporate strategy for IT systems deployment. The IT strategy should sync up with and support the overall corporate goals and objectives. This also aids in establishing organizational IT standards to guide and control the various IT systems; i.e., "consolidate and conquer" should be the theme prevalent throughout an organization. A centralized system that feeds off to various other child systems according to their individual needs is the logical solution.

In IT terms, the Hub and Spoke Architecture provides a centralized data gathering, auditing, transferring, summarizing, and storage platform (see *Figure 2*). This environment consists of a main Data Warehouse — the Hub, which

Figure 2

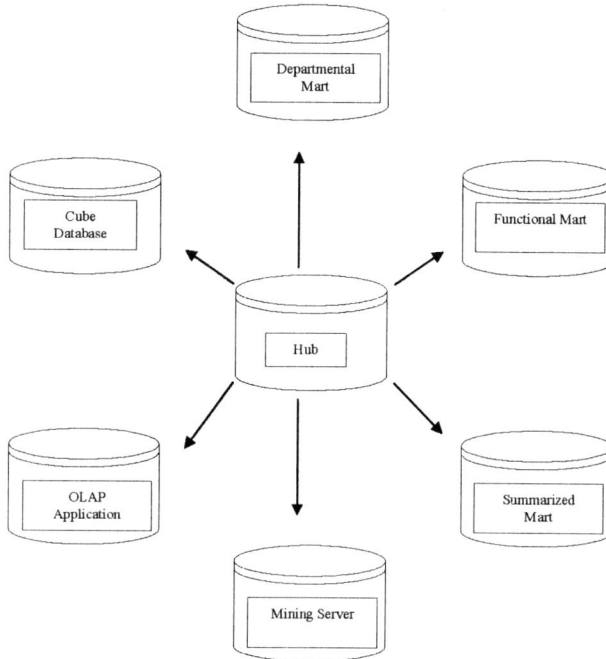

sources data from various sources and maintains the most granular view of data within an organization. The Spokes of this architecture are comprised of the various departmental/functional Data Marts, Data Mining Servers, OLAP, and multi-dimensional/cube applications.

Additionally, the Hub of our architecture houses the most granular form of an organization's data. We can slice and dice, summarize the data in any manner that would deem it beneficial for different departmental and functional purposes, i.e., the data marts, mining servers, OLAP applications, etc. These Spokes of the architecture are often quite smaller than the Hub in terms of holding the historical data and the quantity of data. These are easier to finance and develop once we have our Hub fully sourced and established.

However, in the development of the Hub, an organization not only has to ensure that a single version of data is maintained, but also has to maintain the best quality of data within the system. Inmon (2002) states that there are three basic opportunities for cleansing the data. These can occur in the Extraction, Transformation, and Loading (ETL) steps.

1. Cleanse data at the source, in the application environment, while extracting the data. However, not all application environments can provide the logistics needed to perform such activities. The primary function of the environment is processing transactions, and any additional task can hamper the efficiency of the entire system.

2. Cleanse data in the platform where it's integrated and transformed. This provides the optimal environment for data-cleansing activities. The purpose of this environment is to apply universal business rules and integrate data from multiple sources. And, most importantly, this environment initializes the metadata documentation process.

3. Cleanse data while auditing the loaded data. This should be the final cleansing environment. However, it's best to identify problems and fix them earlier, in the data integration and transformation step.

Thus, upon the completion of the ETL process, the organization should not only have good quality data, but also a full Metadata documentation describing the data.

The Metadata is a very important tool in enabling the quality of analysis within an organization. The analyst/power user/decision-maker's understanding of the data is fully dependent on what data is and how it is used. Thus, within an organization, Metadata should be the only tool to educate users on data usage. Any data analysis conducted at any level or department of the organization should lead to same business metrics and same understanding of the metrics.

One final benefit of the Hub of the Architecture is that data will get archived off one centralized system of the organization, rather than various data elements getting archived off various disjointed systems at different points in time. The benefits of archiving off the central location, rather than in pieces off various locations, are often at the magnitude of data the organization has. For example, a department needs four years of data for some time-series analysis, but the Data Mart and Data Warehouse only house two years of data. The department will have to get the data for the additional two years off the archival system. This archived data will need to be reinstated back to the server (Warehouse or Data Mart), and, in the case of a Hub and Spoke Architecture, it's just a matter of reloading from tape or other archival device. This enables ease of use and speed of access to archived data.

Imagine the logistics involved in reconnecting data that was archived from different systems. In such cases, the task is more tedious, as it will involve not only loading from multiple sources, but also trying to adjust for the differences in time lags when the data was archived. And in the absence of metadata, it will also involve hunting down within the organization the Subject Matter Experts (SME) of the various systems, to understand what the data meant and represented back in a certain date period. This will result in a massive "connect-the-dots" project and, eventually, even with all of these factors taken care of, the results would never be similar to the BI that existed back at a certain point in time. The basic reason for this is that other variables cannot be held constant across the multiple disparate systems. Any attempt to recapture archived BI off multiple sources will be wasted time and effort. Going back to our Hub and Spoke Architecture, which holds the organization's single version of truth (in terms of data/information/business intelligence), retrieving BI from archived data is a much simpler, cleaner, and speedier process.

BUSINESS PROCESS OF BI
WITHIN AN ORGANIZATION

The Business Process is an important component for successful BI within an organization. It's imperative for the Upper Management to understand the Business Process and thus the flow of BI within an organization. Creating a road map of all the Business Processes within an organization is basically tracing all organizational operations from the start to the very end.

For example, for a "Mom and Pop" Bookstore, the Business Process could be as simple as illustrated in *Figure 3*.

This is the process of linking the multiple functions of an organization together, as they function for the organization as a whole and work toward shared common goals and objectives — the corporate goals and objectives. As illustrated in the example given in *Figure 3*, with the Business Processes, there is a continuous flow of BI from one process to another. It is this BI that helps maintain an accurate management focus on the business. Suppose there was a breakdown between "Maintaining an Inventory" and "Stacking Shelves." This would result in some books missing completely from the shelves and not being available for customers. The last thing a business wants to do is turn a customer away, and this is quite possible when there is a breakdown in BI flow.

Over the past decades, developments in IT have enabled organizations to accumulate huge mines of data. And the larger the corporation, the more

Figure 3

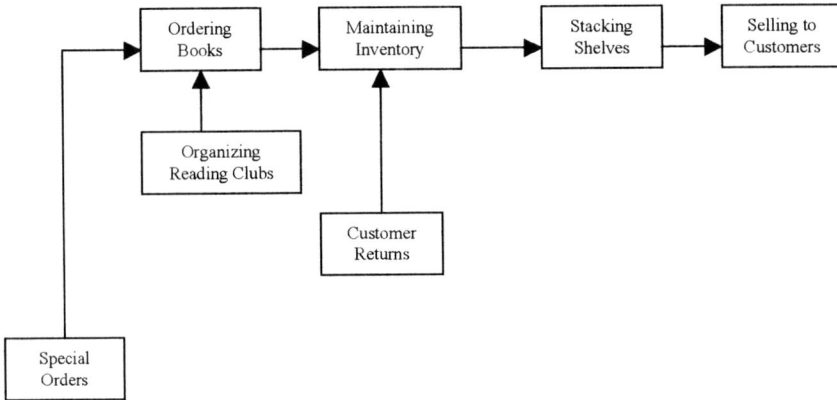

systems of data collection, distribution, and redistribution it has. Imagine a network of data highways, all intertwined, live, and interactive. How can one possibly make sense of these myriad data paths/flows? Business Process documentation is a good solution, as it provides a road map. Organizations can see where there is an overlap and redundancy and thereby eliminate wastage and maximize their valuable resources.

Business Process is both the technical (databases, ETL processes, middleware, etc.) and the nontechnical infrastructure of an organization. And it's the nontechnical infrastructure that most organizations completely neglect (Moss, 2003). Content Management/Business Information Stewardship/ Performance Management groups of an organization can contribute hugely to the overall success of managing the nontechnical aspects of the Business Process. The larger a corporation, the more complicated its Business Processes are. Additionally, there are more acronyms and buzzwords. Many times folks are talking of the same thing and yet completely misunderstand each other.

Referring back to the earlier example of ABC Corp. and XYZ Corp., which level of customer is the most appropriate for the corporation as a whole and its customer strategy? The Sales Department of XYZ Corp. refers to a customer as an "Account/" while the Marketing Department refers to a Customer at a different level. Having similar terminologies and standards within an organization can help eliminate problems of reconciling metrics reported from different departments. The bookstore example represents a small business that is family owned; imagine all the business processes within a large, national retail organization or telecomm.

Simply put, if Department A calls it a square, then Department B too should also deem it a square. There should be standardization of all data and process definitions across the board. The documentation of the Business Processes within an organization provides a start-to-finish view of the entire business. Such views often exist in the minds of "old timers" within an organization. But for the freshmen, the task of relating to the corporate strategy and how the various departments work together can be greatly simplified by gaining understanding of the Business Processes within the organization.

The BI generated from gaining an in-depth understanding of an organization's Business Process also lead to competitive advantages. In the example of ABC and XYZ Corporations, what XYZ Corp. should be tracking is where the decisions in ABC Corp. are made and how it can leverage its relationship across the entire ABC Corp. In *The One to One Future*, Peppers and Rogers (1993) argue that a "Share of a Customer" is more important than a "Share of a Market." Efforts should be made to monopolize the entire ABC Corp. at each and every level; i.e., XYZ Corp. should concentrate on gaining "economies of scope" not "economies of scale" with ABC Corp. Peppers and Rogers state: "Who ever knows a particular customer best has the advantage with that customer." This is only possible by maintaining a "one-to-one" relationship with the customer and can be achieved by clearly understanding all points of interaction with the customer. These points of interaction are sources of valuable BI that only XYZ Corp. has. XYZ has the home-field advantage of storing all the data from its various interactions with ABC Corp. These interactions can be translated into key metrics, such as the entire product/ service basket, point-of-sale decision-makers, etc., that ABC has, thereby personalizing the deal at the corporate level, rather than at the individual account levels.

Additionally, Business Process documentation provides better BI during a reorganization of the corporate structure. Duplication of tasks and processes can be eliminated. And after a reorganization, it is easier for the employees to understand their new roles and how their positions relate to the entire organization.

BI ACCOUNTABILITY

The debacles of Enron, WorldCom, and Anderson have placed BI Accountability in a new light. The Internet Bubble economy has also provided

Figure 4

Month	Existing	Lost	New	Net	Churn
Customer Churn					
Jan	12000	650	450	11800	1.7%
Feb	11800	500	400	11700	0.8%
Mar	11700	500	375	11575	1.1%
Apr	11575	700	550	11425	1.3%
May	11425	550	400	11275	1.3%
Jun	11275	600	400	11075	1.8%
Jul	11075	300	150	10925	1.4%

important lessons for the prudent use of BI through the use of sound business models/economics. Stakeholders on both sides of the corporate fence should be and are demanding accountability from Management.

Assume the above scenario for the XYZ Corporation. Here the metrics being reported are Customer Churn in a competitive environment. Without considering the costs associated with the acquisition and loss of customers, the churn rate would seem considerably low. In addition, the Sales Department can also make a good case that, despite the losses occurring, it is able to reel in at least half of the losses occurring in any given month. This, however, would not show up as a great achievement for the Finance Department, which tracks the overall financial health of the organization. Finance sees only in monetary terms — that the costs (advertising and new customer perks, etc.) associated with acquiring a new customer base are bleeding the bottom line. In such a scenario, it is imperative to step back and look at the larger picture — the impact of decisions on the organization as a whole, rather than the individual departments within the organization.

Thus, BI accountability plays an important role in such scenarios. Most organizations will want to fight churn head-on. But management should stop and consider what is an acceptable cost for retaining customers for XYZ Corporation? Are all customers truly the same in terms of profitability? Some customers cost more to organizations than the revenues they bring in the long term. These customers should be differentiated from the profitable base when retention programs are being designed. On the other hand, management should be wondering if the newly acquired customer base is the same as the embedded base in terms of churn behavior/profitability? Many of the new customers may show a revolving-door behavior when looked at closely, i.e., transitioning

Figure 5

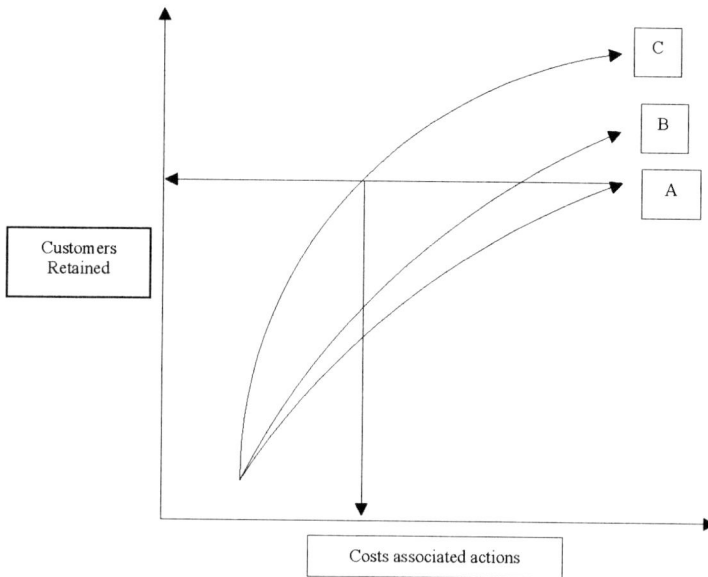

between companies because of the perks they get as new customers. It may not have been a wise judgment on part of the Sales Department.

There are ample tools and techniques available that can help predict and model customer behavior. And BI accountability should be a major control factor in interpreting and distributing these results. For example, with the help of Data Mining, XYZ Corporation may be able to predict the customer base that can be lost. But before the organization embarks on a massive retention campaign to retain those customers, it should also stop to look at the revenue this group is bringing in and the costs associated with the retention campaign. It may not be a wise decision at all to try to retain all customers, and it may be best to let some of them go. Techniques such as the Lift Charts, which are part of most good Data Mining applications, should be prudently put to use. A Lift Chart will show in the financial impact of the retention campaign to the organization (see *Figure 5*).

In *Figure 5*, we have three scenarios:

- A – maintain status quo, things go on as business as usual.
- B – We have a model that we can use. However, for the costs associated with the implementation of the retention program, there is not a significant increase in the customers retained.

- C – shows a remarkable increase in the number of customers retained. The gains in customers retained compared to Plan A is almost double with the implementation of C. Therefore, the model with such results, Plan C, should definitely be implemented by the organization.

Basically, BI accountability has proven to be an important factor for the long-term success of corporate strategy and also for accountability from Management. Upper Management should be sincerely documenting and distributing the key business metrics that support the corporate strategies within an organization. This enables decision-making processes at all levels to stay aligned and support the overall strategy. Decisions made based on the presence or absence of BI have huge repercussions. Organizations with established, documented, and distributed standards make it easier for BI to support corporate accountability. In such cases, BI not only helps achieve accountability, but also helps back it up, all within the legal framework of the organization. The data and information derived can only be transcribed to BI and reports in the form of the most accurate representative of the business, rather than the least preferred.

EXECUTION ON BI

The execution phase is the last crucial step in maintaining a successful cycle of corporate strategy backed by BI. The information derived has to be taken into account and executed, thereby creating the start of a new cycle of BI strategy. Data Mining, Ad hoc analysis, and CRM all enable data-pattern discovery, analysis, and solution generation for competitive customer focus. Again referring back to XYZ Corporation, once a good business model with a reasonably profitable lift has been developed, the scores of the model should be passed onto the hands of the Sales team. These folks are the frontline contact personnel for any organization. They need to be able to distinguish between a good retention and a not-so-good candidate. The information that is provided to them will help them attain the organization's goals for retaining valuable customers and letting go of customers who cost more to serve.

Aiding the BI execution is the continuous development of corporate skills. Obsolete skills and processes within an organization are counter-effective to success. Maintaining tandem with the technological advancement is equally important in the maintenance of a smooth execution of BI. Additionally, it's highly preferable that employees acquire skills in related disciplines or the disciplines of the groups with which they work closely. This will create an environment that aids in communication and synergy: communication, because it's easier to understand the processes and work methodologies of varied background work groups, and synergy because one can intelligently contribute to the task(s) at hand.

Organizations also need to take into effect the "Change" mechanisms/ processes that need to be implemented for BI execution. Ideas developed at the higher echelons of an organization need a definite buy-in for proper execution. Porter (1985) stated quite categorically in 1985, "Change or die." And after close to two decades later, this statement has not lost any of its validity. Change is imperative for organizations to get out of their old mold of doing things and move towards improvement. Flexibility within an organization is often paramount for corporate success.

As stated earlier, the factors discussed in this chapter are not sequential; rather, they go hand-in-hand. For successful change mechanisms to occur (which are, at times, quite important for successful execution of BI), the understanding of the entire organization's business process and its management come into play. The organization should be able to view the complete set of relationships/processes within it; i.e., end to end. This is what makes the entire BI a live, dynamic, and immensely interesting process.

Lastly, though BI is considered to be the most volatile environment and one that merits constant attention, we should not lose focus of other factors. These can be industry competition, government, both internal and external customers, and the economy in general. Various forms of external BI also stem from these sources, and the corporate philosophy should foster a climate that encourages seeking BI, from both the internal and external environments.

CONCLUSION

Technology advances made within the last few decades have enabled organizations to gather huge mines of data. This data, when twisted, turned, sliced, and diced reveals valuable information. Information is knowledge and intelligence. The basic premise of BI is that the intelligence generated is only as good as the data and the systems/people who handle it. Thus, how the business intelligence is gathered, derived, and understood is very important. All the factors discussed above play major roles in harnessing valuable, useful BI. The overall strategic ramifications of using BI are huge for any organization, and management should take into account all the factors, channeling activities that enable an environment of flexibility and gainful harnessing of BI.

REFERENCES

Dresner, H., Linden, A., Buytendijk, F., Friedman, T., Strange, K., Knox, M., & Camm, M. (2002). The business intelligence competency center: An essential business strategy. *Gartner Strategic Analysis Report*, R-15-2248.

Folger, D. (2002). The top ten pitfalls in business intelligence deployments: Web & collaboration strategies. *META Group*. Delta 1143.

Inmon, B. (2002). Enterprise intelligence — Enabling high quality in the data warehouse/DSS environment. White paper. *Vality Technology Incorporated Paper*. Available online at: http://www.vality.com.

Moss, L. (2003). Non-technical infrastructure for BI applications. *DMRReview.com*. January. Retrieved online at: http://www.dmreview.com/editorial/dmreview/print_action.cfm?EdID=6190.

Peppers, D., & Rogers, M. (1993). *The One to One Future: Building Relationships One Customer at a Time*. (pp. 18-51, 140). New York: Currency and Doubleday.

Porter, M. (1985). *Competitive Advantage*. New York: The Free Press.

Smith, M. (2002a). The BI transformation: Innovation and evolution provide new value and opportunity. *IntelligentEnterprise.com*. December. Retrieved online at: http://www.intelligententerprise.com/021205/601decision1_2.shtml.

Smith, M. (2002b). Business process intelligence: BI and business process management technologies are converging to create value beyond the sum of their parts. *Intelligent Enterprise.com*. December. Retrieved online at: http://www.intelligententerprise.com/021205/601decision1_2.shtml.

Stodder, D. (2002). Strategic IT: Key to profitability — The 2002 Intelligent Enterprise Dozen Executive Roundtable debates what makes business/IT synergy thrive. *IntelligentEnterprise.com*. December. Retrieved online at: http://www.intelligententerprise.com/021205/601strategic1_1.shtml.

Tapscott, D. (2003). Knowledge culture: To enact a corporate strategy you have to tell your employees what it is. *Intelligent Enterprise*, (May 13), 12.

Wu, J. (2003). Business Intelligence: Assessing your organization's information. *DM Review Online*. Retrieved online at: http://www.dmreview.com/editorial/dmreview/print_action.cfm?EdID=6543.

Chapter XI

Transforming Textual Patterns into Knowledge

Hércules Antonio do Prado, Brazilian Enterprise for Agricultural Research, Brazil and Catholic University of Brasília, Brazil

José Palazzo Moreira de Oliveira, Federal University of Rio Grande do Sul, Brazil

Edilson Ferneda, Catholic University of Brasília, Brazil

Leandro Krug Wives, Federal University of Rio Grande do Sul, Brazil

Edilberto Magalhães Silva, Brazilian Public News Agency, Brazil

Stanley Loh, Catholic University of Pelotas and Lutheran University of Brazil, Brazil

ABSTRACT

Business Intelligence (BI) can benefit greatly from the bulk of knowledge that stays hidden in the large amount of textual information existing in the organizational environment. Text Mining (TM) is a technology that provides the support to extract patterns from texts. After interpreting these patterns, a business analyst can reach useful insights to improve the organizational knowledge. Although text represents the largest part of the available information in a company, just a small part of all Knowledge Discovery (KD) applications are in TM. By means of a case study, this chapter shows an alternative to how TM can contribute to BI. Also, a discussion on future trends and some conclusions are presented that support the effectiveness of TM as source of relevant knowledge.

INTRODUCTION

In order to help companies to remain competitive, Business Intelligence (BI) requires adequate tools to transform the large amount of information existing in the organizational environment into models that accurately represent the reality. By analyzing and interpreting these patterns, a business analyst can reach interesting insights that lead to a better understanding of the business, to improve internal processes, and to enable more accurate decision making. In this environment, Knowledge Discovery in Databases (KDD) has been shown to be an important approach, providing the methodologies to extract models from large data sets by means of relatively user-friendly tools.

This chapter discusses the application of Text Mining (TM) in the BI realm. TM is part of the broader field of KDD that, departing from a data set relevant to the solution of a specific problem, looks for interesting and previously unknown patterns. After human-specialized interpretation of these patterns, important knowledge that leads to the solution of that problem can be discovered. KDD comprises the preliminary tasks of data collection, cleansing, and transformation, the core task of data mining, and the post-processing pattern interpretation activity. Data Mining (DM) is concerned with the extraction of patterns from structured data. In our point of view, TM is situated at the same level of DM, but is addressed to extract patterns from textual information. The patterns issued by a TM application can provide feedback to the business specialist, triggering the mental process that leads to insights on the business problems.

The next section draws the relations between TM and BI, making clear at which point TM can interfere proactively in the BI process. It also discusses the weak use of TM in an environment in which the majority of the available information is represented in textual form. Next, the methodology applied to guide the case study is presented. After that, a description of some procedures applied to identify clusters in a set of texts is shown. The subsequent section is devoted to discuss the case study carried out in a Brazilian public news agency. Future trends on TM and some conclusions are presented in the last two sections of the chapter.

TEXT MINING IN THE CONTEXT OF BUSINESS INTELLIGENCE

Information about the external environment and organizational processes are among the most worthwhile input for BI. Nowadays, companies have plenty of information in structured or textual forms either from external monitoring or from the corporate systems. In the last years, the structured part of this information stock has been massively explored by means of DM techniques (Wang, 2003), generating models that enable the analysts to gain insights on the solutions for organizational problems. On the TM side, the rhythm of new applications development did not go as fast. For example, in an informal poll carried out in 2002 (Kdnuggets, 2002a), just 4% of the KDD practitioners were applying TM techniques. This fact is as intriguing as surprising if one considers that 80% of all information available in an organization comes in textual form (Tan, 1999).

In his popular model to explain the phases of technology adoption (*Figure 1*), Moore (1999) discusses the existence of a chasm between the "early adopters, visionaries" and the "early majority pragmatists" phases that a technology has to cross in order to become extensively adopted. From our point of view, TM is still crossing this chasm. Despite the offering of mature tools in the market and the increasing number of successful case studies presented (Dini & Mazzini, 2002; Ferneda, Prado, & Silva, 2003; Fliedl & Weber, 2002), it seems that

Figure 1: The Technology Adoption Life Cycle of Moore

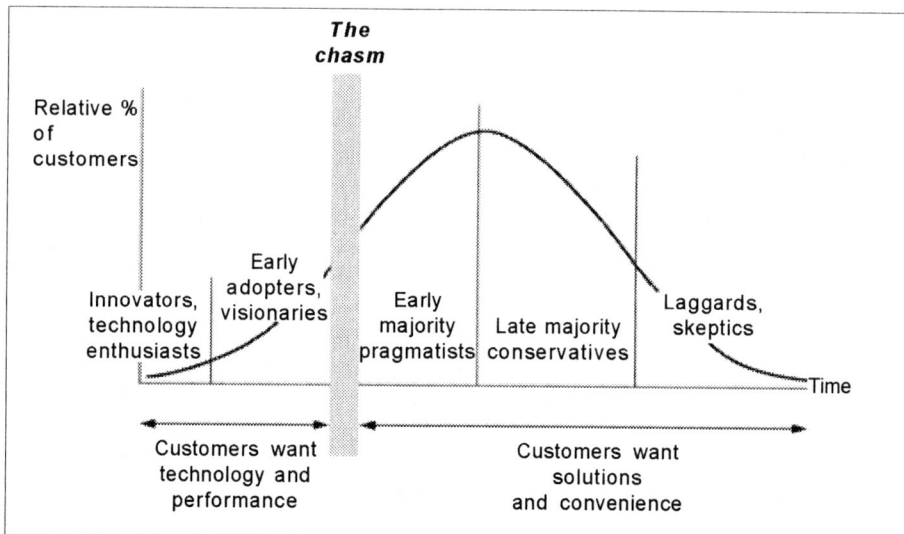

the community is still leaving the second phase. However, the results presented in the case studies point out that the broad adoption of TM will happen in the near future.

When studying the relationship between TM and BI, it is necessary to be aware of an important intermediate layer between them — the Knowledge Management (KM) process. KM refers to the set of activities responsible for carrying the information throughout the organization and making knowledge available where it is necessary.

To clarify the relations between TM and BI, from the point of view of a KM model, we adopted the generic KM model (*Figure 2*) proposed by Stollenwerk (2001), after reviewing many alternatives present in the literature. The model is made up of seven processes:

1. *Identification* and development of the critical abilities;
2. *Capture* of knowledge, skills, and experiences to create and maintain skills;
3. *Selection and validation* that filters, evaluates, and summarizes the acquired knowledge for future use;
4. *Organization and storage* to assure the quick and correct recovery of the stored knowledge;

Figure 2: The Generic KM model of Stollenwerk (2001)

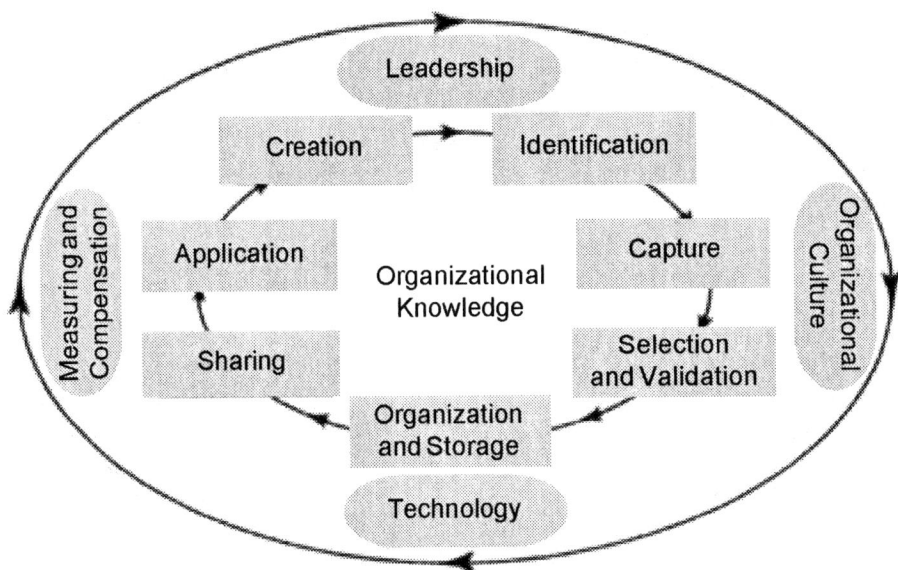

5. *Sharing* that provides easy access to information and knowledge;
6. *Application* in which the knowledge is applied to real situations; and
7. *Creation* that comprises the activities of sharing of tacit knowledge, concept creation, building archetypes, and cross-leveling knowledge.

Involving the mentioned processes, there exist four organizational aspects that condition the model:

1. *Leadership*, that gets commitment and direction from the managers;
2. *Organizational Culture*, referring to the desirable characteristics for a knowledge-based organization, namely, engagement on high performance, focus on the client, focus on improvement and on excellence, high level of competence and knowledge, and high rate of learning and innovation;
3. *Measuring and Compensation* standing by the recognition and reward of the co-workers; and
4. *Technology* that provides the necessary support for the KM processes.

TM is one of the technological factors that support the knowledge creation process, particularly, in the leveraging of the concept formation.

METHODOLOGICAL APPROACH

To conduct the case study, the CRISP-DM method was applied (Chapman et al., 2000) as a general guideline. CRISP-DM is a methodology created to promote the standardization of the KDD process. It encompasses a set of steps and processes that describe the tasks that are necessary to develop a KDD application. The steps of the method are:

- *Business Understanding* – this phase looks for the identification of requirements and objectives of the application from the clients' point of view. Problems and restrictions that can cause a waste of time and effort must be considered. This phase also includes a description of the client background, its business objectives, and a description of the criteria used to measure the success of the achievement.
- *Data Understanding* – identify all information relevant to carry out the application and develop a first approximation on its content, quality, and utility. The initial collection of data helps the analyst learn about its details.

Conflicts related to the expected and the real format and values are identified in this phase. Information about the manner in which data was collected, including its sources, meaning, volumes, reading procedure, etc., can also be of interest since it is a good indicator of the data quality. In this phase the first discoveries are reached.

- *Data Preparation* – this phase consists of the tasks concerned with the acquisition of a final data set from which the model will be created and validated. In this phase, tools for data extraction, cleaning, and transformation are applied to data preparation. Combinations of tables, aggregation of values, and format changing are performed to satisfy the input requirements of the learning algorithms.

- *Modeling* – in this phase the most appropriate data-mining techniques are selected and applied, according to the objectives defined in the first step. Modeling represents the core phase of KDD that corresponds to the choice of the technique, its parameterization, and its execution over a training data set. Many different and complimentary models can be created in this phase.

- *Evaluation* – the evaluation phase consists of reviewing the previous steps in order to check the results against the objectives defined in the business understanding phase. In this phase, the next tasks to be performed are defined. Depending on the results, route corrections may be defined, which correspond to the return to one of the already performed phases using other parameters or looking for more data.

- *Deployment* – sets the necessary actions to make the acquired knowledge available to the organization. In this phase, a final report is generated to explain the results and the experiences useful to the client business.

Regarding to the specific tasks, the works of Wives (2000), Tan (1999), and Halliman (2001) provided the methodological support. These tasks are presented along with the case study.

SOME TECHNICAL ISSUES

In this section, the main clustering methods and algorithms involved in the process of cluster analysis of textual data are described. The objective is to offer to the reader the concepts related to the implementation and use of clustering methods to analyze textual data.

Clustering is a widely employed approach to analyze data in many fields (Everitt, Landau, & Leese, 2001; Jain, Murty, & Flynn, 1999). The idea behind cluster analysis is to find knowledge about previously unfamiliar data. Clustering methods are able to give suggestions about how specific sets of data are organized or correlated. It is possible to identify the similarity and the dissimilarity among many objects or data patterns and, based on that, construct classes or categories. Categories or classes are very important as they are the basic elements on which to build new concepts, and concepts are the basis of the human knowledge (Aldenderfer & Blashfield, 1984).

However, since clustering indicates relationship among objects, it can be used for many other objectives. Aldenderfer (Aldenderfer & Blashfield, 1984), for example, classifies the goals of cluster analysis into four categories:

1.   to develop a typology or classification;
2.   to investigate useful conceptual schemes for grouping entities;
3.   to aid the generation of hypothesis; and
4.   to test hypothesis, verifying that types defined through other procedures are really present in the data set.

But what is clustering? Clustering is a knowledge discovery process that identifies relationships among objects and builds clusters of objects based on these relationships (Jain et al., 1999; Willet, 1988). It is based on the cluster hypothesis (Rijsbergen, 1979), which states that similar objects tend to remain together in the same cluster as a consequence of a specific concept distance metric.

Clustering Types

There are many clustering methods, and this fact generates many types or schemes of clusters. According to Aldenderfer (Aldenderfer & Blashfield, 1984), these methods can be classified into seven families: hierarchical agglomerative, hierarchical divisive, iterative partitioning, density search, factor analytic, clumping, and graph theoretic. Each of them creates a type or scheme of clusters that is very peculiar.

In this chapter, we will classify and detail the clustering methods according to the categories proposed by Schütze and Silverstein (1997) and Everitt, Landau, and Leese (2001). We did so because we believe that any method generates schemes of clusters that fall in one of these categories. These categories are (1) *hierarchical* and (2) *non-hierarchical* (or *partitioning* clustering).

Figure 3: Hierarchic Scheme of Clusters

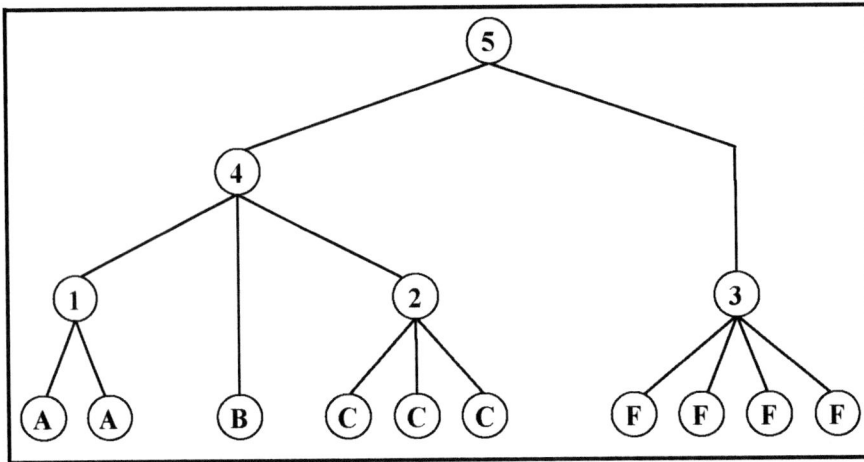

Hierarchical Clustering

In hierarchical clustering, the resulting scheme of clusters is very similar to a tree (see *Figure 3*). Each node represents a cluster. The intermediate clusters are clusters of clusters and the leaves are objects. The relationship among clusters is of paramount importance as it shows the specificities and abstractions among groups of objects. If the user goes up in the tree of clusters, it is possible to identify more abstract or generic groups. On the other hand, if the user goes down, more specific groups will be identified until the objects themselves are reached.

Non-Hierarchical or Partitioning Clustering

When working with non-hierarchical clustering, the objects are allocated in isolated clusters, and no relationship among clusters can be found. This type of clustering is also known as partitional clustering, and it is said that it generates flat (without structure) partitions of clusters (see *Figure 4*).

Clustering Algorithms

As already stated, there are many clustering methods. More detail on these and other clustering methods can be obtained in Aldenderfer and Blashfield (1984), Jain et al. (1999), Kowalski (1997), and Willet (1988). In this section, we describe only the methods provided by the tool used in our experiments —

Figure 4: Flat Partition of Isolated Clusters

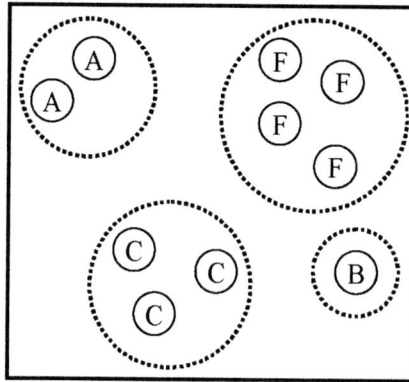

the Eurekha tool (Wives, 1999). The algorithms implemented belong to the graph theoretic family of algorithms and are described next.

Stars

The Stars Algorithm analyzes the objects and tries to find groups of similar elements where the resulting aspect or format is like a star of correlated objects. In this case, the center of the star is the element that has a relationship with all the other objects in the cluster, linking them together. It means that the other elements should be near or similar to this central element but not necessarily to the others. To minimize the dissimilarity among an element that is on one side of the star from another element on another side of the star, it is defined a similarity threshold. A larger threshold among all elements in relation to the center makes the group more coherent. The more they are similar to the center (or near to the center), the more they will be similar to each other.

The algorithm starts selecting any element in the set of elements. This selection can be performed randomly or by any other method. However, the selection order influences the resulting clustering scheme.

The selected element is then elected as the center of the star (the center of the cluster). Then, this element is compared to all other elements not yet clustered (i.e., allocated to a cluster). If a relationship is found — meaning that it is greater than a previously user defined similarity threshold — the element being compared to the center is allocated to the cluster. Once all elements are compared to the star center, another un-clustered element is selected and the process continues until all elements are analyzed. The elements in which the similarity to another element is not greater than the established threshold are said to be un-clustered and are ignored or allocated to an isolated cluster — one to each element.

Best Star

The main problem of the Star Algorithm is that the order in which the elements are selected as centers influences the clustering result. Another problem is that the user has to select a threshold of minimum similarity between objects and the center, and there is not an optimal threshold to be used as a usual value. Each data set may have a different threshold. These are the greatest problems of cluster analysis that uses this kind (or family) of algorithms.[1]

The Best Star Algorithm intends to solve these problems, allocating an element — even if it is already clustered — to the star where it is more similar (the nearest star). Somehow, a side effect is that the user does not need to establish a threshold. In this case, the elements will be reassigned to the cluster where they are more similar (i.e., nearer to the star's center).

Cliques

This algorithm is similar to the Stars Algorithm. However, the elements are added only if they satisfy the threshold of similarity among all elements already in the cluster and not only with the central element. In this case, the elements are more tightly coupled and the quality of the resulting clusters is better.

Full Stars

Sometimes the user must know all the clusters to which an element would be allocated. All the other algorithms discussed in this chapter allocate the element in the best cluster for it, according to its algorithmic restrictions. This algorithm solves this necessity, allocating an element to all clusters to which it has a relationship greater than the threshold established by the user.

CASE STUDY ON A NEWS AGENCY DATA

A case study based on a set of about 57,000 texts generated in 2001 by Radiobrás, the Brazilian Public News Agency, is now presented. The case comprises the complete cycle of CRISP-DM, beyond the specific text-mining methodology. The last phase of the method includes the pattern interpretation required for the generation of organizational knowledge.

Business Understanding

Radiobrás (www.radiobras.gov.br) is a public news agency responsible for establishing a communication channel between the departments of the Federal Government and the Brazilian society. Radiobrás tries to universalize information regarding to the acts and facts of the Federal Republic of Brazil. Its objectives are:

1. To publish accomplishments of the Federal Government in economy and social politics, and to disseminate adequate knowledge about the Brazilian reality abroad, as well as implementing and operating radio stations and exploring broadcasting services of the Federal Government;

2. To implement and operate its repeating networks and the retransmission of broadcasting, exploring its services, as well as promoting and stimulating the formation and the training of specialized staff necessary to its activities;

3. To gather, elaborate, transmit, and distribute — directly or in cooperation with other social communication entities — news, photographs, bulletins, and programs concerned with acts and facts from the Government and other issues of political, financial, civic, social, sportive, cultural, and artistic nature, by means of graphical, photographic, cinematographic, electronic or any other vehicle;

4. To distribute legal publicity from entities directly or indirectly related to the Government; and

5. To perform other activities assigned to the agency by the Chief Ministry of State of the Government Communication Secretariat of the President of the Republic.

By means of this project, Radiobrás aims to obtain indicators related to the distribution of news by subject and the diffusion of news abroad, to estimate the distribution of news throughout government departments, and to check news content regarding the Communication Secretariat. For this purpose, efforts will be focused on measuring the amount of news by type, period, and main topics, extracting the concepts produced and propagated by the agency based on clustering analysis, determining the amount of news about acts and facts of the Government, and studying the degree to which Radiobrás is achieving its objectives.

This work meets these objectives by (1) determining the most important words in the issued news, (2) determining the main correlation between the news and the keywords that compose each cluster, (3) separating news by groups, (4) pointing out the most representative words, (5) discovering the main concepts from the clustering analysis, and (6) elaborating statistics about the news by time, subject, and quantity.

Data Understanding

The data were obtained from the public repository of the agency. Each text file corresponds to specific news. Corrupted, control files, and news files in foreign languages were discarded. We considered just the news produced in the year of 2001. *Figure 5* shows the monthly production of news in that year. After these steps, 55,635 texts remained.

Data Preparation

The selected news, i.e., releases, complete notices, guidelines, presidential agenda, events in course and photos, are prepared according to the cycle depicted in *Figure 6*. In this phase, we found that the January and February production should be considered as outliers and, consequently, discarded. This happened due to problems related to the process of importing text from the repository, causing loss of records.

Figure 5: Monthly Production in 2001

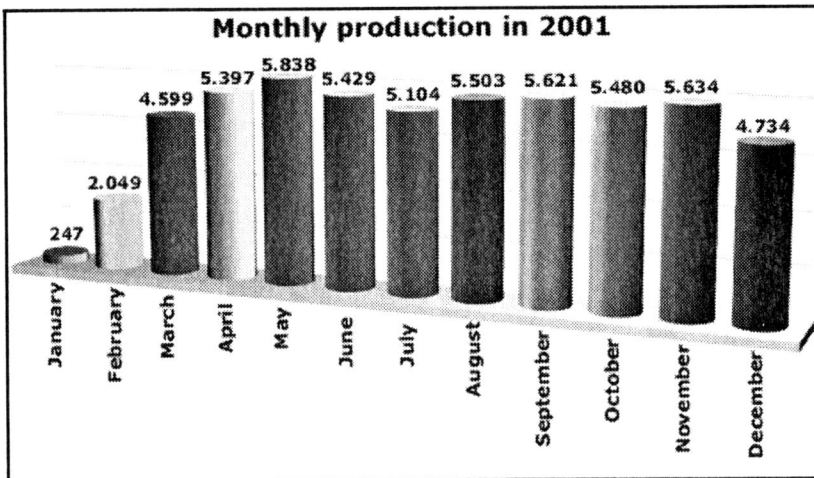

Monthly production in 2001

January	247
February	2.049
March	4.599
April	5.397
May	5.838
June	5.429
July	5.104
August	5.503
September	5.621
October	5.480
November	5.634
December	4.734

Figure 6: Data Preparation

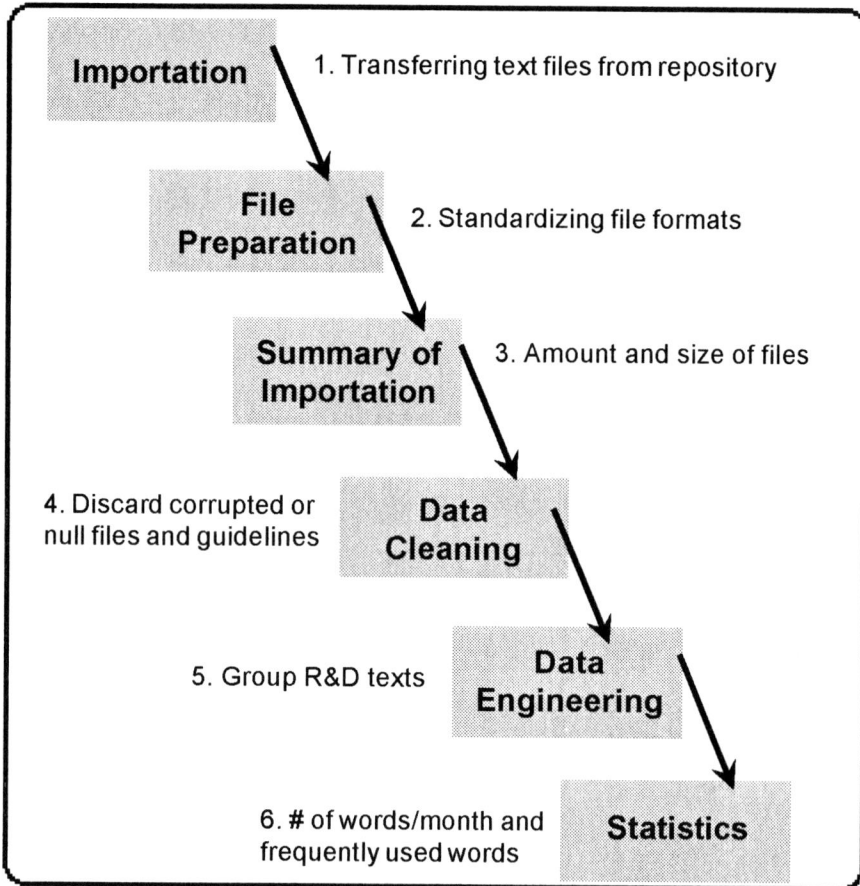

Data Modeling

We carried out the work in this phase by describing and summarizing the data and, then, segmenting the set of texts. Tan's (1999) approach was applied, in which two steps are performed: (1) text refinement, which corresponds to the transformation of texts from the free form to an intermediary form, and (2) knowledge extraction, corresponding to the data mining itself. An example of data description and summarization is shown in *Figure 7*. Results from the segmentation step can be seen in *Figures 8* and *9*. To induce the clusters, we applied the Eurekha tool described by Wives (1999) that had been shown to be well-suited to our purpose since it is versatile and user friendly. Moreover, it provides a variety of algorithms that we did not see in other alternatives. Most of the other tools use the *k*-means or the buckshot algorithm (Cutting, 1992),

Figure 7: Incidence of the Most Used Words

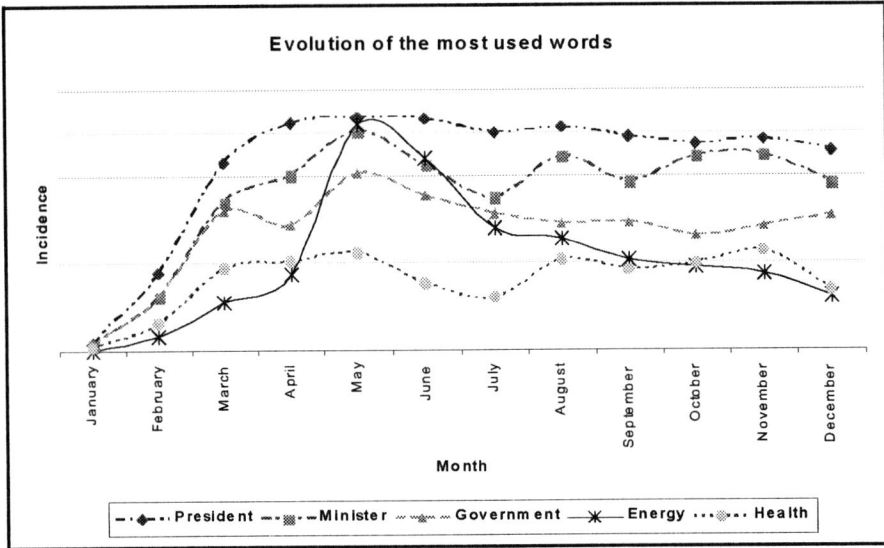

Figure 8: Examples of Categories: 'Presidency' and 'Economy'

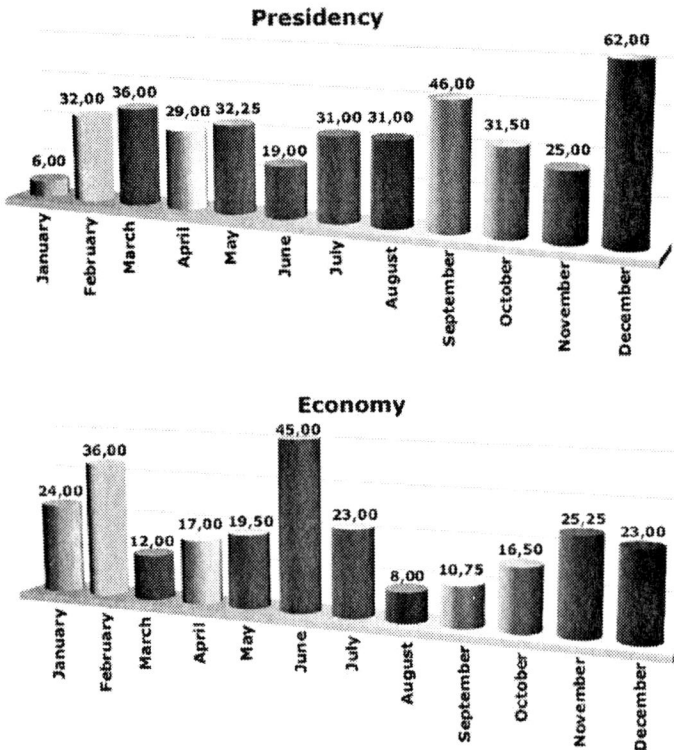

Figure 9: Types of News and Geographic Distribution

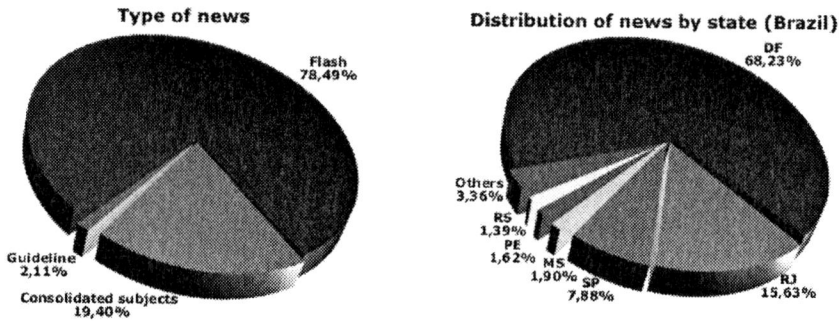

Type of news

Flash
78,49%

Guideline
2,11%

Consolidated subjects
19,40%

Distribution of news by state (Brazil)

DF
68,23%

Others
3,36%

RS
1,39%

PE
1,62%

MS
1,90%

SP
7,88%

RJ
15,63%

in which the user must indicate the number of clusters to be found. Considering that the aim of clustering is to figure out previously unknown categories, it is very difficult to know, a priori, the best number of clusters to be found. The overall process of clustering required for segmentation of the documents in the case is depicted in *Figure 10*.

Model Evaluation

The clusters found in the previous phase were analyzed by an expert in order to discover some meaning in them. After that, a categorization by subject was carried out. This categorization was performed by the application of the methodology introduced by Halliman (2001) that combines cluster analysis with background knowledge.

After analyzing the categories found, five major areas were identified. They are:

1.   *Presidency of Republic* - 30% (president, Fernando, Henrique, Cardoso);
2.   *Economy* - 21% (central bank, monetary values, inflation, stock exchange, dollar rates, interests, national treasure);
3.   *Meteorology* - 21% (time forecast, cloudy, partially, rain);
4.   *Development* - 8% (energy, monetary values, state companies, investment and development); and
5.   *Politics* - 7% (parties acronyms, house of representatives, senators, ministry names, senators names).

Figure 10: Methodology for Clustering in TM

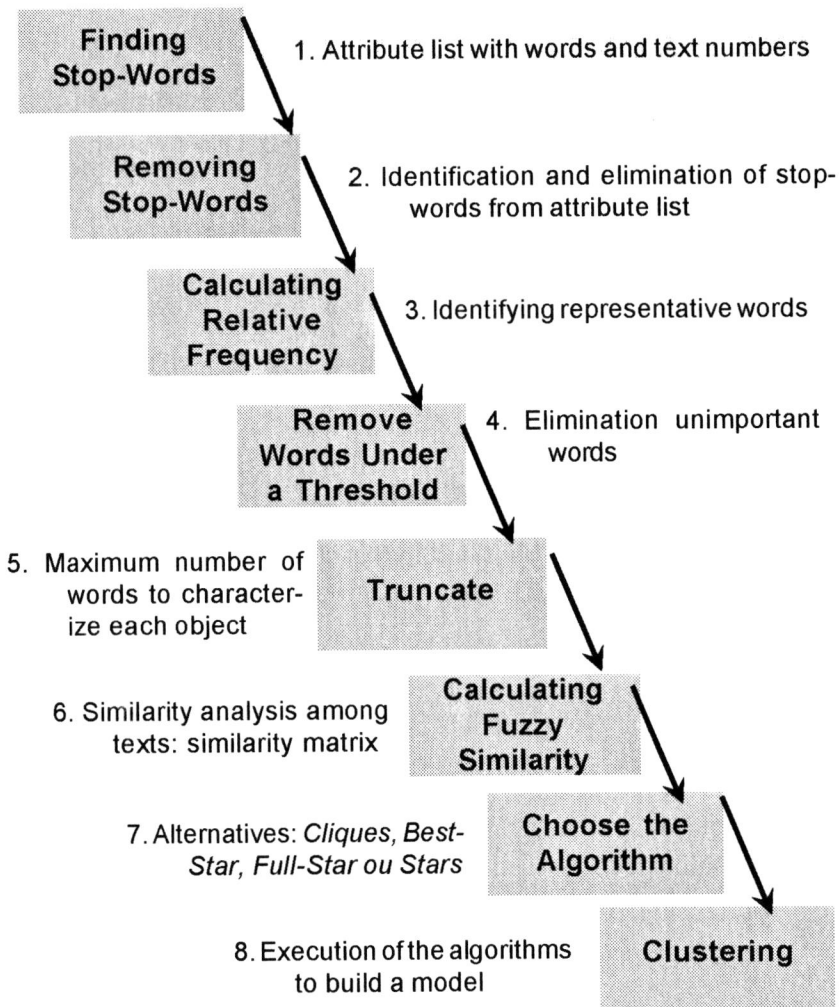

Finding Stop-Words — 1. Attribute list with words and text numbers

Removing Stop-Words — 2. Identification and elimination of stop-words from attribute list

Calculating Relative Frequency — 3. Identifying representative words

Remove Words Under a Threshold — 4. Elimination unimportant words

5. Maximum number of words to character-ize each object — **Truncate**

6. Similarity analysis among texts: similarity matrix — **Calculating Fuzzy Similarity**

7. Alternatives: *Cliques, Best-Star, Full-Star ou Stars* — **Choose the Algorithm**

8. Execution of the algorithms to build a model — **Clustering**

It is important to emphasize that this classification was just a feeling before the present analysis and now has a sound rationale. Almost all news does not have any label that could be used as a category descriptor. Other less frequent categories were also listed that correspond to 13% of the whole text set.

Next, these categories and their corresponding key words are listed:

1.   *Education* (school census, university, national school evaluation);
2.   *Health* (AIDS, HIV, clone, generic medicines, hospital, cholesterol, medicine);

3. *International* (UN, WWF, El Salvador, Mercosul, Palestine, Israel, New York, attempted against, towers, United States);
4. *Security* (federal police, anti-drugs);
5. *Social security* (INSS, social security, deadline);
6. *R&D* (Genome, technology);
7. *Justice* (court, federal, justice, trial, indian, Galdino);
8. *Environment* (environment, birds, ISO, Amazon);
9. *Agriculture* (INCRA, agrarian reform, IBAMA, soil);
10. *Culture* (carnival, art, museum, exhibition, orchestra, symphonic, beautiful, winter festival);
11. *Transportation* (airports, police, bus station, subway, conference, traffic);
12. *Sports* (INTERCOM, ECT, soccer, Nike, CBF, sets, marathon, Vasco, Gama, Cruzeiro, Goiás, Olympic games);
13. *National* (quality, price, meat, accident, P-36); and
14. *Work* (woman, agreement, rural, work, infant, forum, SENAC, SEBRAE).

For a better understanding of the categories, many graphs similar to the one that appears in *Figure 7* were created. That graph shows the most used words during 2001. This graph was interpreted by an expert that issued the interpretations below.

Discussing Figure 7

The constant use of the words "president," "government," and "minister" suggest the approach of actions taken by the central administration. The frequency of the word "healthy" increases as the government and the Health Department make public vaccination and drug prevention campaigns (e.g., against AIDS). The most scored word was "energy," pointing out the effort employed by the central administration to deal with the lack of energy in Brazil during a certain period.

Discussing Figure 8

The categories "presidency," "politics," "development," and "economy" meet the agency objectives regarding the coverage of acts and facts generated by the central administration. They also reflect that, in each month, there is coincidence between the news and important facts. We can mention, for example, financial crisis and "economy," development and "blackout campaign," war and terrorism in USA and "International" and "Security," strike in the metro, bus and trains and "transportation," educational campaigns and "education."

Discussing Figure 9

Almost all news are flashes that do not bring any other information than the pure text (e.g., it is not informed the news focus). It does not allow a more precise evaluation regarding the distribution inside the "slices" of the pie charts. It is also possible to verify that the biggest amount of news came from the cities of Distrito Federal (DF), Rio de Janeiro (RJ) and São Paulo (SP). It concurs with the fact that Brasília and Rio de Janeiro are the headquarters of many public departments and with the economic importance of São Paulo. In this graphic, we can also see the presence of Pernambuco, mainly due to news related to the so-called "polygon of marijuana."

FUTURE TRENDS

Traditional textual clustering approaches use words or keywords, extracted automatically from the text, to represent the elements. But words can lead to semantic mistakes, known as the vocabulary problem, for example, when people use synonyms or word variations.

A recent alternative method proposes the use of an approach that uses concepts instead of words to represent documents. In the conceptual approach for clustering, concepts represent the content of a textual document in a higher level, minimizing the vocabulary problem. Concepts talk about real-world events and objects and are used by people to express ideas, ideologies, thoughts, opinions, and intentions through language (e.g., in talks, texts, documents, books, messages, etc.).

In previous works (Loh, Oliveira, & Gastal, 2001; Loh, Wives, & Oliveira, 2000), concepts were used with success in mining processes of textual documents. Thus, using concepts as document attributes in the clustering process helps to generate better results than using words, since the resulting clusters have elements with more cohesion, besides being more understandable.

CONCLUSION

The advent of the Knowledge Society has imposed an important change in the context of organizations. The business competitiveness is significantly affected by the availability of knowledge about the organizational processes and the external environment. The importance of the information existing in the organizations as a raw material to create knowledge has been recognized since the late eighties. As a matter of fact, the use of such knowledge for leveraging business has led to an increasing number of KDD applications. However, the majority of these applications have been addressed to process structured data, rather than unstructured, which is, by far, the biggest part of the organizational information.

The existence of mature tools to develop TM applications and the amount of textual information available in the organizations seems to be a strategic opportunity that cannot be ignored. In this chapter, the role of TM in BI was discussed, and the interface between them was clarified. The case study presented, with the methodological approach described and an adequate tool, can be used to guide an analyst in developing other applications and provide the business specialists with important inputs to their problem-solving activities. The disclosing of the algorithmic aspects that work behind the scene in a conceptual rather than technical approach brings an important knowledge. This knowledge is usually kept hidden to non-technical people. By presenting such conceptual description, our aim is to allow the analyst to know how the models are being generated, instead of believing in a "black box."

REFERENCES

Aldenderfer, M., & Blashfield, R. K. (1984). *Cluster Analysis.* Beverly Hills, CA: Sage.

Chapman, P., Kerber, R., Clinton, J., Khabaza, T., Reinartz, T., & Wirth, R. (2000). *The CRISP-DM Process Model.* Retrieved October 2002 from: http://www.crisp-dm.org.

Cutting, D. (1992). Scatter/Gather: A cluster-based approach to browsing large document collections. Paper presented at the *Annual International ACM-SIGIR Conference on Research and Development in Information Retrieval.* New York.

Dini, L., & Mazzini, G. (2002). *Opinion classification through information extraction.* Paper presented at the Third International Conference on Data Mining (Data Mining III).

Everitt, B., Landau, S., & Leese, M. (2001). *Cluster Analysis (4th ed.).* New York: Oxford University Press.

Ferneda, E., Prado, H., & Silva, E. (2003). *Text mining for organizational intelligence*. Paper presented at the Fifth International Conference on Enterprise Information Systems (vol. 2). Angers, France.

Fliedl, L., & Weber, G. (2002). "NIBA – TAG" – A tool for analyzing and preparing German texts. Paper presented at the Third International Conference on Data Mining (Data Mining III).

Halliman, C. (2001). Business intelligence using smart techniques: Environmental scanning using text mining and competitor analysis using scenarios and manual simulation, Information Uncover, Houston.

Jain, A., Murty, M., & Flynn, P. (1999). Data clustering: A review. *ACM Computing Surveys*, 31(3), 264-323.

Kdnuggets (2002a). Poll: Which data mining techniques do you use regularly? Retrieved June 25, 2002 from: http://www.kdnuggets.com/polls/2002/data_mining_techniques.htm.

Kowalski, G. (1997). *Information Retrieval Systems: Theory and Implementation*. Boston, MA: Kluwer Academic Publishers.

Loh, S., Oliveira, J., & Gastal, F. (2001). Knowledge discovery in textual documentation: Qualitative and quantitative analysis. *Journal of Documentation*, 57(5), 577-590.

Loh, S., Wives, L., & Oliveira, J. (2000). Concept-based knowledge discovery in texts extracted from the WEB. *ACM SIGKDD Explorations*, 2(1), 29-39.

Moore, G., & McKenna, R. (1999). *Crossing the Chasm: Marketing and Selling High-Tech Products to Mainstream Customers*. New York: HarperBusiness.

Rijsbergen, C. V. (1979). *Information Retrieval (2nd ed.)*. London: Butterworths.

Schütze, H., & Silverstein, C. (1997). Projections for efficient document clustering. Paper presented at the Annual International ACM-SIGIR Conference on Research and Development in Information Retrieval, Philadelphia, PA, USA.

Stollenwerk, M. (2001). Knowledge management: Concepts and models. In K. Tarapanoff (Ed.), *Organizational and Competitive Intelligence*, Brasilia (Brazil: Editora Universidade de Brasilia (in Portuguese).

Tan, A.-H. (1999). Text mining: The state of the art and the challenges. Paper presented at the Workshop on Knowledge Discovery from Advanced Databases (PAKDD'99), Beijing.

Wang, J. (ed.) (2003). *Data Mining, Exposed and Examined*. Hershey, PA: Idea Group Publishing.

Willet, P. (1988). Recent trends in hierarchic document clustering: A critical review. *Information Processing & Management*, 24, 577-597.

Wives, L. K. (1999). *A study about arrangement of textual documents applied to unstructured information processing using clustering techniques.* Master Thesis. PPGC/Federal University of Rio Grande do Sul, Porto Alegre, RS — Brazil (in Portuguese).

Wives, L. K. (2000). Technologies for knowledge discovery in texts applied to competitive intelligence. Qualification Exam. PPGC/Federal University of Rio Grande do Sul, Porto Alegre, RS — Brazil (in Portuguese).

ENDNOTES

[1]   Another problem, already stated, is related to the algorithms that do not work if the user does not indicates the number of clusters that must be found (*k-means* and *buckshot*). This indication or selection is not necessary in the algorithm described and in all the algorithms of the graph theoretic family.

Chapter XII

Understanding Decision-Making in Data Warehousing and Related Decision Support Systems:

An Explanatory Study of a Customer Relationship Management Application[1]

John D. Wells, Washington State University, USA

Traci J. Hess, Washington State University, USA

ABSTRACT

Many businesses have made or are making significant investments in data warehouses that reportedly support a myriad of decision support systems (DSS). Due to the newness of data warehousing and related DSS (DW-DSS), the nature of the decision support provided to DW-DSS users and the related impact on decision performance have not been investigated in an applied setting. An explanatory case study was undertaken at a financial services organization that implemented a particular type of DW-DSS, a Customer Relationship Management (CRM) system. The DSS-

decision performance model has provided some theoretical guidance for this exploration. The case study results show that the decision-making support provided by these systems is limited and that an extended version of the DSS-decision performance model may better describe the factors that influence individual decision-making performance.

INTRODUCTION

The significant investments in data warehousing that began in the 1990s and continue today were motivated by the belief that more information would enable business users to make better decisions resulting in improved returns. Data warehousing-related decision support systems (DW-DSS) were built to assist business users in analyzing the vast amounts of data that originate from heterogeneous data sources. These business intelligence systems utilize tools such as OLAP, data mining, and query management, enabling businesses to pursue organizational strategies such as customer relationship management (CRM), business process management, and supply-chain management. While businesses have been eager to invest in DW-DSS applications, many appear to have overlooked the relationship between the efficient use of these investments and a user-oriented approach to developing and maintaining these systems (Gardner, 1998; Glassey 1998). Some companies investing in these initiatives have already noted that it is difficult to translate the information provided by these systems into positive business results (Hoffman, 2001). Obtaining the necessary information is an important hurdle, but how the information is presented and used for decision-making purposes is equally important.

The purpose of the research project reported in this chapter is to investigate the decision-making support provided in the complex, heterogeneous decision environment of DW-DSS and to focus on the decision-makers' perceptions of this support. An explanatory case study of a Fortune 500 company that is utilizing a CRM application, an instance of a DW-DSS, was conducted to understand these issues. While many organizations claim to have developed systems that support this customer-centric strategy, there has been little research on the functionality and decision support provided by these systems. An investigation of this decision-making support should extend the body of research on decision-making support systems in general, as well as the multi-billion dollar CRM sector. The goal of this case study is to investigate how DW-DSS provide decision support to individual decision makers by (1) documenting the decision-making support provided in a large-scale DW-DSS application, (2) explaining these decision-making scenarios in the context of Todd and Benbasat's (1999) DSS-decision performance model, and (3) identifying the specific DW-DSS characteristics that may influence decision performance.

In the first section of the chapter, we review the relevant data warehousing and DSS literature and introduce our research questions, noting how these questions address significant gaps in the literature. We then discuss our research methodology, a case study approach, and describe our case study protocol. In the next section, the findings motivated by the research questions are presented. Lastly, the lessons learned as well as opportunities for future research are described.

LITERATURE REVIEW AND RESEARCH GOALS

Given the domain and context of this study, the literature on the DW-DSS infrastructure and decision-making seemed most relevant in developing the research questions for this study. The three components of the DW-DSS infrastructure are first described to highlight the different types of decision support that can be provided. Next, the literature on decision-making in DSS is summarized, and the theoretical model used to guide some of our investigation is presented. Lastly, the unique characteristics of the DW-DSS environment are discussed.

DW-DSS Infrastructure

Historically, organizations have leveraged information assets to make decisions that will improve productivity, effectiveness, and efficiency. These information assets were derived from the resulting data of an organization's internal (e.g., inventory management) and external (e.g., sales) operations and used to support unstructured and semi-structured decisions (Keen & Scott Morton, 1978; Sprague & Carlson, 1982). As the ability to gather, store, and distribute such data has matured and the number of data sources has increased, organizations began to build an information infrastructure that would provide a holistic view of its business operations, partners, and customers. Key components of this infrastructure are shown in Figure 1 and include (1) core technologies (i.e., data storage), (2) enabling technologies (i.e., analytic processing), and (3) application solutions (i.e., decision support systems)

Figure 1: DW-DSS Infrastructure (adapted from Kalakota & Robinson, 1999)

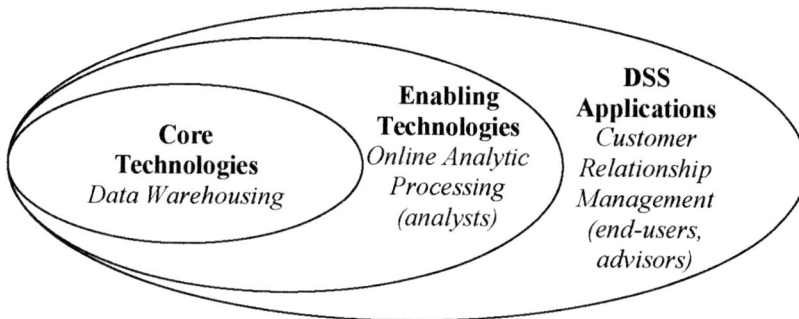

(Kalakota & Robinson, 1999). The following sections briefly describe each of these components in the context of a heterogeneous, decision environment and how these components can support decision-making.

Core Technologies. The early data sources for DSS applications were sequential flat files and, over time, evolved to relational databases. As data sources continued to increase, the complexity of integrating this data became an issue (Rudensteiner & Zhang, 2000). Data warehousing emerged as a core technology for supporting an organization's heterogeneous, decision-making environment. A data warehouse (DW) is a database system designed to support organizational decision processes and is separate from traditional transaction processing systems (Gray & Watson, 1998; Inmon, 1992, 1998).

Enabling Technologies. The heterogeneity of these decision environments has stimulated the need to explore more effective techniques for mining and presenting data in a meaningful format (Shaw, Subramaniam, Tan, & Welge, 2001). These enabling technologies include techniques such as OLAP (Datta & Thomas, 1999) and statistical data-mining algorithms (Drew, Mani, Betz, & Datta, 2001) to produce information that can improve performance. Effective execution of these techniques enables an organization to detect weaknesses (e.g., customer dissatisfaction) as well as hidden opportunities (e.g., customer segmentation). Decision makers, or *analysts*, with a technical orientation typically work with this component of a DW-DSS.

Application Solutions. As noted by Wixom and Watson (2001), most end-users do not access the DW directly, and instead access the numerous decision support applications that are dependent on the warehouse. For example, a sales staff can receive decision support for deciding which customers to target, what products they are most likely to buy, and what products will be most profitable for the company. In the context of a DW-DSS environment, support can be provided to hundreds of decision makers, or *end-users*, with little technological expertise, as compared to previous DSS that were more limited in scope.

Decision-Making Support in Each DW-DSS Component. Organizations establish a DW-DSS infrastructure to support individual decision-making. While the effectiveness of this type of infrastructure has been discussed from conceptual and technical perspectives, less focus has been applied to how a DW-DSS infrastructure and its three components actually facilitate decision-making. The current literature describes how each component *can* support decision-making but does not document the support being provided in real DW-DSS. The following research question focuses on how decision-making is supported by the DW-DSS infrastructure components.

R1: How are the components of a DW-DSS infrastructure being used to facilitate and support decision-making?

The next section reviews theory-based research on individual decision-making in DSS and the factors that may influence decision-making performance.

Decision-Making with DSS

For more than three decades, researchers in the multi-disciplinary, DSS area have investigated how information systems can provide support to organizational decision-makers. While early research focused on system capabilities, more recent research has focused on the decision-maker and on identifying the factors that affect individual decision performance and user perceptions.

The DSS-Decision Performance Relationship. Through a recent series of experiments, Todd and Benbasat (1991, 1992, 1993, 1994a, 1994b, 1999) developed an extended model of the relationship between DSS capabilities and performance measures such as effectiveness and efficiency. The DSS-decision performance model, shown in Figure 2, was based upon earlier DSS research and the cost-benefit framework of cognition (Payne, 1982). This model was used to guide some of our investigation of a specific DW-DSS environment, and the model description that follows provides some necessary background information for the discussion of our findings.

Figure 2: DSS-Decision Performance Model (Todd & Benbasat, 1999)

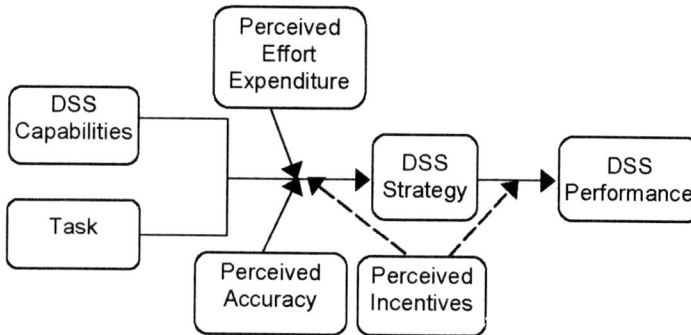

The model incorporates some aspects of the task-technology fit perspective (Goodhue & Thompson, 1995) by including the two factors, DSS capabilities and task. The capabilities factor represents the *features or type* of DSS while task represents the *characteristics or requirements* of the decision-making task. Decision performance can be interpreted as the effectiveness (quality, accuracy) and/or efficiency (reduction in effort or time) of the decision-making process. Capabilities and task are believed to individually influence performance and to jointly influence performance to the extent that the capabilities matched the decision-making task. In Todd and Benbasat's model, the effect of capabilities and task on decision performance is fully mediated by decision strategy in accordance with Jarvenpaa's (1989) work on information processing strategies and decision performance. Strategy is described in the DSS context as "the way in which the DSS is appropriated by the decision-maker to handle the task" (Todd & Benbasat, 1999, p. 358). A strategy that utilizes all of the available information is believed to be better than one that eliminates alternatives (and the related information) based upon certain attribute values.

The model also includes the decision-maker's *perceived effort expenditure* and *accuracy* as moderating influences on the selected decision strategy based upon the cost benefit framework of cognition (Payne, 1982). Empirical research from this cognitive perspective suggests that decision-makers attempt to maximize accuracy while minimizing effort, and that effort has a stronger influence than accuracy. *Incentives* were also included as a moderating influence in the model as performance-based incentives were believed to increase "the decision-maker's sense of involvement with the task," leading to a higher level of performance (Todd & Benbasat, 1999, p. 360). The results of these experiments, however, did not support the influence of incentives on either decision strategy or performance. Given the equivocal findings on the influence of incentives, these relationships are shown with dotted lines in Figure 2 (Todd & Benbasat, 1999).

The DSS-Decision Performance Model in an Applied Setting. The DSS-decision performance model was developed and validated in a controlled, experimental setting. Because the model has not been operationalized in an applied setting, the dimensions for each construct have not been identified. For example, in the experiments, the capabilities and task constructs were held constant or controlled, and individual dimensions for these constructs were not developed. The following research question addresses the external validity of this model and represents an initial step towards operationalizing the model in a DW-DSS environment.

R2: Do the constructs and relationships in the DSS-decision performance model adequately explain the decision-making processes within a DW-DSS?

By applying the DSS-decision performance model in this case study, we can observe how well the model's constructs apply to a DW-DSS context as well as gaining insight into other characteristics that may be significant in this environment.

Characteristics of DW-DSS Decision Environments

DW-DSS applications represent a complex, heterogeneous decision-making environment and possess unique characteristics. During our review of the literature, three characteristics emerged that are specific to the DW-DSS environment as compared to a traditional DSS environment. First, the heterogeneity of the data sources that populate a data warehouse has prompted the need to correctly interpret these data, particularly at the analytical user level. The primary means for accomplishing this goal is through the use of metadata, which is descriptive data about the data available in an information system. Practitioners and researchers continually stress the importance of metadata in a data warehousing environment (Gardner, 1998; Inmon 1998; Sen & Jacob, 1998), and have observed that without it, users will avoid using the data warehouse or will use it inefficiently (Watson & Haley, 1998).

Second, as data are pushed out to end user decision-makers, these end users require more *explanations* of the data. Explanations are formal, more high-level descriptions of the data and support provided by a system, and in the context of the DW-DSS, frequently contain metadata content. Research on the use and construction of explanations in DSS and other intelligent systems has highlighted the impact of explanations on DSS performance and user perceptions (Gregor & Benbasat 1999; Ye & Johnson 1995). The complexity and volume of information in DW-DSS suggest that explanations may play an even greater role for users of these systems. Explanations are also important for interpreting the qualitative data gathered in DW-DSS.

Finally, CRM and other DW-DSS domains highlight the inherent need to populate a DW with qualitative and quantitative data derived from transactional and non-transactional sources (Wells, Fuerst, & Choobineh, 1999). The issue of qualitative data is particularly challenging as it comes in an unstructured and uncategorized format. Options for data storage include: (1) leave it in its original form which is difficult to query and analyze, or (2) transform it to a discrete format (Huck & Cormier, 1996) that can be queried and include the original data as explanatory metadata. While there has been research on the issues of mapping qualitative data to a quantitative format (Ngwenyama & Bryson, 1999) and using fuzzy logic to address qualitatively oriented decisions (Bolloju, 1996; Zeleny, 1983), the use of these data for decision-making purposes is largely undocumented. While subjective, qualitative data is eventually applied to a data warehouse in a discrete, quantitative format, the primary challenge for utilizing this type of data in a DW-DSS environment is maintaining the explanatory power of the data in its original form.

By considering the unique characteristics of a DW-DSS environment, further insight can be gained into how the decision-making process is affected by such issues. Our third research question addresses how these three characteristics may influence the decision-making process.

R3: How do the DW-DSS characteristics of metadata, explanations, and qualitative data affect an individual's decision-making process?

As a form of DW-DSS, CRM applications exhibit these characteristics. CRM provides decision-making support for activities that range from market basket analysis to one-to-one marketing (Makos & Schmarzo, 1997). Unlike traditional decision tasks such as inventory management, CRM-related decisions are extremely complex because they must take into consideration subjective, human factors such as attitudes and preferences (Romano & Fjermestand, 2002). This creates a need to store, process, and distribute transactional (e.g., products purchased) as well as non-transactional (e.g., complaints) data.

The research methodology presented in the next section describes a case study design focusing on decision-makers utilizing a real CRM application to answer the research questions we have described above.

RESEARCH METHODOLOGY

The case study research methodology was selected based upon the nature of the research questions, the inability to control the users of an actual DW-DSS, and the focus on current rather than historical events, as suggested by Yin (1994). The research questions were explanatory in nature and the focus on users of an actual DW-DSS made it difficult to manipulate or control the users' behavior. Other researchers have similarly noted that a case study approach is appropriate when the project goal is description or classification (Bonoma, 1985) and the phenomenon of interest should be studied in its natural setting (Benbasat, Goldstein, & Meade, 1987).

Case Study Protocol

The case study protocol defined in Yin (1994) was used in our case study research design. The general goal of this project, to investigate how DW-DSS provide decision support to individual decision makers, requires a *unit of analysis* at the individual decision-maker level. Individual decision-makers using a live DW-DSS were thus the subjects of our analysis. A *multiple case study design* was used to improve reliability given the numerous external, uncontrolled conditions that could influence each individual's decision-making behavior. The study was *replicated* eight times, as four users of the enabling technologies component (analysts) and four users of the applications solution component (end-users) served as case study subjects. Care was taken to include both experienced and inexperienced decision-makers in our case study as experience has been shown to influence user perceptions.

Data triangulation, collecting different types of data, was used to improve construct validity. Each of the individual case study subjects, both analysts and end-users, was interviewed using the case study instrument described below. In addition, these individuals were observed using the DW-DSS for decision-making purposes, and archival records, such as screen prints and daily reports, from the decision-making process were collected when possible. In addition, four individuals that were not decision-makers but had knowledge of the DW-DSS and the decision-making activities of the analysts and end-users were interviewed using the same instrument. Interviews with these individuals, data warehouse administrators and strategic directors provided additional support for the self-reported perceptions of the decision-makers. Both investigators on this project were present during all data collection procedures and all interviews were recorded and documented in writing.

Case Study Instrument. Open-ended interview questions were developed for each of the three research questions. For R1 *(How are the components of a DW-DSS infrastructure being used to facilitate and support decision-making?)*, multiple questions were developed regarding the functionality and the type of decision-making support provided in each infrastructure component. For R2 *(Do the constructs and relationships in the DSS-decision performance model adequately explain the decision-making processes within a DW-DSS?)*, multiple questions were developed for each of the constructs in the DSS-decision performance model. For R3 *(How do the DW-DSS characteristics of metadata, explanations, and qualitative data affect an individual's decision-making process?)*, multiple questions were developed for each of the specific characteristics identified. Given the open-ended, unstructured nature of the questions, and the number of questions, each interview took approximately two hours. Observation of the actual decision-making process required additional time with the decision-makers.

Problem Domain. CRM applications, the specific problem domain for this study, are an accurate instance of a DW-DSS and provide a fertile context for addressing this study's research questions. CRM applications often encompass a number of different tools (i.e., OLAP, data mining, etc.) and are designed to support a range of decision-making activities (Cooper, Watson, Wixom, & Goodhue, 2000). All three components of the DW-DSS infrastructure were present in the specific CRM application studied. Two distinct groups of decision-makers were present, the analysts and the end-users (also referred to as personal financial advisors) in conjunction with the two infrastructure components that directly support decision-making. In addition, the specific characteristics of DW-DSS identified from the literature review were present and the decision-makers were familiar with these characteristics. Additional information about the DW-DSS, the individual decision-makers, and the business organization is provided in the next section.

CASE STUDY RESULTS

The case studies were conducted at a Fortune 500 financial services organization (FS) that was utilizing a CRM-related DW-DSS application to enhance decision-making. Due to the competitive sensitivity of the results, the identity of this organization will remain confidential. The following sections provide a detailed discussion of the observed decision-making support in the context of this study's three research questions.

Background Information on FS

The organization that participated in this case study competes in the Financial Services sector and utilizes CRM functionality to generate sales leads, enhance customer service, and improve profitability through customer segmentation. FS has pursued this initiative by gathering data from different sources to create a comprehensive view of it customers in its DW. Both the DW and the CRM application were developed in-house. The DW was developed in DB2 and, initially, its sole function was to support CRM functionality. The DW is populated via approximately 40 data sources including account master files, transaction log files, and customer service files. These data are mined and analyzed to identify potentially profitable customers. This information is then leveraged to contact the right customer at the right time with in-depth insight into his/her financial needs and, hence, offer a financial service that is congruent with that customer's needs. Currently, the DW infrastructure has been used exclusively for the CRM application, but other functional areas (e.g., Fraud/Risk Management) have requested access to the DW. More than 1,500 personal financial advisors utilize the *applications* component of the system and approximately 75 analysts utilize *enabling technologies* in the DW-DSS infrastructure.

FS's performance assessments of the DW and related CRM application are based on a number of metrics including account balance, new accounts, and success per contact. Customer surveys are distributed in an effort to gauge customer satisfaction, and FS plans to implement a measure of customer retention. Ideally, FS would also like to measure and track the lifetime value of each customer, but has yet to operationalize this metric.

As previously noted, interviews were conducted with the actual decision makers, both customer segment *analysts* and personal financial advisors (*end users*), along with data warehouse administrators and strategic directors, who play critical roles in FS's CRM initiatives. The following discussion describes in more detail the decision-making scenarios supported by the DSS application and enabling technology components of the DW-DSS infrastructure. Managerial issues mentioned by DW administrators and project managers are also described.

DW-DSS Infrastructure (R1)

This research question addressed how the DW-DSS infrastructure was being used to support individual decision-making. The results from this question are categorized based upon the three infrastructure components.

Core Technologies. DW administrators noted several challenges with the DW and the related decision-making support systems. Two of the challenges related to the heterogeneity of the data sources. First, the dynamic nature of the data (i.e., multiple formats) makes it more cumbersome to transform to a usable format. For instance, the customer service files are populated by a Voice Recognition Unit (VRU) application and proper transformation rules are imperative if these files are to be placed in the DW in a usable format. Second, and somewhat related to the first issue, is the need to incorporate current, descriptive information (i.e., metadata) about the data stored in the DW. Such information includes transformation rules, business rules, and calculation descriptions.

Initially, FS concentrated on populating its DW with primarily quantitative data. The majority of the qualitative, non-transactional data was stored and processed offline by the system users. While these users expressed an urgent need to incorporate qualitative data in the DW, DW administrators expressed concerns about adding this type of data. An example of qualitative data that has been transformed and stored in the warehouse is 'customer disposition'. After contacting a customer and discussing potential product offerings, personal financial advisors are prompted to enter an assessment of 'customer disposition' (e.g., interested, disinterested, etc.). The advisors choose from predetermined, discrete categories, and these data are used for future customer segmentation. DW administrators, however, expressed concerns with regard to incorporating qualitative data, principally because of the unstructured original form of these data and the transformation process required before the data can be stored in a structured format.

A high-ranking executive further supported the need for more qualitative data in the context of a key piece of qualitative data that FS is attempting to leverage, customers' primary life events. To effectively segment its customers, FS feels that it is essential to gather and store accurate data on these primary life events (e.g., marriage, childbirth, etc.), but is having difficulty in collecting and utilizing these data. Contact personnel are not provided with incentives to identify and input these events, and thus these qualitative data are not being consistently recorded.

Decision-Making Support from Enabling Technologies. Customer segment analysts use the enabling technologies of the DW-DSS infrastructure to perform largely unstructured tasks including target model identification, direct marketing list creation, customer retention analysis, and various data mining functions. Because of the unstructured, novel nature of the tasks, the analysts noted that their decision-making efforts required a high degree of offline processing and a lot of effort on their part. Also, tasks were described as somewhat novel and required a high degree of offline processing. The analysts are also provided with a metadata application to derive the query criteria for their various tasks. This application is user-invoked and primarily presents text-based information in a GUI interface. The analysts expressed dissatisfaction with metadata quality, particularly with respect to business descriptions and transformation rules. One analyst estimated that they spend '20-50% of their time tracking down accurate metadata'.

Decision-Making Support in the CRM Application. Personal financial advisors access the CRM application for sales leads. Each week, the application provides a list of 60 customer leads along with a *single* product/service recommendation for each lead. The advisors use the CRM application, other bank systems, and their own private, offline customer files to support their decision-making in trying to sell customers the appropriate products.

Advisors expressed a disconnect between the structure of the decision task provided by the DW-DSS and the actual nature of the decision. The CRM application provides the advisor with a sales lead along with a *single* product recommendation, and the advisors believe it is inappropriate to only offer one product recommendation. Interestingly, the decision task was considered to be more unstructured (and the disconnect greater) as the experience level of the advisor increased. One advisor expressed concern regarding the effect that this product recommendation has on novice advisors. It was observed that a novice advisor contacts a customer with the system-generated product recommendation without researching the customer profile for other potential product offerings. Conversely, more experienced advisors pay little attention to the product recommendation and instead, research customer needs and derive a short list of potential products. The advisors also noted that the descriptive information (or explanations) provided by the CRM application were fairly straightforward, but limited (i.e., primarily field descriptions). They noted that additional explanations or descriptions of the information and recommendations provided by the application would be useful. In summary, the interviews and subsequent analysis revealed that the system was providing a minimal level of decision support and users were utilizing external data and processes to gain additional support.

DW-DSS Decision-Making and the DSS-Decision Performance Model (R2)

The response to this question is organized based upon the constructs in the DSS-decision performance model: task, capabilities, perceived effort, perceived accuracy, incentives, strategy, and performance. A summary of these findings is provided in Table 1.

Task. The *Task* types differed considerably among the infrastructure components and the corresponding groups of users. Analysts using the enabling technologies were involved in less structured, novel decision-making tasks, while advisors supported by the application solutions were completing more structured, routine tasks. Due to the disparity in the nature and structure of these tasks, the decision-making characteristics for these two groups of users were investigated separately and both perspectives will be discussed.

Table 1: Summary of T&B DSS-Decision Performance Assessment

Constructs	Analysts	Advisors (End Users)
Task	-Highly unstructured -More Novel -Heavy offline processing	-Structured to semi-structured -More Routine -Moderate offline processing
DSS Capabilities	-Very lacking, required heavy offline processing	-Somewhat lacking, required moderate offline processing
Perceived Accuracy	-Spent a considerable amount of time tracking down missing information (e.g., metadata) to increase decision accuracy	-Novices were unable to effectively judge decision accuracy -Experts altered strategy to increase decision accuracy
Perceived Effort	-High effort attributed to missing metadata and unstructured tasks	-Novices reported low effort -Experts reported high effort
Perceived Incentives	-Nothing outside of job description and task visibility	-Nothing outside of job description and task visibility
Decision Strategy	-Unguided	-Guided
Decision Performance	- # of New Accounts, Lifetime Value of Customer	-Account Balance, # of New Accounts, Success per Contact

DSS Capabilities. As with task types, the DSS capabilities varied greatly between the two types of applications and user groups. For the analysts, it was observed that the capabilities of the DSS did not adequately support the less structured, novel decision-making tasks as was evident by the amount of offline processing (e.g., tracking down metadata) that was required. Some of the advisors similarly felt that their application did not provide sufficient support. The level of advisors' experience with their job (selling banking products) seemed to affect how the capabilities of the DSS were perceived. The more experienced advisors would readily question the results being produced by the DSS and engage in more offline processing based upon their knowledge and experience with customers. Conversely, the less experienced advisors would take the results produced from the DSS at face value, not perform offline processing, and be satisfied with the capabilities of the DSS.

The Effect of Perceived Accuracy, Effort, and Incentives on Strategy Selection. In the DSS-decision performance model, accuracy, effort, and incentives were included as moderating influences on strategy selection. In FS's DW-DSS, the dynamics of these factors varied greatly among the two decision-making scenarios, the CRM application used by the personal financial advisors and the enabling technology component used by the customer segment analysts.

With respect to the personal financial advisors, the application guides the users in a specific decision strategy by providing a listing of customers that are likely to buy additional products and by suggesting a single product that each customer is likely to purchase. Customer characteristics and product profitability are used to generate these recommendations. The system attempts to guide the advisors in their customer selling efforts by readily providing these recommendations and thus reducing the *effort* of these users. At this time, FS does not provide any specific *incentives* to the advisors for using the system generated recommendations, and the advisors' level of involvement in each customer call is relatively low as they typically contact more than 20 customers in a day. FS does not monitor the specific products sold by the advisors, and as a result, there is no information on how often the recommended products are actually sold.

During interviews with the advisors, it became apparent that some advisors were choosing to ignore some of the recommendations provided by the system. While most advisors accepted the recommended customers as good leads, the more experienced advisors often lacked confidence in the *accuracy* of the product recommendation (i.e., incorrect product recommendation) or felt that a recommendation of only one product was insufficient. As a result, these more experienced advisors would put forth additional effort by consulting both on-line and off-line information about the customer to increase the quality and volume of their recommendations and resulting sales. Conversely, the less-experienced advisors would often minimize their effort by using only the single product recommendation provided by the system in their selling efforts. One explanation for the difference in strategy selection could be that the less experienced advisors failed to assess the inaccuracy or insufficiency of the product recommendation.

The analysts use the enabling technologies to support a high effort, comprehensive data analysis strategy, and the task duration is relatively long, with some tasks taking days or weeks to complete. The analysts' high level of accountability for each task, along with the duration of each task, results in a strong sense of involvement in each decision task. And while FS does not explicitly provide *incentives* for the use of a better strategy, the analysts' level of involvement implicitly creates an incentive. Thus, the analysts were willing to pursue a better decision strategy (i.e., using all of the available information even when it was difficult to obtain) that required a higher degree of *effort* because it also provided a higher degree of *accuracy* and ensured that the analysts would achieve high decision quality.

Decision Performance. While FS's management was quick to provide a list of performance metrics demonstrating how sales and profitability had been improved by the implementation of their DW-DSS environment, FS was not currently monitoring decision-makers' strategy selection. There appeared to be no effort to measure the effectiveness of the decision support provided by these systems independent from the data access provided. At the employee level, there were no efforts to monitor the advisors' utilization of the appropriate recommendations and decision strategy or the analysts' pursuit of the best decision strategy. As a result, in the case of advisors who had fewer incentives, the recommendations and strategies were not used.

Specific Characteristics of a DW-DSS Decision Environment (R3)

The third research question focuses on exploring three specific DW-DSS characteristics that may influence decision performance (i.e., characteristics that were not explicitly included in the Todd & Benbasat model). As the three characteristics of metadata, explanations, and qualitative data were brought up during the interviews, the decision makers repeatedly noted the DW-DSS was weak in these areas and noted the negative influence these weaknesses had on various aspects of decision performance. The discussions of these three DW-DSS characteristics are summarized in Table 2 and described in more detail in the next three sections.

Metadata. As noted in the literature review, *metadata*, descriptive data about the data available in an information system, plays an important role in the complex, heterogeneous DW-DSS environment. Very little is known, however, about how metadata quality influences users' decision-strategy and decision performance. With regard to the DSS-decision performance model, metadata facilities would correspond to the DSS *capabilities* construct and thus could serve as an important dimension of this construct and influence decision performance.

Within FS's DW-DSS, the analysts generally had poor perceptions of *metadata* quality. While the initial metadata facilities established appeared to be adequate, these facilities were not maintained as the DW design and sources changed. For the analysts, the poor quality metadata did not appear to influence the decision strategy used but did affect the efficiency of the decision process. The analysts had sufficient involvement to ensure that they selected the best decision strategy and achieved the best decision quality despite the loss of efficiency.

Unlike the analysts, the advisors were not familiar with the term metadata. Instead, they appeared to rely on *explanations* of the data provided by the

Table 2: Summary of Specific DW-DSS Characteristics

Characteristics	Analysts	Advisors (End-Users)
Metadata	-Stand-alone, GUI application -Low confidence in metadata accuracy -When poor, users sought supplemental information	-Limited use of metadata (primarily field descriptions) -When poor, users sought supplemental information -Primarily viewed as explanations
Explanations	-Primarily thought of in terms of metadata	-Considered to be lacking in current DSS environment
Qualitative Data	-Not used -Need transformation to complete, discrete categories	-No incentives for accurate data capture/storage -Desire to use rich, unstructured data

system, unaware that these explanations are often based upon metadata. The relationship between metadata and explanations was readily apparent during the interviews, and a more detailed description of explanations is provided in the next section.

Explanations. The advisors at FS noted that better *explanations* or descriptions could be provided for some of the information included in the application solutions. For example, the experienced advisors noted that they did not use the information or recommendations provided by the system because they were unsure of its source or derivation. Instead they chose to rely on their off-line information, which they assumed to be more accurate. Novice advisors did not have enough experience to question the system output and simply accepted the recommendations provided. Again, the provision of *explanations* in DSS appears to be strongly linked to metadata, as it is typically the core content of the explanations provided. While analysts may use metadata to answer the questions that they have about the data in a DW-DSS environment, the advisors use higher-level, more formal *explanations* for the how, when, why, and what questions that they may have in using a DW-DSS environment.

A lack of metadata generally appeared to result in a lack of adequate explanations. Conversely, the presence of metadata did not ensure adequate explanations. Explanation type (content, format, and provision mechanism) is believed to influence explanation use (frequency, extent of use), which subsequently influences DSS performance (Gregor & Benbasat, 1999). In this context, the presence and type of explanations could significantly affect decision performance. Explanations could be considered a DSS *capability* in terms of the DSS-decision performance model and thus would be considered a dimension of the *capability* construct.

Qualitative Data. While some *qualitative*, non-transactional data was provided in FS's DW-DSS, the presence and use of this data was limited. DW administrators appeared to avoid it whenever possible due to the unstructured nature of the data and the requisite transformation process, which may account for its absence. When qualitative, non-transactional data existed, both analysts and advisors stated that a lack of descriptive information on the data context and discrete transformation process affected the frequency of use and increased their effort when using the data. The decision-makers, however, unanimously agreed that additional qualitative data would strengthen the decision-making support provided and were eager to have more of it included in the DW.

Given the difficulty that analysts and advisors seem to have in interpreting qualitative data in its raw format and after conversion to a discrete format (e.g., through categorization), the addition of qualitative data may require more explanations during the decision-making process. The storage or accessibility of qualitative data could be interpreted as a DSS *capability* in the context of DW-DSS and thus may be an important determinant of this construct in the DSS-decision performance model. Future research opportunities with qualitative data in DW-DSS are described in the next section.

LESSONS LEARNED AND FUTURE RESEARCH

This explanatory case study reveals that while organizations are successfully automating the retrieval and input of data for front-end users, there are a number of decision support issues that need improvement and could benefit from further investigation. In the organization studied, decision-making support is provided to advisors (end users) using the front-end application, but the advisors do not understand how the supporting recommendations are generated, and are not given the explanations or incentives that would encourage them to utilize this support. The analysts, utilizing the enabling technologies component, are similarly not provided with explicit incentives and must seek out the needed metadata and explanations. Interestingly, the analysts generally utilize the preferred decision strategy while the advisors do not. Further, the organization studied does not monitor or measure the use of these recommendations. Based upon discussions with other organizations, this lack of decision support evaluation is commonplace.

The three specific DW-DSS characteristics identified, (1) metadata, (2) explanations, and (3) qualitative data, each appear to be a significant dimension of the DW-DSS *capability* construct and have a significant effect on decision performance. These DW-DSS capabilities repeatedly surfaced during the interviews because the capabilities (or lack thereof) did not fit the decision task required of the user. In the case of metadata, it appears that this capability does not meet the task needs of the users due to insufficient resources. The users and administrators seem to understand what *metadata* capabilities are needed, but sufficient resources are not currently allocated to create and maintain these capabilities. Capabilities related to *explanations* and *qualitative data* may be more difficult to achieve because the required capabilities have not been readily identified. Thus, both sufficient resources are required and research is needed on how to provide these capabilities.

The difference in strategy selection between the two groups of users, analysts and advisors, appeared to be related to incentives. While neither group of users was provided with explicit incentives to pursue the desired strategy, implicit incentives in the form of task involvement appeared to moderate strategy selection. Analysts were highly involved in their tasks due to the lengthy nature of the task and their high accountability for the decision outcome. As a result, they were willing to select a more effortful strategy that would improve the quality of their decision. The advisors, however, were not as involved due to the shorter duration of the task and a lower level of accountability for the task outcome. Thus, in some cases, these advisors would select a strategy requiring less effort rather than a more effective one.

The observation that incentives do influence strategy selection may appear to differ from Todd and Benbasat's experimental findings (1999). In their study, incentives were explicitly manipulated by varying the reward for completing the task, but because it was an experimental task, it was difficult to create a high level of involvement. The user's experience level also seemed to affect strategy selection. Based upon these findings, the DSS-decision performance model could benefit from an additional construct in the task-technology fit research stream, *individual characteristics*. This construct includes the dimension of user expertise and could offer a theoretical explanation for the equivocal evidence on the influence of incentives. Further research on incentives, the desired level of involvement, and individual characteristics would provide more insight into how companies can better ensure the desired decision performance.

This explanatory case study provides some needed insight into how organizations are using large-scale decision-making support systems to provide decision-making support and illuminates future areas of research. While the DSS-decision performance model provides some descriptive and prescriptive insight on individual decision-making in DW-DSS, it appears that the explanatory power of the model could be improved by adding *individual characteristics* as a construct and incorporating metadata, explanations, and qualitative data as explicit dimensions of the DSS *capability* construct. A first step in future research should be the identification and validation of the construct dimensions in an extended version of the DSS-decision performance model. Additional areas of exploration could include the (1) moderating effect of incentives on decision strategy and performance, (2) understanding the types of explanations that are most effective for certain tasks, (3) developing appropriate methods for capturing, transforming, and interpreting qualitative data, and (4) a more detailed analysis of task-technology fit in DW-DSS.

REFERENCES

Benbasat, I., Goldstein, D., & Meade, M. (1987). The Case Research Strategy in Studies of Information Systems. *MIS Quarterly*, 11(3), 369-386.

Bolloju, N. (1996). Formulation of Qualitative Models Using Fuzzy Logic. *Decision Support Systems*, 17(4), 275-299.

Bonoma, T. (1985). Case Research in Marketing: Opportunities and Problems. *Journal of Marketing Research*, 22(2), 199-208.

Cooper, B., Watson, H., Wixom, B., & Goodhue, D. (2000). Data Warehousing Supports Corporate Strategy at First American Corporation. *MIS Quarterly*, 24(4), 547-467.

Datta, A. & Thomas, H. (1999). The Cube Data Mode: A Conceptual Model and Algebra for On-Line Analytical Processing in Data Warehouses. *Decision Support Systems*, 27(3), 289-301.

Drew, J., Mani, D., Betz, A., & Datta, P. (2001). Targeting Customers with Statistical and Data-Mining Techniques. *Journal of Service Research*, 3(3), 205-219.

Gardner, S. (1998). Building the Data Warehouse. *Communications of the ACM*, 41(9), 52-60.

Glassey, K. (1998). Seducing the End User. *Communications of the ACM*, 41(9), 62-69.

Goodhue, D. & Thompson, R. (1995). Task-Technology Fit and Individual Performance. *MIS Quarterly*, 19(2), 213-236.

Gray, P. & Watson, H. (1998). *Decision Support in the Data Warehouse*. Upper Saddle River, NJ: Prentice Hall PTR.

Gregor, S. & Benbasat, I. (1999). Explanations from Intelligent Systems: Theoretical Foundations and Implications for Practice. *MIS Quarterly*, 23(4), 497-530.

Hoffman, T. (2001). Conference Attendees: CRM Initiatives May Miss Their Marks. *ComputerWorld*, 35(9), 7.

Huck, S. & Cormier, W. (1996). *Reading Statistics and Research*. New York: HarperCollins.

Inmon, W. (1992). *Building the Data Warehouse*. New York: Wiley.

Inmon, W. (1998). Enterprise Meta Data. *DM Review*. Retrieved February 11, 2002: http://www.dmreview.com/master.cfm?NavID=198 &EdID=2480.

Jarvenpaa, S. (1989). The Effect of Task & Graphical Format Congruence on Information Processing Strategies & Decision Making Performance. *Management Science*, 35(3), 285-303.

Kalakota, R. & Robinson, M. (1999). *e-Business: Roadmap for Success*. Addison-Wesley.

Keen, P. & Scott-Morton, M. (1978). *Decision Support Systems: An Organizational Perspective*. Reading, MA: Addison Wesley.

Makos, R. & Schmarzo, B. (1997). *Retail Decision Support Solutions*. Beaverton, OR: Sequent Computer Systems.

Ngwenyama, O. & Bryson, N. (1999). Eliciting and Mapping Qualitative Preferences to Numeric Rankings. *European Journal of Operational Research*, 116(3), 487-497.

Payne, J. (1982). Contingent Decision Behavior. *Psychological Bulletin*, 92(2), 382-402.

Romano, N. & Fjermestand, J. (2002). Electronic Commerce CRM: An Assessment of Research. *International Journal of Electronic Commerce*, 6(2), 61-114.

Rudensteiner, A. & Zhang, X. (2000). Maintaining Data Warehouses Over Changing Sources. *Communications of the ACM*, 43(6), 57-62.

Sen, A. & Jacob, V. (1998). Industrial-strength data warehouse. *Communications of the ACM*, 41(9), 28-31.

Shaw, M., Subramaniam, C., Tan, G., & Welge, M. (2001). Knowledge Management and Data Mining for Marketing. *Decision Support Systems*, 31(1), 127-137.

Sprague, R. & Carlson, E. (1982). *Building Effective Decision Support Systems*. Englewood Cliffs, NJ: Prentice Hall.

Todd, P. & Benbasat, I. (1991). An Experimental Investigation of the Impact of Computer-Based Decision Aids. *Information Systems Research*, 2(2), 87-115.

Todd, P. & Benbasat, I. (1992). An Experimental Investigation of the Impact of Computer-Based DSS on Processing Effort. *MIS Quarterly*, 16(3), 373-393.

Todd, P. & Benbasat, I. (1993). Decision-Makers, DSS, and Decision Making Effort: An Experimental Investigation. *INFORS*, 31(2), 1-21.

Todd, P. & Benbasat, I. (1994a). The Influence of DSS on Choice Strategies: An Experimental Analysis of the Role of Cognitive Effort. *Organizational Behavior and Human Decision Processes*, 60(1) 36-74.

Todd, P. & Benbasat, I. (1994b). The Influence of DSS on Choice Strategies Under Conditions of High Cognitive Load. *IEEE Trans. on Systems, Man, and Cybernetics*, 24(4), 537-547.

Todd, P. & Benbasat, I. (1999). Evaluating the Impact of DSS, Cognitive Effort, and Incentives on Strategy Selection. *Information Systems Research*, 10(4), 356-374.

Watson, H. & Haley, B. (1998). Managerial Considerations. *Comm. of the ACM*, 41(9), 32-37.

Wells, J., Fuerst, W., & Choobineh, J. (1999). Managing Information Technology (IT) for One-to-One Customer Interaction. *Information & Management*, 35(1), 53-62.

Wixom, B. & Watson, B. (2001). An Empirical Investigation of the Factors Affecting Data Warehousing Success. *MIS Quarterly*, 25(1), 1-25.

Ye, L. & Johnson, P. (1995). The Impact of Explanation Facilities on User Acceptance of Expert System Advice. *MIS Quarterly*, 19(2), 157-172.

Yin, R. (1994). *Case Study Research Design & Methods*. Sage Publications.

Zeleny, M. (1983). Qualitative Vs. Quantitative Modeling in Decision Making. *Human Systems Management*, 4(1), 39-42.

ENDNOTES

[1]   Some of the literature and concepts described in this chapter were presented at the Hawaii International Conference on System Sciences Meeting, Big Island, Hawaii, January 7-10, 2002.

This work was previously published in the Information Resources Management Journal, 15(11), 16-32, Oct-Dec © 2002.

Chapter XIII

E-CRM Analytics:
The Role of Data Integration

Hamid R. Nemati, University of North Carolina, USA

Christopher D. Barko, University of North Carolina, USA

Ashfaaq Moosa, University of North Carolina, USA

ABSTRACT

Electronic Customer Relationship Management (e-CRM) Analytics is the process of analyzing and reporting online customer/visitor behavior patterns with the objective of acquiring and retaining customers through stronger customer relationships. To better understand the role of data integration in achieving the goals of e-CRM, the authors conducted a study by means of a survey. The results of this study propose that although online, offline and external data integration has its complexities, the value added is significant. This survey of CRM professionals is composed of two parts. The first part investigated the nature of the data integrated and the data architecture deployed. The second part analyzed the technological and organizational value added with respect to the e-CRM initiative. The findings suggest that organizations that integrate data from various customer touch-points have significantly higher benefits, user satisfaction and return on their investment (ROI) than those that do not. Additional insights are also presented exploring the role of data integration in e-CRM projects at both business to business (B2B) and business-to-consumer (B2C) firms. For organizations implementing e-CRM, this study reveals that data integration is worth their time, money and efforts.

INTRODUCTION

With the advent of the World Wide Web (web) and electronic commerce (e-commerce), there has been a dramatic change in market dynamics in that customers, both end users and businesses, can check prices and buy from suppliers around the globe, regardless of time and distance (Stephens, 1999). Due to this surge in purchasing power, companies must view their data in a more strategic light. In addition, there is a growing trend of organizations leveraging their data resources by developing and deploying data mining technologies to enhance their decision-making capabilities (Eckerson & Watson, 2001). To address this need, organizations are implementing Organizational Data Mining (ODM) technologies, which are defined as technologies that leverage data mining tools to enhance the decision-making process by transforming data into valuable and actionable knowledge to gain a competitive advantage (Nemati & Barko, 2001). ODM spans a wide array of technologies, including but not limited to e-business intelligence, data analysis, CRM, EIS, digital dashboards, information portals, etc.

As a result of these marketplace trends, organizations must begin implementing customer-centric metrics as opposed to solely adopting product-centric metrics (Cutler & Sterne, 2001). This scenario has triggered increased interest in the implementation and use of customer-oriented ODM technologies such as Customer Relationship Management (CRM) systems. CRM can be defined as the adoption, through the use of enabling technology, of customer-focused sales, marketing, and service processes (Forsyth, 2001). CRM is the process that manages the interaction between a company and its customers. The goal of CRM is to create a long-term, profitable relationship with all of an organization's customers. It is more than just a software package — it is a business process enabled by technology. CRM vendors label these packages as CRM systems because their main goal is to analyze customer behavior and identify actionable patterns. This information is then used to improve goods and services offered to customers while increasing profitability through better relationships. CRM software provides the functionality that enables a firm to make the customer the focal point of all organizational decisions. CRM technologies incorporate some of the best-in-class processes for features such as customer service, product configuration, field service, and customer analysis.

CRM has become a key process in the strengthening of customer loyalty and in helping businesses obtain greater profit from low-value customers. The manner in which companies interact with their customers has changed tremendously over the past few years. Customers no longer guarantee their loyal patronage, and this has resulted in organizations attempting to better understand them, predict their future needs, and decrease response times in fulfilling their demands. This is extremely important to retaining customers since, according to common industry knowledge, the cost of acquiring a new customer is typically much higher than retaining an existing one.

Most companies are now realizing and understanding the value of collecting customer data but are faced with the challenges of using this knowledge to create intelligent pathways back to the customer. Most data mining technologies and techniques for recognizing patterns within data help businesses sift through the meaningless data and allow them to anticipate customers' requirements and expectations, manage channel partnerships and other relationships more profitably. These technologies also enable companies to maintain customer privacy and confidentiality while gaining the benefits of profiling, calculating the economic value of the CRM tool, and discovering the key factors that would make or break the CRM project. By integrating these data mining tools with CRM software, organizations are able to analyze very large databases to extract new customer insights for stronger and more profitable relationships. Data mining by itself is not a business solution; it is just an enabling technology. However, by assimilating data mining technology with CRM, organizational data can be transformed into valuable knowledge to enhance business decisions that optimize customer interactions. For example, consider a catalog retailer that wants to determine to whom they should send current information about new products. The information integrated into the data mining and CRM process is contained in a historical database containing prior customer transactions along with their demographic and lifestyle attributes. This information is collected each time there is any type of interaction with the customer, whether it be through sales, calls, or complaints (Teerlink, 1999).

Similarly, e-CRM can be defined as the process of acquiring a thorough understanding of an organization's online visitors/customers in order to offer them the right product at the right price. e-CRM analytics is the process of analyzing and reporting online customer/visitor behavior patterns with the objective of acquiring and retaining customers through stronger customer relationships. Prior research has found that in order to understand online customers, a company must integrate its data from both online and offline sources (Mena, 2001). In similar fashion, our study also demonstrates that a company cannot thoroughly understand its customers if it neglects integrating its customers' behavioral data from both the online and offline channels. In order to have this complete customer viewpoint, it is imperative that organizations integrate data from each customer touch-point. Our chapter elaborates on this critical issue of integrating data from multiple sources and its enabling role in facilitating successful and valuable e-CRM analytics.

In exploring these issues, we first conduct a literature review and provide a foundation for our research. Then we present our research framework and associated propositions. Next we detail our research methodology utilized in our study. Finally, we present and discuss our findings and their organizational implications.

RESEARCH FOUNDATIONS AND FRAMEWORK

Several studies (Brancheau, Janz & Wetherbe, 1996; Neiderman, Brancheau & Wetherbe, 1991; Brancheau & Wetherbe, 1987; Dickinson, Leithesier, Wetherbe & Nechis, 1984; Ball & Harris, 1982; Martin, 1982) show that data has been ranked as one of the top priorities for IS executives. With the emergence of web technologies, the collection and storage of data, both internal and external to an organization, has increased dramatically. Internal data refers to data generated from systems within an organization, such as legacy and online transactional processing (OLTP) systems. External data refers to data that is not generated by systems within an organization, such as government census data, industry benchmark data, consumer psychographic data and economic data. For instance, consumer demographic and psychographic data is available for each of the 200 million adults in the United States, and product-based data is available for the 18 million businesses in the United States. If this data is collected, integrated, and formatted properly, it can prove to be immensely beneficial to a firm in better understanding its customers (Rendlemen, 2001). External data should be leveraged in a CRM system to the extent that it adds additional value to the already existing internal organizational data.

Companies approach consumers through various marketing channels. Traditionally, each channel or functional area has been managed separately, and all data pertaining to a channel is housed in its own system in a proprietary format (Eckerson & Watson, 2001; SAS Institute, 2001). Technically, data integration can be defined as the standardization of data definitions and structures through the use of a common conceptual schema across a collection of data sources (Heimbigner & McLeod, 1985; Litwin, Mark & Roussopoulos, 1990). This implies that data is accessible across functional areas, making data in different corporate databases accessible and consistent (Martin, 1986). For example, if a traditional 'bricks and mortar' company deploys a website and decides to integrate the web data with its legacy systems, it has to consider various technological and design issues such as data requirements, data quality, data inconsistencies, synchronization, security, etc. Once these issues are addressed, an organization must present the data in a way that is consistent and conducive to viewing across heterogeneous enterprise departments (Johnson, 2000). In a B2C company, an example of data integration might be creating an integrated customer database to enable the sales and manufacturing departments to access a single source of customer information even though they each require their own view of the customer.

The volume of data in an organization is estimated to double every 18 to 24 months (Experian Corporation, 2002). Issues arise when determining which piece of information about a particular customer is accurate, up to date and relevant. In deciding on which parts of the data should be used for analysis, the issues of inconsistent data formats, metadata inconsistencies, different levels of data granularity and other such data inconsistencies need to be resolved. This is a complex and continuous procedure that requires a significant amount of resources.

Even though data integration is such a complex task, organizations successfully tackling this issue have derived immense benefits from it. For example, Staples Inc. (SAS Institute, 2001) integrated all customer and sales data from their store, catalog and online efforts into a common database. Integrating all this information allows Staples' marketers to monitor and predict how customers migrate from one channel to another or how they utilize the channels to get what they need. Staples can identify what products are purchased at a store versus their Staples Direct catalog or through their online store. This valuable information gives Staples an edge over its competition and allows marketers to (1) target specific products to customers through preferred channels, and (2) give them the ability to perform cross- and up-selling to customers across multiple channels.

A recent survey from Forrester Research (Baudisch, 2000) suggests that marketing professionals spend 44 percent of their website promotion budgets on offline media. This finding raises a number of allocation questions. How do organizations determine: (1) which marketing media to use, (2) where their customers spend most of their time, and (3) what their customer's lifestyles are? To better answer these questions, it is essential for online marketers to get a 360-degree (holistic) view of their customers (Experian Corporation, 2002). This holistic view requires organizations to integrate their data to track every customer transaction (customer purchases, returns and complaints) in all customer touch-points (e-mail, phone, online and direct mail).

A survey by Jupiter Media Metrix (Collins, 2001) revealed that 70 percent of online customers would not shop at the offline store if they received poor service at the website. Further, the survey found that only 18 percent of the clicks 'n bricks retailers (those with both online and traditional operations) offered customers the convenience of integrating their online and offline accounts, as well as the ability to buy online and pick up or return merchandise at the company's local store. Since customer service via e-mail is poor in the case of most retailers, customers want to voice their concerns offline (Collins, 2001).

In another study (Mena, 2001), online retailers spend an average of $100 to $250 to acquire a new customer. On average, this customer will spend about $24 with the retailer, and then more than likely never return as a patron. It was found that only 35 percent of buyers make a second purchase at a site they initially purchase from. These grim figures suggest that if you want to survive in today's competitive online marketplace and be profitable, you need to go beyond cookies and meta tags — you need to learn what your online customers are like offline (Mena, 2001).

Case studies (Doll & Torkzadeh, 1988) have shown that data integration is useful and cost justifiable under two circumstances: (1) when the interdependence between functional units increases, and (2) when the tasks and environment under which these sub-units operate is more or less fixed, that is, there will not be short-term changes to the functional information systems to address changing needs. In today's dynamic economy and rampant increase in the number of customer attritions, organizations must be cognizant of customer preferences and demands to optimally manage their delicate yet vital relationship with them. This leads us to our first two propositions.

Proposition 1: The more data sources a company integrates, the better the customer insight, thus creating more value for the company.

Proposition 2: Integrating online data with data from the firms' offline operations will lead to better customer insight, thus creating more value for the company.

Timeliness of data is an important component of user satisfaction (Doll & Torkzadeh, 1988; Ballou, Wang, Pazer & Tayi, 1998; Adams & Song, 1989). Users need to have up-to-date information about customers' needs and preferences (Swift, 2002) to thoroughly understand and satisfy those needs. Traditional measures of customer-centric metrics such as recency, frequency and monetary statistics need to be incorporated into the analysis. Without integrated data (from online and offline sources), these statistics will not be accurate. Traditionally, it was acceptable for organizations to update their customer database on a monthly or quarterly basis. But in today's fast-paced electronic economy where critical decisions are made daily, companies strive for more current information, requiring systems to update their databases much more frequently (daily, hourly, or in real time). This leads us to our next proposition.

Proposition 3: Data that is more frequently refreshed will lead to better customer insight, thus creating more value for the company.

Past experiences or product quality are not the only reasons why customers make purchases. There are factors external to an organization such as new marketplace competitors, economic factors, competitor promotions and other similar factors that alter our buying preferences. In his book *Web Farming*, Richard Hackathorn (1998) advocates that organizations must integrate external data into its data warehouse to gain a complete picture of its business. Sources of external data may include government databases of customer demographics, census data, zip codes and weather data. This leads us to our next proposition.

Proposition 4: Integrating external data with internal data will lead to better customer insight, thus creating more value for the company.

A recent Data Warehousing Institute Industry Report (Eckerson & Watson, 2001) found that organizations are challenged when integrating web technologies into their existing systems. A few of the reasons behind this challenge are scalability issues, managing large clickstream databases, immaturity of technology, lack of experience, and the complexity of modeling web data for analysis. But despite the integration challenges, the benefits to be realized are enormous.

In a recent survey of 800 information technology executives by the Meta Group, four out of five companies did not have a 360-degree view of their customers even though 92 percent of the firms surveyed ranked increasing customer knowledge as a top priority (Cooke, 2000). This study goes on to report that although business and information technology managers in these companies are interested in obtaining customer knowledge, a number of serious obstacles prevent them from doing so, i.e., building the right data architecture and obtaining useful analytical tools to integrate and use this data effectively.

For successful CRM analytics, an enterprise-wide, customer-centric data repository should be utilized rather than a channel specific data repository (Beck & Summer, 2001; Swift, 2002; Johnson, 2000). Vasset (2001) suggests an enterprise-wide, customer-centric data warehouse should be the foundation of any CRM initiative. This leads us to our last proposition.

Proposition 5: Deploying an enterprise-wide data warehouse as the CRM backbone will lead to better customer insight, thus creating more value for the company.

Research in CRM is growing as it is gaining greater acceptance within organizations. CRM has received considerable attention from researchers in many diverse disciplines. Although there is a growing pool of literature that addresses many aspects of the application of CRM for business solutions, there are few scholarly publications that focus on the study of CRM from an e-commerce perspective. Given the complexity of the issues involved in data integration, the enormous benefits that e-CRM can offer and the role data integration plays in achieving e-CRM's goals, we developed an e-CRM Value Framework (see Figure 1) to study data integration issues and their impact on the overall value attained from e-CRM projects. Through this framework, we empirically test our five propositions to determine the impact each factor has on creating e-CRM value for an organization. The results from four of the five factors support this new framework.

RESEARCH METHODOLOGY

Our study comprised two parts. The first part was a literature review where we looked at the results of previous studies on data integration and its

Figure 1: The e-CRM Value Framework

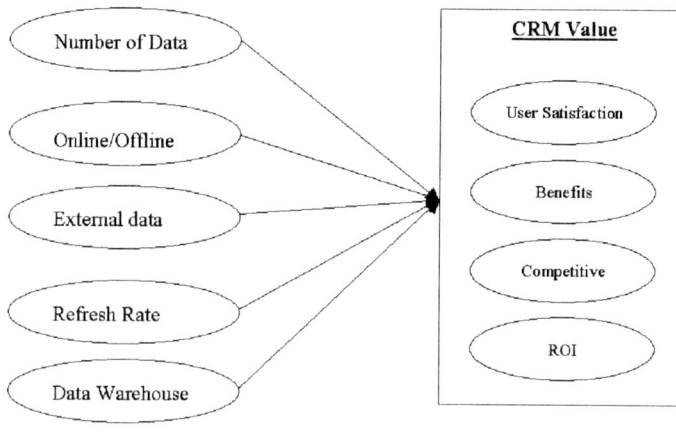

inherent complexity. Based on this literature review, we designed a questionnaire to explore organizational data sources, how these data sources are integrated, the data architectures utilized for this integration and the key integration issues organizations faced. The second part of the survey addressed e-CRM topics such as specific benefits realized, ROI expectations, user satisfaction levels and the creation or absence of a new competitive advantage. Demographic information was also collected on respondents and their organizations.

An initial survey instrument containing 17 questions was reviewed by three industry professionals to ensure appropriate and unambiguous content. The objective of this survey was to gain an insight into the various data sources organizations integrate and to reveal that data collection and integration for e-CRM, despite its complexity, can create value for an organization. Respondents were asked to identify benefits they had achieved or expected to achieve from their e-CRM project. Specifically, we probed responders on specific data integration procedures in their organization such as number of data sources integrated, integration of online and offline sources, integration of external data, data refresh rates and whether these data sources were centralized (data warehouse) or decentralized.

Additional survey questions solicited information regarding ROI, user satisfaction levels, competitive advantages, and both the quantity and types of data sources integrated in respondents' e-CRM projects. These questions utilized a Likert scale to allow users to rate the success of their e-CRM initiative based on four equally weighted factors — ROI, competitive advantage, business benefits attained and user satisfaction.

Next we transformed the responses from the questions about ROI, user satisfaction, competitive advantage and benefits realized into a derived measure representing Total Value to an organization. We defined Total Value as being a combination of ROI, competitive advantage, business benefits attained and user satisfaction. The equally weighted scores obtained from these questions were added together and used as a measure of overall value generated by the e-CRM initiative. This Total Value figure was calculated as follows: Total Value = total benefits + user satisfaction + competitive advantage + ROI. The total benefits figure was calculated by summing the total number of benefits reported. This value ranged from 0 to 12. Some of the benefits reported were the increased ability to cross-sell/upsell to customers, enhanced product/service customization, increased customer retention, and better customer service and inventory management. User satisfaction of the new e-CRM system ranged from 1 (not satisfied) to 7 (very satisfied). Measuring competitive advantage was calculated as the likelihood (1 = very low, 7 = almost certain) the e-CRM project enabled the company to achieve a sustainable competitive advantage. And measuring ROI was calculated as the likelihood (1 = very low, 7 = almost certain) the e-CRM initiative generated the expected ROI.

In measuring each organization's Total Value, we argue that a larger number represents more total value to the organization than a smaller number. For example, an organization with an e-CRM system that delivered eight benefits (8), created very satisfied users (7), enabled a competitive advantage (7), and delivered close to expected ROI (6) (for a Total Value = 28) would be much more valuable to an organization than a system which delivered three benefits (3), unhappy users (1), an unlikely competitive advantage (1) and unsatisfactory ROI (1) (for a Total Value = 6). Using this basis for Total Value, we conducted statistical analyses using ANOVA to determine the correlation between our framework's five e-CRM factors (propositions) and the Total Value the project created for the organization.

A website was developed for the survey and hosted at the Department of Information Systems and Operations Management at The University of North Carolina at Greensboro. A request to complete the survey was distributed to about 340 entities in the Information Systems and Operations Management Department database of organizations. This database contains data about organizations, consultants, and professionals specializing in CRM technologies. A total of 115 useable responses were received and analyzed from both U.S. and international organizations, providing a 34 percent response rate.

RESULTS AND DISCUSSIONS

Demographics

Figure 2 reveals demographic information from the survey respondents. Respondents work in a wide variety of industries with the majority (48%) from CRM consulting/vendor firms and 30 percent from the technology, transportation, healthcare, advertising and financial industries. Job categories for respondents range from top management to business managers with the majority employed as CRM professionals (55%) followed by analysts (17%). Organizational revenues represent a fair mix of both small and large companies. Forty-four percent reported sales of less than a $100 million while 37 percent reported sales of greater than $500 million. In regards to CRM project statuses, the majority of respondents (39%) had begun their CRM initiative over a year ago while 24 percent had started their CRM initiative less than three months ago. The majority of respondents (65%) were also clicks 'n bricks (web and store) companies while 23 percent were purely web retailers. In addition, 45 percent of respondents worked for organizations whose primary web operations were B2B (business-to-business) while 35 percent worked for organizations classified as B2C (business-to-consumer).

Figure 2: Respondent Demographics (N=115)

Industry	% Responders
Technology - Software/Services	48%
Financial	12%
Transportation	5%
HealthCare	4%
Advertising	4%
Utilities	3%
Publishing	2%
Other	20%

Position	% Responders
CRM Professional/ Consultant	55%
Analyst	20%
CIO	8%
DBA	8%
Business Manager	6%
CEO	2%
Other	9%

Revenue	% Responders
<100 million	44%
101 - 500 million	19%
501 - 1 billion	11%
>1 billion	26%

Website Type	% Responders
B2B	45%
B2C	35%
C2C	1%
Other	19%

Figure 3: B2B vs. B2C Analysis (N = 115)

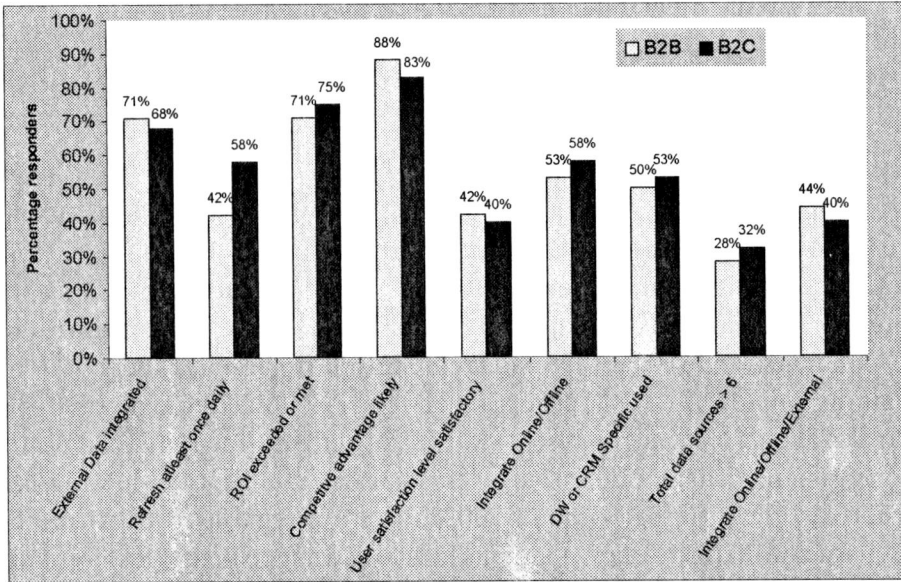

B2B vs. B2C

Next we conducted a cross-tabular analysis to gain better insights into B2B and B2C organizations. As previously noted, 45 percent worked for B2B companies and 35 percent were from B2C companies. There was one C2C (consumer-to-consumer) firm while the remainders comprised the "other" category, which we presume were information-based companies such as news agencies and magazines whose revenue is primarily supported through advertising.

The survey data were analyzed across nine categories (see Figure 3). The only category that showed a significant difference between the two types of firms was the data refresh rate. Forty-two percent of B2B companies refreshed their data at least once a day while 58 percent of B2C companies did the same. The other categories revealed very similar results when comparing the two types of firms.

Next we looked at the sources of data integrated by B2B and B2C firms (see Figure 4). Figure 4 reveals that, in general, B2B firms integrate more data than B2C firms. The top four sources of data collected were customer demographics, online sales, offline sales and customer communication data such as call center data, e-mail data, etc.

Figure 4: B2B vs. B2C Data Sources (N = 115)

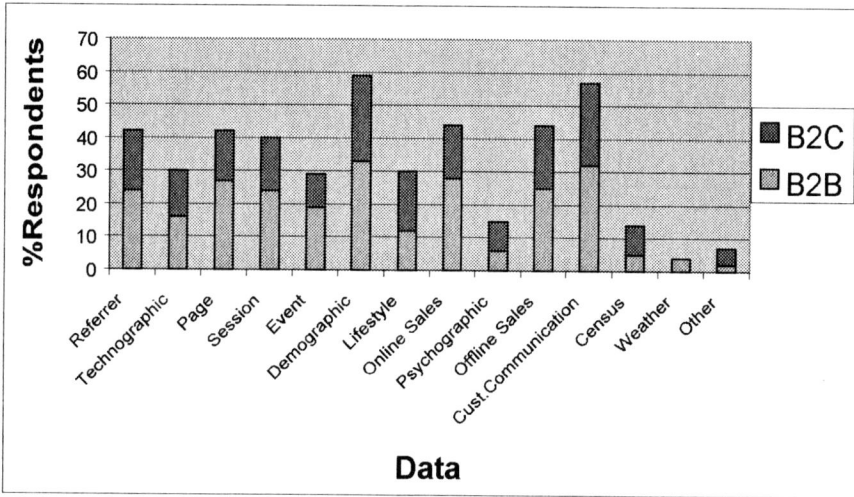

Next we compared the challenges and problems encountered between the firms (see Figure 5). What we observed was that the top three problems faced by B2C firms were lack of planning, change management and organizational politics. The top three problems B2B firms faced were change management, organizational politics and lack of user buy-in. It is interesting to note that all

Figure 5: B2B vs. B2C Problems (N = 115)

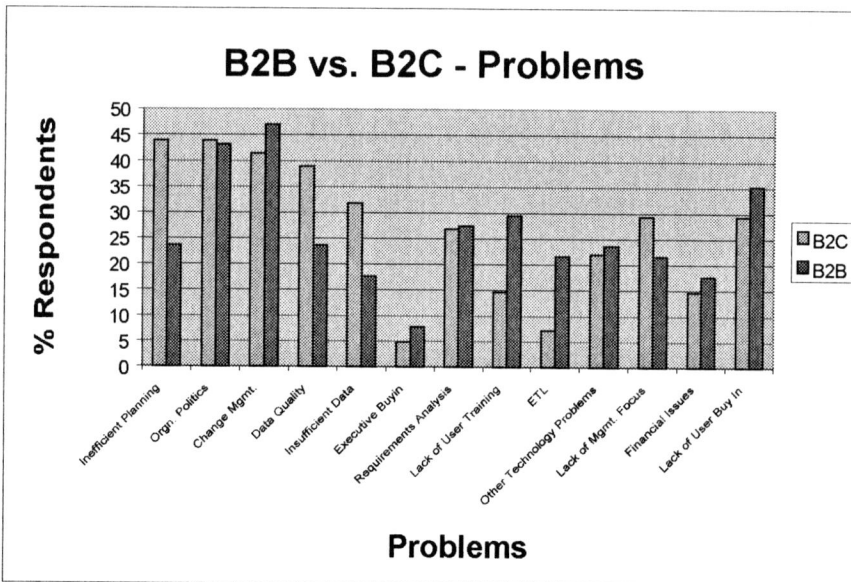

Figure 6: B2B vs. B2C Benefits (N = 115)

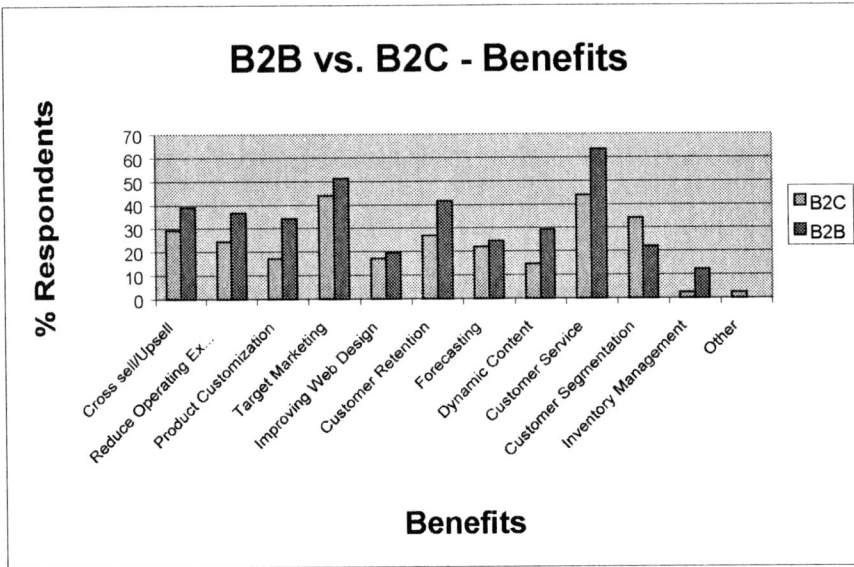

of the top three problems of both B2B and B2C firms are organizational problems, not technical. As far as technical problems, 25 percent of B2B firms versus 40 percent of B2C firms identified data quality as a problem. In addition, 30 perent of B2B firms lack user training while only 15 percent of B2C firms reported the same problem.

Figure 6 displays the benefits attained between the two types of firms. In general, more B2B firms benefit from their CRM implementations than B2C firms. One interesting findings is that 55 percent of B2B firms reported customer service benefits while only 38 percent of B2C firms reported the same benefit. Apparently B2B organizations are more effective at servicing their customers than B2C companies, which might be due to the less complexity in servicing the relatively lower volumes of business customers in comparison to the much larger numbers of consumer customers. We previously reported that one of the biggest problems with B2C firms' CRM projects was lack of planning. This problem may be a key reason behind the overall lower benefits realized in B2C firms. Although Figure 5 shows that 35 percent of B2B firms reported users not buying into the project, Figure 6 implies that in general, B2B firms achieve significantly more benefits from their CRM projects.

Table 1: ANOVA results (N = 115); Correlation of Measure vs. Total Value

Measure	DF	Sum of Squares	Mean Squares	F Ratio	Prob > F	Significant ($p <= 0.05$)
(1) Number of Sources	13	924.13	71.09	2.376	0.008	Yes
(2) Integrate Data	1	189.90	189.90	5.713	0.019	Yes
(3) Daily Refresh	1	35.03	35.03	1.012	0.317	No
(4) External Data	1	132.26	132.26	3.919	0.050	Yes
(5) DW or CRM database	1	219.10	219.10	6.643	0.011	Yes

Proposition Testing

See Table 1 for ANOVA results and proposition findings. All propositions were found to be significant ($p <= 0.05$) in their relationship to Total Value except for proposition 3, which proposes more Total Value if data is refreshed daily. A more detailed explanation and analysis of each proposition follows.

For proposition 1, respondents were asked to specify the number of data sources they integrated into the data repository for the purposes of their e-CRM project. The total number of data sources integrated was calculated. Using ANOVA, we determined the relationship between the total number of data sources integrated, and the Total Value was significant ($p = 0.008$). This finding suggests that Total Value increases as organizations integrate more data sources in their e-CRM projects.

An interesting insight was that only 22 percent of respondents integrated all four dimensions of clickstream data, as described by Ralph Kimball and Richard Merz (2000), namely session, page, event and referrer. The session data type is a high-level diagnosis of the complete web session. Examples of segmenting web sessions by customer behavior includes "Product Ordered," "Quick Hit and Gone," "Unhappy Visitor" or "Recent, Frequent and Intense Return Shopper" (Kimball, 2000). Referrer data identifies how the website visitor arrived at the website. A simple descriptive analyses of the percentages of different ways a visitor arrived at a website provides valuable information about how to better allocate an organization's advertising budget. The page dimension stores data about the various attributes of each web page visited. For example, some attributes would be the page name (Product X Description, Payment Page, etc.), when it was visited, how long the user stayed on that page and where the user went from that page.

For Proposition 2, respondents were asked whether or not they integrated offline data with their online data. Sixty-two percent said they integrated these data sources while 30 percent did not. The remaining 8 percent were unsure. Using ANOVA, we determined the relationship between those who integrated offline and online data and Total Value was significant ($p = 0.019$). Therefore, we propose that organizations that integrate both online and offline data in their e-CRM projects have significantly more benefits than organizations that do not integrate their data.

For Proposition 3, respondents were asked how often they updated/refreshed the data in their data repositories. We segmented all responses into two groups — those who refreshed their data at least once a day and those who did not. Using ANOVA, we determined the relationship between frequently refreshed data (at least daily) and Total Value was not significant ($p = 0.317$). Therefore, we propose that organizations that refresh their data at least once a day do not have a significantly higher value than organizations that refresh their data less frequently. This proposition was rejected.

For Proposition 4, respondents were asked whether or not they integrated external data into their data warehouse. Seventy-four percent integrated external data in some form while 26 percent did not. Of those who did integrate, 62 percent said that external data comprised less than 20 percent of the total data used for analysis. Using ANOVA, we determined the relationship between integrating external data and Total Value was significant ($p = 0.050$). Therefore, we propose that organizations that integrate external data in their e-CRM projects enjoy significantly more benefits than organizations that do not integrate external data.

For Proposition 5, respondents were asked to identify the data repository used for their e-CRM systems. Fifty-one percent of companies implemented legacy databases, operational data stores (ODSs) or data marts as their data repositories, while forty-nine percent implemented CRM specific databases or data warehouses as their data repositories. Using ANOVA, we determined the relationship between the Total Value derived by these two segments was significant ($p = 0.011$). We discovered the total value derived by the group using a data repository was significantly lower than the group who used a data warehouse or CRM specific database. Therefore, we propose that organizations that implement a data warehouse or CRM-specific database as their e-CRM data repository enjoy significantly more benefits than organizations that do not implement these types of data repositories.

In summary, the above propositions show that data integration is essential to accurately assessing customer needs and thus allowing the firm to achieve greater CRM and organizational value. Therefore, we propose our e-CRM Value Framework (minus Proposition 3 — daily data refresh) is a model for generating greater total benefits for organizations engaging in e-CRM projects. To achieve the greatest amount of benefits, we suggest organizations use a data warehouse as their e-CRM data repository. This data warehouse should contain a healthy number of data sources and house all integrated data including online, offline and external data. With this architecture in place, companies are able to achieve greater profitability by obtaining a better understanding of its customers and its relationships with them.

CONCLUSION

We have presented a new e-CRM Value Framework to better examine the significance of integrating data from all customer touch-points with the goal of improving customer relationships and creating additional value for the firm. Various issues such as number of data sources: integrating offline, online and external data; and data architectures are discussed. We also compared and contrasted the CRM efforts of B2B versus B2C organizations and revealed some of the challenges and opportunities each faces. Our findings suggest that despite the cost and complexity, data integration for e-CRM projects contributes to a better understanding of the customer and leads to higher ROI, greater number of benefits, improved user satisfaction and a more likely chance of attaining a competitive advantage. Thus, when all else is equal, a company's Total Value increases when a company integrates data from online, offline and external sources.

We hope that our empirical research and findings can assist practitioners and managers in identifying more efficient and effective ways of creating CRM value through data integration. It should be noted that we have only discussed the data-related issues of integration. Future research on this topic should investigate and identify managerial, financial, environmental and strategic issues that affect organizational value. In addition, other technical issues to explore include the impact of data quality and the integration role of web services.

REFERENCES

Adams, C. R. & Song, J. H. (1989). Integrating Decision Technologies. *MIS Quarterly,* (June), 199-209.

Ball, L. & Harris, R. (1982). SMIS Member: A Membership Analysis. *MIS Quarterly*, 6(1), 19-38.

Ballou, D., Wang, R., Pazer, H., & Tayi, G.K. (1998). Modeling Information Manufacturing Systems to Determine Information Product Quality. *Management Science*, 44(4), 462-484.

Baudisch, P. (2000). Getting to E-Yes: Building Customer Relationships Online. www.entreworld.org.

Beck, B. & Summer, J. (2001). Data Warehousing Horizons: CRM: Not Just Operational and Collaborative. *DMReview*, (September).

Brancheau, J.C. & Wetherbe, J.C. (1987). Key Issues in Information Systems Management. *MIS Quarterly*, 11(1), 23-46.

Brancheau, J.C., Janz, B.D. & Wetherbe, J.C. (1996). Key Issues in Information Systems Management: 1994-95 SIM Delphi Results. *MIS Quarterly*, 20(2), 225-242.

Collins, A. (2001). Customer Service counts. March 21, Business 2.0.

Cooke, B. (2000). Companies in the Dark about Customers. *Information Week*, (May 1).

Cutler, M. & Sterne, J. (2001). *E-Metrics: Business Metrics for the New Economy*. NetGenesis Corp. www.netgen.com/emetrics.

Eckerson, W. & Watson, H. (2001). Harnessing Customer Information for Strategic Advantage: Technical Challenges and Business Solutions. Industry Study 2000, Executive Summary, The Data Warehousing Institute.

Experian Corporation. (2002). *CRM Whitepaper*. www.uk.experian. com/assets/crm_whitepaper1.pdf.

Dickinson, G.W., Leithesier, R.L, Wetherbe, J.C. & Nechis, M. (1984). Key Information Systems Issues for the 1980s. *MIS Quarterly*, 8, 135-159.

Doll, W.J. & Torkzadeh, G. (1988). The Measurement of End-User Computing Satisfaction. *MIS Quarterly*, (June), 259-274.

Forsyth, R. (2001). *Successful CRM: Global Trends*. (June 22). http://www.crm-forum.com/library/conf/con-031/.

Hackathorn, R. (1998). *Web Farming for the Data Warehouse*. San Francisco, CA: Morgan Kaufmann Publishers.

Heimbigner, D. & McLeod, D. (1985). A Federated Architecture for Information Management. *ACM Transactions on Office Information Systems*, 3(3), 253-278.

Johnson, B. (2000). Fault Lines in CRM: New E-Commerce Business Models and Channel Integration Challenges. *CRM Project*, 1(January 1).

Kimball, R. (2000). The Special Dimensions of the Clickstream. *Intelligent Enterprise*, 3(2).

Kimball, R. & Merz, R. (2000). *The Data Webhouse Toolkit: Building the Web-Enabled Data Warehouse.* NJ: John Wiley & Sons.

Litwin, W., Mark, L., & Roussopoulos, N. (1990). Interoperability of Multiple Autonomous Databases. *ACM Computing Surveys*, 22(3), 267-293.

Martin, E.W. (1982). Critical Success Factors of Chief MIS/DP Executives. *MIS Quarterly*, 6, 1-9.

Martin, J. (1986). Information Engineering, Savant Research Studies, Carnforth, Lancashire, UK.

Mena, J. (2001). Beyond the Shopping Cart. *Intelligent Enterprise*, (March 8).

Neiderman, F., Brancheau, J.C. & Wetherbe, J.C. (1991). Information Systems Management Issues for the 1990s. *MIS Quarterly*, 15, 474-500.

Nemati, H. R. & Barko, C. D. (2001). Issues in Organizational Data Mining: A Survey of Current Practices. *Journal of Data Warehousing*, 6(1), 25-36.

Rendleman, J. (2001). Customer Data Means Money. *Information Week*, (August 20).

SAS Institute. (2001). Staples: Loyal Customers and Killer Marketing. *SAS COM Magazine*, (September/October). www.sas.com.

Stephens, D. (1999). The Globalization of Information Technology in Multinational Corporations. *Information Management Journal*, 33(3), 66.

Swift, R. (2002). Analytical CRM Powers Profitable Relationships: Creating Success by Letting Customers Guide You. *DMReview*, (February).

Teerlink, M. (1999). Beyond Consumerism: Know Your Customers' Needs, Before They Do! (July 26). http://www.crm-forum.com/library/art/art-022/brandframe.html.

Vasset, D. (2001). Using the Data Warehouse to Drive your CRM Effort. (February 23). CIO.com.

This work was previously published in the Journal of Electronic Commerce in Organizations, 1(3), 73-89, July-Sept © 2003.

Glossary

Application Service Provider (ASP): Describes the third-party vendors that host a company's software applications. It's a form of outsourcing.

Balanced Scoreboard: Developed in the early 1990s by international strategy consultant, David Norton and Harvard Business School Accounting Professor, Robert Kaplan. It is a means to measure performance and formulate future strategy for a company. The objectives and measures view organizational performance from four perspectives: financial, customer, internal business process, and learning and growth.

Browser: Software application through which users access the Web; these applications communicate via HTTP, manage HTML, and display certain data types for graphics and sound.

Business Process Reengineering (BPR): The process of introducing a major innovation into an organization's structure or business processes, resulting in possible overhaul of the organization's technological, human, or organizational dimensions.

B2B: Abbreviation for "business to business." It is used to describe software interaction between business partners.

B2C: Abbreviation for "business to consumer."

Cascade Style Sheet (CSS): Enhancement of HTML that adds page layout features to Web documents by specifying a template for graphic elements that can be placed on the page.

Client/Server Architecture: A form of distributed processing in which several computers share resources and are able to communicate with many other computers. A client is a computer used to access shared network resources, and a server is a machine that is attached to the same network that provides clients with these services.

Collaborative Filtering: A personalization service available to Web users that polls their preferences on products and then delivers customized information to the users.

Competitive Intelligence: The activities of an organization in gathering information on its competitors, markets, technologies, and government action.

Customer-Focused Approach: A business approach that pays close attention to customers and their preferences.

Data Manipulation Language (DML): Instructions used with higher-level programming languages to query the contents of a database, store or update information therein, and develop database applications

Data Mart: A database containing data extracted and often summarized from one or more operational systems or from a data warehouse and optimized to support the business analysis needs of a particular unit.

Data Mining: A component of business intelligence decision-support process in which patterns of information in data are discovered through the use of a smart program that automatically searches the database, finds significant patterns and correlations through the use of statistical algorithms, and infers rules from them.

Data Warehouse: A form of data storage geared towards business intelligence that integrates data from various parts of a company. The data in a data warehouse is read-only and tends to include historical as well as current data so that users can perform trend analysis.

Database Management System (DBMS): The software used to specify the logical organization for database and access it.

Decision Support System (DSS): Used in the 1970s and 1980s to describe business systems.

Distributed Data Management: Client/server structure in which all three application components are in the client, with database management distributed between the client and the server.

Distributed Logic: Client/server structure in which the data management is on the server and presentation logic is on the client.

Drill Down/Up: A component of OLAP analysis. The term *drill down*, in the context of data analysis, refers to the process of navigating from less-detailed aggregated information to more granular data. Moving in the opposite direction is called *drill up*.

EFT/POS: A form of electronic funds transfer in which the purchaser is physically at the point of sale (POS). Operates using either debit or credit card.

Enterprise Deployment: Term used in the computer industry to describe hardware and software configurations aimed to address the corporation as a whole as opposed to a single department.

Enterprise Network: The interconnection of multiple LANs and WANs to form a network that completely spans an entire organization.

Enterprise Resource Planning System (ERP): It enables a company to integrate data used throughout the organization in functions such as finance, operations, human resources, and sales. This system extends the pool of information for business intelligence.

Executive Information System (EIS): Customized views of business data with access limited to the senior executives. These systems were difficult to build and were expensive, hence, slow to adapt to the rapidly changing modern corporations.

Executive Support System: Comprehensive executive information system that may also include analytical communication and intelligent capabilities.

Extensive Markup Language (XML): Industry standard for the design and formatting of web documents. More powerful and flexible than HTML.

External Database: A database that exists outside an organization.

Extraction, Transformation, and Loading (ETL) of Data: Data is selected from the source(s) based on specific criteria and often transformed from its original state. Extracts may be output to various media.

Extranet: Variation of the word *Internet*. The company can share information with external customers and/or suppliers through a web-based application.

Fiber-Distributed Data Interface (FDDI): Data transmission technology that passes data around a ring at high speeds; based on speed and capacity of fiber optics but can use any transmission medium.

Firewall: A security device located between a firm's internal and external networks; regulates access into and out of the firm's IT system.

Fuzzy Logic: A method of working with "fuzzy" information, that is, incomplete or ambiguous information.

Group Document Database: A powerful storage facility for organizing and managing all documents related to a specific team or group.

Intelligence: First step in decision-making process where a problem, need or opportunity is found or identified.

Intranet: Variation of the word *Internet*. A web-based application that allows sharing information with a firm's employees.

Knowledge Base: The collection of data, rules, procedure, and relationships that must be followed to achieve value or the proper outcome.

Knowledge-Based System: Also called an expert system. An artificial intelligence system that applies reasoning capabilities to reach a conclusion.

Knowledge Management: Application for any business to create, maintain, and share company knowledge. The challenge of capturing collective experience, core values, and expertise of an organization.

Linking: Data manipulation that combines two or more tables using common data attributes to form a new table with only the unique data attributes.

Local Area Network (LAN): A network that connects computer systems and devices within the same geographical area.

Management Security Service Provider (MSSP): An organization that monitors and maintains network security hardware and software for its client companies.

Metadata: The information a database or application stores to describe an organization's business data and the applications that support it. Refers to the information used to describe a set of data.

Multidimensional Analysis: A type of analysis by which users combine data from many different perspectives in order to test conclusions or compare alternative strategies.

Net Markets: Also known as *ehubs, online trading exchanges.* They bring together a huge number of sellers and buyers through the Internet. They also increase the number of choices available.

Online Analytical Processing (OLAP) Method: Developed by Microsoft Corporation. Enables access to data from any application, regardless of which database management system (DBMS) is handling the data.

Online Transaction Processing (OTLP) Database: Refers to databases designed to handle a large volume of concurrent updates from a large number of users.

Open Database Connectivity (ODBC): Standards that ensure that software can be used with an ODBC-complaint database.

Planned Data Redundancy: A way of organizing data in which the logical database design is altered so that certain data entries are combined; summary totals are carried in the data record rather than calculated from elemental data; and some data attributes are repeated in more than one data entity to improve data performance.

Portal: Entry point. Describes the entry point for users to access information available throughout the World Wide Web.

Push Technology: Automatic transmission of information over the Internet rather than making the users search for it with their browsers.

Replicated Database: A database that maintains multiple copies of information in different locations.

Sales Force Automation (SFA): Software that helps management of sales forecast and enables sales teams to coordinate activities.

Semantic Layer: A software layer that insulates business users from the technical intricacies of database. It provides data as familiar business terms.

Set-Based Analysis: A recent method that uses groups of sets. It facilitates the examination and comparison of data.

Slice and Dice: Another term for *multidimensional analysis*. When data has three (or more) dimensions, it can be thought of as being arranged in a cube (or hypercube), with each side representing a dimension. When the data is analyzed, part of the cube can be "sliced" off or "diced" to get to an individual cell.

Source Data Automation: Capturing and editing data, where the data is originally created in a form that can be directly input to a computer, thus ensuring accuracy and timeliness.

Structured Query Language (SQL): Industry standard database protocol introduced by IBM.

Supply Chain: A complex network that organizations maintain with trading partners.

Total Quality Management (TQM): Meeting customers' expectations through continuous improvement.

Virtual Private Network (VPN): A public network that guarantees availability to an organization, but does not provide the organization with a dedicated line or communication media.

Wireless Application Protocol (WAP): Industry standard that allows the projection of Internet data onto the small screen on a wireless device such as a cellular phone.

About the Authors

Mahesh Raisinghani is a program director of e-Business and a faculty member at the Graduate School of Management, University of Dallas (USA), where he teaches MBA courses in Information Systems and e-Business. Dr. Raisinghani was the recipient of the 1999 UD Presidential Award and the 2001 King Haggar Award for excellence in teaching, research, and service. He has consulted with several well-known organizations such as IBM, Nokia, Petroleum Mexicanos, SwissAir, U.S. Government Services Administration, and the National Science Foundation. His previous publications have appeared in *Information and Management, Information Resources Management Journal, Journal of Global IT Management, Journal of E-Commerce Research, Information Strategy: An Executive's Journal, Journal of IT Theory and Applications, Enterprise Systems Journal, Journal of Computer Information Systems, and International Journal of Information Management*, among others. He serves as an associate editor and on the editorial review board of leading information systems/e-commerce journals and on the Board of Directors Sequoia, Inc. Dr. Raisinghani is included in the millennium edition of *Who's Who in the World, Who's Who Among America's Teachers* and *Who's Who in Information Technology*.

*   *   *   *

Andi Baritchi has been practicing in the computer industry for more than 10 years. He holds a master's in Computer Science and Engineering and is a Certified Information Systems Security Professional. His current research interests include information security, fraud detection, and telecommunications, each of which play a role in the PhD dissertation he is currently developing. Besides work and research, Andi is an avid automobile and motorsports enthusiast.

Christopher D. Barko is an Information Technology professional at Laboratory Corporation of America. His IT industry experience spans many years in various consulting, business intelligence, software engineering and analyst positions for a number of Fortune 500 organizations. He received his BBA in Computer Information Systems from James Madison University and MBA from the University of North Carolina at Greensboro where he specialized in Decision Support Systems. His current research interests include organizational data mining, business intelligence and customer relationship management and how these technologies can enhance the organizational decision-making process to optimize resource allocation and improve profitability. His research has been published in several leading journals such as the *Journal of Data Warehousing, Journal of Computer Information Systems,* and others. He is also president of Customer Analytics, Inc., a consultancy that leverages advanced analytics to deliver profitable database marketing solutions.

Clare Brindley is principal lecturer/deputy head of Department at Manchester Metropolitan University, UK. Prior to embarking on an academic career, Clare worked in marketing management roles both in the private and public sectors. Clare is a member of the editorial advisory boards of the *Journal of Internet Research* and the *Cyprus International Journal of Management.* She is a member of the Chartered Institute of Marketing, the Academy of Marketing, and the Institute for Small Business Affairs. The themes prevalent in her research are risk, entrepreneurship, supply chain management, relationship marketing, and ICT developments, particularly in a gendered context. Clare has published in a range of management journals including: *Management Decision, Marketing Intelligence and Planning, Education and Training, Journal of Internet Research,* and *Integrated Manufacturing Systems.* She is a founding member of the International Supply Chain Risk Management Network.

Edilberto Casado is an independent consultant in Information Technology and Business Performance Management with more than 10 years of experience working with Peruvian organizations and multinational companies. He holds an MBA from Escuela de Administración de Negocios Para Graduados (ESAN) in Lima, Perú. His areas of interest include business intelligence, the application of system dynamics for business and strategic management, and information technology project management. Currently, he is an associate professor at Gerens, a management training and consulting firm based in Lima, Perú, and is also a member of the System Dynamics Society.

Somya Chaudhary has an MBA Marketing, and an MPA (Master of Public Administration) in Urban Planning and Development. She has multifaceted work experience from the public, private, and non-governmental organization sectors. She has also worked for the United Nations as a policy maker. More recently, she was a management consultant for Fujitsu. Last year, she took a full-time position with a major telecommunications firm in the Southeast U.S. She specializes in data warehouses, business intelligence, and strategic planning. She has a wonderful husband, an energetic toddler son, and a delightful baby daughter, keeping her otherwise engaged. She can be reached at somya@bellsouth.net.

Edilson Ferneda was a senior professor at the Federal University of Paraíba from 1986-2000 and is now a full-professor at the Catholic University of Brasília and an associated researcher at the University of Brasília. He graduated in Systems Analysis at the Technological Institute of Aeronautics (1977-1979), received his MSc in Computing and Systems from the Federal University of Paraíba (1984-1988) and a DSc in Computer Science from University of Montpellier II, France (1988-1992). His current research interests are machine learning, knowledge acquisition, knowledge-based systems, and scientific reasoning. He has published 87 scientific papers, supervised 19 MSc dissertations, and three PhD theses.

Ulfert Gartz is a principal consultant working for the Systems Integration & Solution Group of PA Consulting Group, Germany. After studying business economics and computer sciences, he has been working for several large enterprises and consulting companies leading data warehouse and business intelligence projects. At PA he is responsible for business intelligence and large-scale information management solutions.

Traci J. Hess is an assistant professor of Management Information Systems at Washington State University, USA. Her research interests include the design and use of decision support systems and software agents. She has published her research in such journals as *Decision Sciences and Decision Support Systems*. She received a PhD and Masters in Information Technology from Virginia Tech and a BS from the University of Virginia.

Jeffrey Hsu is an assistant professor of Information Systems at the Silberman College of Business Administration, Fairleigh Dickinson University, USA. His research interests include human-computer interaction, e-commerce, groupware, distance learning, and business intelligence (CRM, data mining, etc.). He is the author of six books and numerous papers and articles, and has professional experience in the IT industry. Hsu holds a PhD in Management Information Systems from Rutgers University, three master's degrees, and several professional certifications. Dr. Hsu is always interested in discussing opportunities for research and other scholarly activities, and can be reached via e-mail at jeff@fdu.edu.

Lakshmi Iyer is an assistant professor in the Information Systems and Operations Management Department at the University of North Carolina at Greensboro, USA. She obtained her PhD in Business Administration from the University of Georgia, Athens. Her research interests are e-commerce, global issues in IS, intelligent agents, decision support systems, knowledge management, and cluster analysis. Her research work has been published or accepted for publication in *CACM, Annals of OR, DSS, JGITM, Journal of Scientific & Industrial Research, Encyclopedia of ORMS, Journal of Information Technology Management, Journal of Data Warehousing,* and *Industrial Management and Data Systems*.

Stanley Loh is a professor at the Lutheran University of Brazil (ULBRA) and at the Catholic University of Pelotas (UCPEL). He has a bachelor's and a master's in Computer Science and obtained his PhD in Computer Science in 2001 at the Federal University of Rio Grande do Sul (UFRGS). He is also a director of the enterprises ADS Digital (www.adsdigital.com.br) and InText Mining (www.intext.com.br). His research is focused on knowledge discovery and text mining, information retrieval and information systems for business intelligence.

Ashfaaq Moosa is a data analyst at Upromise, Inc., a firm that helps families save for college. He has worked on various customer-focused data integration and data mining projects for various industries including retail, real estate, and financial. He graduated with a Masters of Science in Information Technology and Management from the University of North Carolina at Greensboro.

John H. Nugent brings more than 25 years of industry and academic experience to the classroom. Dr. Nugent served as president of several firms engaged in developing information systems tools and products, including having served as president and a board of directors member of several AT&T subsidiaries involved in designing and manufacturing secure communications components, products, and systems supporting more than 90 countries and many multinational corporations with their IA requirements. Dr. Nugent is the director of the Information Assurance Concentration and cross-teaches in the Telecommunications Concentration. He headed a firm that became a subsidiary of AT&T. It developed more than 100 information security components, products, and systems ranging from encryption chips to secure radios, phones, fax encrypters, secure data devices, key management systems, and switches to secure satellite and national command and control communication systems serving more than 90 governments and many large commercial enterprises around the world. Under Dr. Nugent's leadership, his firm was chosen by Defense Electronics magazine for its "10 Rising Stars" list. The Republic of France also honored him in 1988 with Diplome de Citoyen D'Honneur for his work in France.

José Palazzo Moreira de Oliveira is a full professor of Computer Science at Federal University of Rio Grande do Sul - UFRGS (Brazil). He has a PhD in Computer Science from Institut National Politechnique - IMAG (1984), Grenoble, France, an MSc in Computer Science from PPGC-UFRGS (1976) and graduated in Electronic Engineering in 1968. His research interests include information systems, e-learning, database systems and applications, enterprise conceptual modeling, applications of database technology, and distributed systems. He has published approximately 160 papers and been advisor to 10 PhD and 45 MSc students.

Hamid R. Nemati is an assistant professor of Information Systems at the Information Systems and Operations Management Department of the University of North Carolina at Greensboro, USA. He holds a doctorate in Management Sciences and Information Technology from the University of Georgia and a Master of Business Administration from the University of Massachusetts. He has extensive professional IT experience as an analyst and has consulted with a number of major corporations. Before coming to UNCG, he was on the faculty of J. Mack Robinson College of Business Administration at Georgia State University. His research specialization is in the areas of Organizational Data Mining, Decision Support Systems, Data Warehousing, and Knowledge Management. He has presented nationally and internationally on a wide range of topics relating to his research interests. His research has been published in a number of top tier scholarly journals.

Hércules Antonio do Prado is a researcher at the Brazilian Enterprise for Agricultural Research – Embrapa, a lecturer at the Catholic University of Brasília, and an associated researcher at the University of Brasília. He received his DSc in Computer Science from the Federal University of Rio Grande do Sul in 2001, and his MSc in Systems Engineering from the Federal University of Rio de Janeiro. He graduated in Systems Analysis in 1976 from the Federal University of São Carlos. His research interests are data mining, neural networks, knowledge-based systems, and knowledge management. He has published 27 scientific papers and supervised two MSc theses. He develops artificial intelligence applications in Embrapa.

Bob Ritchie is head of the Business and Management Department, Manchester Metropolitan University, UK. He is the author of best selling books, *Managing Business Risks* and *Business Information Systems*. Bob is a regular contributor to a number of leading journals and conferences such as IPSERA, BAM and ISBA. In 2002 he won a Literati Award for his paper with Clare Brindley on information and risk published in *Marketing Intelligence and Planning*. He is editor of the *Cyprus International Journal of Management* and acts as a reviewer for ESRC in the area of risk management.

Al Salam is an assistant professor in the Information Systems and Operations Management Department at the University of North Carolina at Greensboro, USA. He earned both his MBA and PhD from the State University of New York at Buffalo. His research interests include e-business and emerging technologies, intelligent systems in e-business, and information technology management. His research has been published in the *CACM, Information Systems Journal*, and *Journal of Information Technology Cases and*

Applications. He has served as a co-guest editor of a Special Issue of the *JECR* and a Special Section on Internet and Marketing in the *CACM*.

Edilberto Magalhães Silva is a lecturer at the UNIPLAC College and a systems analyst at RADIOBRÁS - Brazilian Public News Agency. He has graduated in Computer Science from FIPLAC College (1992-1996) and received an MSc in Knowledge and Information Technology Management from the Catholic University of Brasilia (1999-2002). He currently works with information technology for the Brazilian government. His current interests are decision support systems, data mining and text mining. He has published four scientific papers.

Rahul Singh is an assistant professor in the Information Systems and Operations Management Department at the University of North Carolina at Greensboro, USA. He obtained his PhD in Business Administration from Virginia Commonwealth University. His research interest is in the area of the design of systems that apply intelligent technologies to business decision systems. Specific interests include intelligent agents, knowledge management systems, data mining and machine learning systems. His research work has been published or accepted for publication in *CACM, International Journal of Production Engineering, Journal of Decision Systems, Socio-Economic Planning Sciences* and *The Encyclopedia of Information Systems*.

James E. Skibo is an adjunct professor of Engineering Management at the University of Dallas (USA), Graduate School of Management, and is also pursuing his PhD at the Fielding Graduate Institute, Santa Barbara, CA. He is the director of Co-operative Advertising for the Army & Air Force Exchange Service, Dallas, TX, and is also a consultant in private practice. His areas of expertise include operations management, process management, trade allowance management, and consulting.

Dan Sullivan is president of The Ballston Group (USA), specializing in evaluating, designing, and implementing enterprise content management and unstructured data management systems. Dan is the author of *Proven Portals* (Addison Wesley, 2003) and *Document Warehousing and Text Mining* (Wiley, 2001). He is a columnist with *DM Review* and www.business intelligence.com and has published more than 25 articles in leading industry publications such as *Intelligent Enterprise* and *e-Business Advisor*. He is a contributing author to *Text Mining and Its Applications* (WIT, 2003).

John D. Wells is an assistant professor of Management Information Systems at Washington State University, USA. He received his BBA in Management from the University of Oklahoma and MS/PhD degrees in Management Information Systems from Texas A&M University. His active research areas are electronic commerce and IT strategy. He has worked as a systems engineer/consultant for Electronic Data Systems and the Oklahoma State Senate.

Leandro Krug Wives is an assistant professor of Computer Science at Centro Universitário Feevale (Feevale College). He is finishing his DSc in Computer Science at Federal University of Rio Grande do Sul - UFRGS, has a master's degree in Computer Science from UFRGS (1999), and has graduated in Computer Science (1996) at the Catholic University of Pelotas. His research interests include text mining (with emphasis on cluster analysis of textual data), information retrieval, and competitive intelligence.

Index

O

online analytical processing (OLAP)
    52, 143, 196
online transactional processing (OLTP)
    254
organizational culture 211

P

PA Consulting Group 49
partitioning clustering 214
PeopleSoft 32
personal goals 16
personalization 153
personalized web agents 155
phenomenal data mining 168
privacy concerns 45
proof-of-performance 113
purchase order (PO) 120
purchasing systems 118
push agents 26

R

regression 40
relational database management
    systems (RDBMS) 145
relationship management 82
resource description framework (RDF)
    81
retail point of sale (RPOS) 117
return on investment (ROI) 251
risk assessment 1
risk insulating tool 10
risk management 13, 170
risk management consequences 13
risk perceptions 1, 14
risk resolution 3
rule constraints 168
rule induction 128

S

sales force automation (SFA) 99
second generation data-mining system
    147
sequence data mining 166

ShareKnowledge behavior 91
simple object access protocol (SOAP)
    87
site modification 153
socio-economic changes 3
soft variables 133
spatial data mining 165
spreadsheets 45
SPSS Clementine 44
stars algorithm 215
stock-and-flow diagrams 132
stop words 102
subject matter experts (SME) 199
summarization 41
system dynamics 126
system dynamics approach 130
system dynamics society 130
system improvement 153

T

technology adoption 209
telecommunications market 100
term extraction 100
term frequency (tf factor) 102
text categorization 158
text data mining 156
text mining (TM) 98, 207
text-mining techniques 100
textual patterns 207
third generation data-mining systems
    147
time availability 16
time series data mining 166
timeliness 31
top-down approach 42
trade allowance identification 111
trade allowance system 119
trade allowances 111
transformation 39
turfdoms 195

U

ubiquitous data mining (UDM) 160
unfiltered information 31

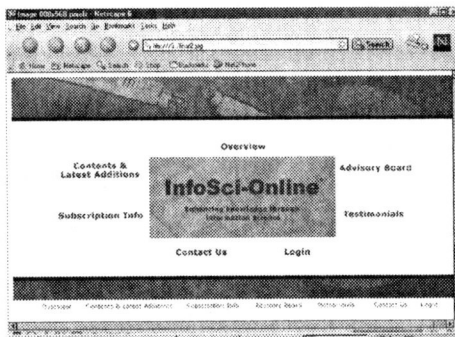

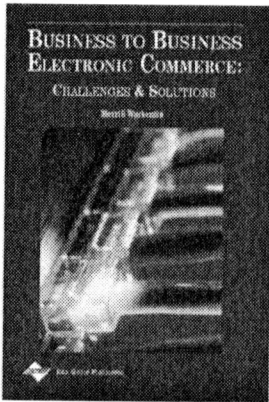